ROBERT MCAFEE BROWN

MODERN SPIRITUAL MASTERS SERIES

ROBERT McAFEE BROWN

Spiritual and Prophetic Writings

Selected with an Introduction by
PAUL CROWLEY

ORBIS BOOKS

Maryknoll, New York 10545

Founded in 1970, Orbis Books endeavors to publish works that enlighten the mind, nourish the spirit, and challenge the conscience. The publishing arm of the Maryknoll Fathers and Brothers, Orbis seeks to explore the global dimensions of the Christian faith and mission, to invite dialogue with diverse cultures and religious traditions, and to serve the cause of reconciliation and peace. The books published reflect the views of their authors and do not represent the official position of the Maryknoll Society. To learn more about Maryknoll and Orbis Books, please visit our website at www.maryknollsociety.org.

Library of Congress Cataloging-in-Publication Data
Brown, Robert McAfee, 1920–2001.
    [Works. Selections]
  Robert McAfee Brown : spiritual and prophetic writings / selected with an
  introduction by Paul Crowley
      pages   cm. — (Modern spiritual masters series)
    Includes bibliographical references and index.
    ISBN 978-1-62698-007-5 (pbk.: alk. paper)
    1. Christianity—History—20th century. 2. Church and social problems.
  3. Ecumenical movement. I. Crowley, Paul G. II. Title.
  BR481.B762 2012
  230′.51–dc23   2012034196

*Righteous men dream dreams
that cannot always be fulfilled
yet . . .*

— Colin Masashi Ehara

To Sydney Thomson Brown

3. THE STRUGGLE FOR HUMAN RIGHTS   118

    Why I Made This Trip   118

    *Theological and Biblical Foundations:
        Christian Responsibility in Human Rights*   121

    *Christian Responsibility in the Human Rights
        Struggle*   130

    Faith in Humankind   133

    Proposition 187—and the Fears of Children   137

    Gay and Lesbian People in the Church   139

4. PEACEMAKING   148

    The Splinter and the Plank   148

    Turning in the Draft Cards   152

    Christianity and Violence   156

    Christmas Eve 1972   163

    Reconciliation: A Christian Approach   170

    Memorial for Those Who Died in Vietnam   175

    Gulf War Prayer   178

5. INTERFAITH SOLIDARITY   179

    Uniting the Church for a Fractured World   179

    *Vocation and the Theology of Work: Resources for
        Dealing with a New Situation*   186

    A Protestant Critique of a Catholic Pastoral Letter   197

    Elie Wiesel: A Jew's Message to Christians   209

On Speaking about Israel: An Ongoing Problem for Jews and Christians 217

Ground Rules for Ecumenical (and Multicultural) Exchange 225

A Concluding Word: On Not Knowing Where We Are Going 230

Further Reading 238

Notes 239

Acknowledgments

I wish to thank the following people and institutions for their support of the preparation of this book: Santa Clara University for the gift of a sabbatical; Robert Benedetto, director of the Flora Lamson Hewlett Library at the Graduate Theological Union, Berkeley, who first suggested this project; for the hospitality of the library he extended to me as a guest scholar, and for his editorial help; David Stiver of the Hewlett Library for help in finding obscure items in the Brown archives; and Caryl Wolfe, Hewlett Library administrative assistant, for attending to practical details of my work there. I would also like to thank Jenny Johnson, Stanford University Libraries, for locating the 1972 Christmas Eve Sermon, and Luis Calero, S.J., of Santa Clara University for help with a translation. Thanks are also due to Vicky Gonzalez, administrative assistant in the Religious Studies Department at Santa Clara for help in obtaining student typists for this project, and to Denise Carmody and Billy Robb for editorial assistance. And I would be greatly remiss to fail to thank Robert Ellsberg and Maria Angelini at Orbis Books for help along the way and seeing this book to publication. Finally, and not least, I wish to thank Sydney Thomson Brown and Peter, Mark, Alice, and Tom Brown for granting approval to work through Bob's papers so that this book could become a reality.

Preface

A celebration of the life and work of Robert McAfee Brown was held at the Graduate Theological Union in Berkeley, California, on October 6, 2010. The celebration brought together Paul Crowley and Judith Dunbar, both students of Robert Brown and now faculty members at Santa Clara University, and Diana Gibson, who was pastor of the Palo Alto Presbyterian Church, where Brown worked as parish associate and who now also teaches at Santa Clara. Several members of the Brown family were also present, including Brown's wife, Sydney Thomson Brown, who gave closing remarks. The papers that were read, and the panel discussion afterward, reinforced in the minds of the audience the continuing relevance of Robert Brown as a master theologian and spiritual guide, and continuing reflection by the participants of that celebration has led to the production of this anthology of Brown's "spiritual writings."

The Brown celebration coincided with the gift of the Robert McAfee Brown Papers to the Flora Lamson Hewlett Library. These papers are a treasure trove of material related to the issues that dominated theological conversation and activity in the last half of the twentieth century and the first decade of the twenty-first century. Among these issues are the civil rights movement and race relations, the ecumenical movement, the Holocaust and Jewish-Christian relations, liberation theology and narrative theology, Marxism, the politics and governments of Central America and Cuba, world poverty, the changing shape of Protestant theology, the Second Vatican Council and Protestant-Catholic relations, and the Vietnam War and the antiwar movement. While this anthology draws from the Brown Papers and also from his published writings, it by no means exhausts Brown's manuscript material and the published and unpublished writings found in his thirty boxes of papers. These papers, which are now open for research, are an enduring legacy that will be studied and quoted for years to come.

Robert McAfee Brown was fully engaged with the issues of his time and for that reason he might be called "an activist." His was not a quiet spirituality born of retreat and contemplation. The times in which he lived did not allow for that. His times were tumultuous: loud, excited, emotional, and polarizing; they were characterized by years of war, political demonstration and protest, and social, political, and religious upheaval. His spirituality was molded by the biblical texts and then pounded on the hard anvil of contrarian leadership. His was no easy spirituality, or what Protestant martyr Dietrich Bonhoeffer called a "cheap grace." Rather, Brown's spirituality was the result of a lifetime of sacrificial engagement with the problems and possibilities of his times. It is this "active spirituality" that characterized his life and is what now qualifies Robert McAfee Brown as a contemporary spiritual master.

ROBERT BENEDETTO
Director of the Flora Lamson Hewlett Library
The Graduate Theological Union
Berkeley, California

Foreword

The following are excerpts from an address given by Judith Dunbar, a professor of English at Santa Clara University, on the occasion of the dedication of the Robert McAfee Brown Collection at the Flora Lamson Hewlett Library of the Graduate Theological Union, Berkeley, on October 6, 2010. The address was entitled, "Robert McAfee Brown: Man of Courage, Justice, Compassion—and Music."

I am grateful to join my deeply valued colleague at Santa Clara University, Paul Crowley, in honoring Bob Brown. That our sharing the platform is also representative of Bob's vital role in dialogue between Protestants and Roman Catholics would, I think, give Bob joy. After his time in 1963 as an invited Protestant observer at the Second Vatican Council, which gave rise to his book *Observer in Rome*, as well as for his prophetic theological works and action for social justice, Bob was granted honorary doctorates by a number of Roman Catholic universities, the first of which, in 1964, was the University of San Francisco (USF). The question came up: what degree would a Catholic university find fitting to give to a Protestant? At the time it seemed, Bob had written, a "doctorate in theology" would have been "out of the question." USF asked which degree he would prefer. Knowing it was really USF's choice, Bob quipped that perhaps, as one of the "*separated* brethren," and because of the journalism involved in his writing from Rome about the Council, he could be given a new kind of degree named for "separated journalists," so that he could call himself "Robert McAfee Brown, SJ."[1] In the end, USF honored him with a LittD, as a Doctor of Letters. When,

almost thirty years later, in 1992, Santa Clara University gave
him an honorary doctorate, Bob was moved to discover it was
as a Doctor of Sacred Theology (STD). He wrote of that marker
of ecumenical progress: "We have come a long way."[2]

Thus to the title of my tribute to Bob Brown, I want to add a
word—humor: Man of Courage, Justice, Compassion, Music—
and Humor. Humor was integral to that endearing humility evident in the ways he treated all who knew him with warmth,
unpretentious humanity, compassion, and respect. He took seriously the issues with which he engaged, but never inflated his
own role, prophetic as it was on the national and international
stage. One of his titles for himself, indeed, was St. Hereticus, in
his column that ran especially in the 1960s and 1970s in the
journal *Christianity and Crisis*, a column that yielded many
pieces for his book, *The Collected Writings of St. Hereticus*, a
book he described (in its sequel, *The Hereticus Papers*), as "a
significant attempt to keep theologians humble."[3] St. Hereticus
nailed in his witty critiques a whole range of social, political,
and religious issues. The inclusion of humor among Bob's qualities is, indeed, recognized in the words his family chose for his
memorial stone:

> Beloved husband, father, grandfather, friend
> Writer, teacher, theologian
> Courageous activist for justice and peace
> Man of love, wisdom, music, humor, and conscience.

In Bob, these aspects of his life and work were integrally con-
nected; the "courageous activist for justice and peace" was at
one with the theologian.

Courage "may be the most important Christian word for our
times,"[4] Bob wrote, and a similar statement is also inscribed
on his memorial stone. His words are, furthermore, written in
the hearts of those who heard his prophetic speech and have
encountered the compelling clarity of his prophetic writing. In
a small, handwritten sign above his typewriter in Bob's study in

his Palo Alto home was Elie Wiesel's statement, from Wiesel's *Legends of Our Time*: Words can *"sometimes, in moments of grace, attain the quality of deeds."*[5] Bob's words had just such a quality, and even more power because of the extraordinary congruence of his words and his actions.

Bob's courage made him a major religious leader in the public sphere. The 2003 Pacific School of Religion Earl Lectures, "Reclaiming Theology as a Public Resource," honored what the planners called Bob's "faithful and insistent spirit—this belief that theology must add value to the public square" (quotation from the brochure for the 2003 Earl Lectures). And he walked his talk. I was drawn to hear him speak when I first came to Stanford and it was announced, in the fall of 1962, that he, a professor from Union Theological Seminary and a Freedom Rider, had come to teach at Stanford in Religious Studies. For civil disobedience in protesting segregation together with ministers, priests, and rabbis, black and white, he was in jail in 1962 in Tallahassee, Florida, when his appointment as a Stanford faculty member was approved by the Stanford Trustees. "I have sometimes wondered whether," Bob wrote later, "if they had known this, it would have swayed their decision, and if so, in which way."[6]

Word quickly got round among the students about the power of Bob's teaching; his course enrollments grew from an average of 15 his first term (Fall 1962) to 250 the very next term (Winter 1963) for the course in theology and contemporary literature for which I subsequently served as his teaching assistant.[7] With engaging intellectual and spiritual courage, he laid bare for discussion his own presuppositions, welcoming questioning, as he explored both overtly Christian writers like W. H. Auden, Graham Greene, and Alan Paton, and non-Christian writers like Albert Camus and Samuel Beckett.

When Bob Brown preached in the Memorial Church at Stanford, he helped us see the defining moments of crisis and opportunity, of *kairos*, in our midst, as he called us to work for justice on multiple fronts, including civil rights, the support of migrant farm workers, and the protest against U.S. policies during the Vietnam War. His call to action was the more powerful since he led through his own active engagement. On the national level, Bob in 1967 co-founded—with other religious leaders, including Abraham Joshua Heschel—Clergy and Laity Concerned about Vietnam, which had an important role in critiquing U.S. policy in Vietnam.[8] On Christmas Eve, 1972, Bob gave a sermon in the packed Memorial Church, joined by approximately two thousand marchers from a candlelight vigil in downtown Palo Alto who had been protesting U.S. saturation bombing of North Vietnam, bombing that Bob compared to Herod's slaughter of the innocents.[9]

Bob brought knowledge to bear on the discernment of contemporary events, and he did so, as in all his teaching and writing—with extraordinary clarity. His was an apostolate of the pen and of the spoken word, as well as of deeds. He had an ability to distill complex ideas into language accessible to wide audiences and, moreover, gave us insight into root causes so we could work for structural change. That Bob's courage of active solidarity in the struggle for justice was at one with his intellectual courage as a theologian shows, strikingly, in two further examples.

The first is his shift of emphasis from formal systematic theology to liberation theology—a theology rooted in tradition, but working from the ground up, a theology of the people, and a theology with deep attention to economic and social analysis. When, in 1972, Bob first read Gustavo Gutiérrez's *A Theology of Liberation*, he confronted himself: "If this is right, I have to start my theological life all over again."[10] Bob's deep engagement with Gutiérrez' work led to his great friendship with Gutiérrez, to teaching summer courses with him at the Graduate Theological Union, and to Bob's writing his substantial, splendidly lucid book, *Gustavo Gutiérrez: An Introduction to Liberation Theology* (1990), that has helped to make Gutiérrez's work accessible to many.

That Bob *lived* his solidarity with those struggling for justice, in conditions of danger, in Central America, was also striking in his 1990 accompaniment of Medardo Gómez, Salvadoran Lutheran bishop-in-exile, on Bishop Gómez's courageous visit back to San Salvador. For his advocacy of the poor and for his political critique, Bishop Gómez had been put in prison and tortured; threats against his family had forced them to leave the country; and when death threats against him intensified, he was counseled by Catholic and Protestant supporters to go into exile.[11] Bob put his life on the line, in the wager that the Salvadoran authorities would find it harder to arrest, harm, or kill Gómez with such accompaniment as he and eleven other North American Christians offered.

For his participation in a protest in 1985 at the San Francisco federal building against U.S. covert support for the *contras* in the war in Nicaragua, Bob—wearing his clerical collar—was arrested. At his trial, he offered prophetic witness. His sentence was almost comically ironic: "eighteen hours of community service."[12] Bob asked the clerk at the courthouse how literally he was to take the admonition not to gather with people involved in protest issues, as he was about to have lunch with one or more of them, me included. He then asked if he could do his community service with the chaplaincy at Dartmouth, where he was that fall a visiting professor. The clerk, embarrassed, gave permission. As it turned out, the Dartmouth staff member who would supervise Bob was a former student of Bob's from Union seminary days. Some hours of Bob's community service supported building a shanty-town type structure on the Dartmouth green to protest the U.S. failure to break economic ties sufficiently with the apartheid regime in South Africa.

How Bob's active concern for justice was at one with his courage as a theologian shows in a further example. From 1970 onward he confronted himself with difficult theological questions involving the Holocaust, questions of suffering and of evil, in his encounter with the work of Elie Wiesel. Bob taught courses on the work of Wiesel at Stanford, Union Theological Seminary, and the Pacific School of Religion, and articulated his deeply authentic interfaith explorations and questions in his book *Elie Wiesel: Messenger to All Humanity*.

Bob never ceased to learn from dialogue and had the courage to challenge, strongly, his own perspectives. His dialogue with Wiesel led to a profound friendship, and Bob's commitment to issues involving the Holocaust was recognized in an invitation from President Carter to be a member of the Holocaust Memorial Council, to be headed by Wiesel. In 1979, he accompanied Wiesel on his visit to European Holocaust memorials—including Wiesel's return to Auschwitz-Birkenau. An intense silence fell on them and their small group as they stood on the roof of one of the ruined crematoria at Birkenau. Then, quietly at first, Wiesel's voice began to lead them: "*Shema Yisroel, Adonai Elohenu, Adonai Echod*" ("Hear, O Israel, the Lord our God, the Lord is one.") As Bob later wrote: "At the place where the name of God could have been agonizingly denied, the name of God was agonizingly affirmed—affirmed by those with the most right to deny. . . . I affirmed, but *with them, not alone.*"[13]

No wonder it was Bob whom Wiesel invited to Stockholm in 1985 on the occasion of Wiesel's receiving the Nobel Peace Prize. When Wiesel heard of Bob's death, Wiesel said: "I shall miss him every day when writing every page. I have rarely met a man of such faith, integrity, and compassion. As a teacher, he influenced generations. As a friend, he was the best one can dream of. As a Jew, I saw in him the nobility of what Christianity has to offer."[14]

Those qualities of "faith, integrity, and compassion" that could be so strongly sensed in Bob's presence and his actions also appear as motifs in the wide range of his writing. In his later years, he explored his love of literature, and of the theological power of stories, in fresh ways, by writing his novel *Dark the Night, Wild the Sea*. As Sydney Brown puts it, what she did not know when first she married Bob is "that, after writing twenty-eight theological books, at seventy-eight he would write a magical and beautiful Hebridean-based novel, a tale of love crossing time, poignant and compelling."[15]

In his later years Bob also embraced his life-long love of music in a new way: he learned to play the cello beginning at age sixty.[16] By the time of his retirement from Pacific School of Religion only about six years later, he was able to play one of his favorite pieces, the Andante Cantabile, from Beethoven's Archduke Trio, op. 97.

Music accompanied Bob in his last days. He listened to music by Stanford Professor Stephen (Steve) Sano, whom Bob had known since Steve was a young boy. He listened to the Bach Mass in B minor. And wonderfully, when the family, gathered around his bedside, sang to him, he harmonized with them.

Bob's ashes, those that were taken to the Hebridean island of Colonsay, were scattered both inside and outside of a chapel on the adjacent island of Oronsay, and through the chapel's windows—thus making the connection between church and world as he did in life.[17]

May this collection of his papers and books, in his honor, be an ongoing way Bob's prophetic work and spirit may continue to be leaven in the world, and his legacy be present among us.

Would you join me in remembering Bob in the way those who died in the struggle for justice in Central America are honored: Robert McAfee Brown—*¡Presente!*

JURITH DUNBAR
Santa Clara University

NOTES TO THE FOREWORD

1. Brown, *Reflections over the Long Haul,* 216–17.
2. Ibid., 217.
3. *Hereticus Papers,* 145.
4. Brown, Reflections, 91.
5. Wiesel, *Legends,* viii; italics as in Wiesel's book.
6. Brown, Reflections, 115.
7. Ibid.,118.
8. Ibid.,149.
9. Ibid., 162–63.
10. Brown, *Gustavo Gutiérrez,* xix.
11. Brown, "Ecumenism of the Threatened," *Christianity and Crisis* 50, no. 2 (February 19, 1990): 28.
12. Brown, *Reflections,* 194–95.
13. Ibid., 223; cf. *Elie Wiesel: Messenger to All Humanity,* 189–90.
14. Wiesel is quoted by Thomas C. Fox, in "He Banished 'Lazy Christianity,' Robert McAfee Brown, Obituary," *National Catholic Reporter*, September 14, 2001.
15. "Tributes," 11.
16. Brown, *Reflections,* 277.
17. Cf. Sydney Brown, in ibid., 303–4.

WORKS CITED IN THE FOREWORD

Brown, Robert McAfee. *The Collected Writings of St. Hereticus.* Ed. Robert McAfee Brown. Philadelphia: Westminster Press, 1964.

———. "Ecumenism of the Threatened," *Christianity and Crisis* 50, no. 2 (February 19, 1990): 28.

———. *Elie Wiesel: Messenger to All Humanity.* Notre Dame, Ind.: Universiry of Notre Dame Press, 1983.

———. *Gustavo Gutiérrez: An Introduction to Liberation Theology.* Maryknoll, N.Y.: Orbis Books, 1990.

———. *The Hereticus Papers (being Volume II of The Collected Writings of St. Hereticus).* Ed. Robert McAfee Brown. Philadelphia: Westminster Press, 1979.

———. *Observer in Rome: A Protestant Report on the Vatican Council.* London: Methuen, 1964.

———. *Reflections over the Long Haul: A Memoir.* Louisville, KY: Westminster John Knox Press, 2005.

Fox, Thomas C. "He Banished 'Lazy Christianity'—Robert McAfee Brown—Obituary," *National Catholic Reporter*, September 14, 2001.

"Tributes from His Family." [Brown family members]. Booklet, privately printed, ca. 2002.

Wiesel, Elie. *Legends of Our Time.* New York: Avon Books, 1968.

Introduction

Robert McAfee Brown was one of the leading voices of a prophetic Christianity in the latter half of the twentieth century. The "prophetic" emphasis is derived from the prophets of the Old Testament and the gospel of Jesus, who preached a message of social justice and peace. It was also characterized by an engagement with the world on the basis of this prophetic stance—a stance that was world affirming but at the same time sharply critical of anything opposed to the prophetic gospel message, such as racism, war, economic injustice, or sexism. It was a Christianity that demanded of him clear choices and positions; he never remained neutral, whether the issue was rooted in society or in the church, or both.

THE JOURNEY OF ROBERT McAFEE BROWN

Born on May 28, 1920, in Carthage, Illinois, Brown was the son of a Presbyterian minister who was a pacifist and who became general secretary of the American Bible Society before returning to parish ministry. His mother came from a distinguished line of Presbyterian ministers, and her father had served as moderator of the General Assembly of the Presbyterian Church. Brown's home life was religiously moderate and politically progressive, with strong leanings toward the Social Gospel, a movement of the late nineteenth and early twentieth-century American Protestantism that stressed the social dimensions of the gospel, and obligations of Christians toward the poor.

After high school, Brown moved on to Amherst College, where he earned a B.A. in philosophy in 1943. By the time he graduated, three things were clear to him: (1) Christian faith was insufficient without correlative action in the world, (2) pacifism was the only path he could take in a world ridden with war, and (3) he loved Sydney Thomson, a Smith student, and wanted to marry her. That he eventually did, and in the following years they had four children: Peter, Mark, Alison, and Tom.

For Christians, and particularly Catholics, who came of age during the 1960s and the era of the Second Vatican Council, Brown was first known as an ecumenical leader, an officially appointed Protestant observer at the second session of the Council, representing the World Alliance of Reformed Churches. While his movement into Christian interfaith relations was gradual, he emerged from the Council as a leading interpreter of the promise and challenges that lay ahead for both American Protestants and Catholics. Among progressive Catholics, Brown had become their "favorite Protestant."

However, Brown's developing vocation was to leave some Protestants scratching their heads. His embrace of the prophetic message of Christianity challenged some of the established assumptions of the right ordering of the church with respect to wider society. In his earliest sermons Brown inveighed against a comfortable Christianity that refrained from taking on the social and political issues of the day, from racial segregation and anti-Semitism to the scourge of McCarthyism in the 1950s. His participation in the Eugene McCarthy congressional campaign in 1952—a Catholic and a strong opponent of the tactics of Senator Joseph McCarthy—led several Protestants to demand that Brown be fired from his position at Macalester College as instructor and chaplain. This kind of reaction to Brown's social and political activities was to become familiar as his visibility grew. Indeed, by the mid-1960s, as his activities in civil rights and anti-Vietnam War protests increased, he would earn the dignity of an FBI file. The basis for his stance was a prophetic Christianity rooted in the prophets and in the gospel of justice and peace—in sharp contrast to an inward-looking, sectarian, or socially conservative ideology prevalent in the 1950s and in some quarters even today.

Following Amherst, and unwilling to enlist in the military because of his pacifist convictions, Brown enrolled in 1943 at Union Theological Seminary in New York, which was then the citadel of mainline Protestant theology in the United States, with a very distinguished faculty, including Paul Tillich, Samuel Terrien, and Henry Emerson Fosdick. Brown befriended all of these leading Protestant lights and was, in various ways, shaped by them. At the same time, he decided early on that he would not be content as an academic theologian alone. While he could muster tenure at Union, he did not want to be confined to academic debates, publishing only in academic journals. He yearned for a career where the "apostolate of the pen" would dovetail with a prophetic stance as a Christian in the world, and where, at the same time, he could teach and thereby help raise up a new generation of Christian witnesses.

In keeping with this kind of commitment, two Union theologians would greatly influence Brown: John Bennett and Reinhold Niebuhr. Bennett was a leading ethicist and social progressive who eventually became president of Union. His blend of solid theology with courageous social activism and preaching was to prove a model for Brown, and their friendship was to be lasting and deep. But Niebuhr's influence in particular would mold Brown's personal and theological positions, especially in the early years of his career. First, Niebuhr helped Brown nuance his pacifism, which seemed necessary in the face of the monstrous evil that had emerged in Germany under the Nazis. Niebuhr's own position was closer to a "selective pacifism," a position Brown eventually adopted. This development helped Brown move toward actually serving as a Navy chaplain during World

War II. Second, Niebuhr's realism, and his serious attention to sin not only as a personal reality but as a social reality, was to give a permanent stamp to Brown's theological foundations for an active, worldly Christianity. As Brown later embraced the methods and principles of liberation theology, he would develop the Niebuhrian theology of sin into the concept of "structural sin," a notion especially apt in his critiques of American military power in Latin America.

It was at Union that he would read the important Protestant theologians: not only Calvin, of whom he became an expert interpreter, but also the Swiss theologians Emil Brunner and Karl Barth. Brunner's approach to the relationship between nature and grace was far from the dualism of classical Calvinism. For Brunner, there was a cooperation between the two that led to an emphasis upon human freedom before the sovereignty of God. This was quite different from the view that the function of grace was to conquer a depraved human nature. This relatively hopeful view of human nature, and consequent emphasis on human responsibility in the world, was to influence Brown's political thinking. Ever the realist, he was also determined, by faith, to live in hope.

Brown developed an early enthusiasm for Barth, whom he read in a way not common in his time (or now, for that matter). He knew that Barth had drafted the famous Barmen Declaration, which condemned Nazism and in essence established the anti-Nazi "Confessing Church" of Germany during World War II. Among Brown's unpublished notes is an excerpt from Barth's *Church Dogmatics* (II/1): "God always stands unconditionally and passionately on this side and on this side alone: against the lofty and on behalf of the lowly; against those who already enjoy right and privilege and on behalf of those who are denied it and deprived of it." And, from Barth's collected writings, *Against the Stream*, Brown preserved the following text:

The Church is witness of the fact that the Son of Man came to seek and to save the lost. And this implies that . . . the Church must concentrate first on the lower and lowest levels of human society. The poor, the socially and economically weak and threatened, will always be the objects of its primary and particular concern, and it will always insist on the State's special responsibility for these weaker members of society.

That it will bestow its love upon them [is] the most important thing; but it must not concentrate on this and neglect the other thing to which it is committed by its political responsibility; the effort to achieve such a fashioning of the law as will make it impossible for "equality before the law" to become a cloak under which strong and weak, independent and dependent, rich and poor, employers and employees, in fact receive different treatment at its hands: the weak being unduly restricted, the strong unduly protected. The church must stand for social justice in the political sphere. (*Against the Stream*, p. 36)

Although Brown was to move later on in life to other theological influences, these theological foundations were to shape Brown's public career as theologian and ordained servant of the gospel. And they were essential to what we are calling his "spirituality."

However, the most enduring theological influence upon Brown throughout his life came from a theologian-martyr, Dietrich Bonhoeffer, whom Brown vividly describes in a sermon included in this book. Bonhoeffer's courage to stand up to the Nazis, even to the point of execution, stirred Brown's heart and imagination in the years following his seminary days at Union. And Bonhoeffer's theology, particularly his ethics but also his spirituality (as evidenced in *Letters and Papers from Prison*) would shape Brown in fundamental ways. Bonhoeffer's name would lace Brown's sermons and public pronouncements in many political and ecclesiastical contexts through the years.

After seminary, the Navy, and a teaching stint at Amherst, Brown enrolled in a doctoral program in religion at Columbia, where he wrote a dissertation on the nineteenth-century British theologian, P. T. Forsyth, whom he called a prophet for the twentieth century. In Forsyth he found many of the themes that would sound in his own life and work in the years to come, particularly an understanding of faith that could not evade activity within the world. Christianity could not be world-shunning but had to engage the world as we find it. Fortified by his Niebuhrian realism, Brown was to develop a world-engaging theology in the early years of his pastoral and academic career, both at Macalester and later at Union, where he became a member of the faculty shortly after his dissertation was finished.

To the West Coast and a New World

Fourteen years at Stanford were to follow Union, a wrenching move for him and for Union, as well as for the Brown family. The transition from a seminary environment to the halls of a great secular university was both challenging and freeing, as was the move from the East Coast to the West Coast. This was the height of the "secular Christianity" movement, and the idea of being sent from the church into the world spoke powerfully to Brown. Almost instantly he became a much-sought-after teacher, due not only to his teaching style, but to his approach to religion, which was far from archly academic or churchy. His courses on Christianity and literature drew scores of students who were reading Camus alongside the Bible.

His arrival at Stanford coincided with two other involvements that were to mark his career. The first was his participation in the civil rights movement. Brown had already participated in the Freedom Rides of 1961 and had been arrested with others for his actions. And in 1963 he would travel to Selma to participate in the preparations for the historic march to Montgomery. So he was already being seen by Stanford students, many of whom held no particular religious affiliation, as a courageous and committed Christian whom they respected and admired for his civil rights activities and fresh approach to Christianity's engagement with the world. (The opinions of some faculty and conservative alumni were another matter.) Second, Brown had hardly arrived at Stanford before he was traveling to Rome to attend the Council. There developed a minor celebrity around the professor from Stanford, confirmed by the January 3, 1966, issue of *Newsweek*, which carried his picture on the cover.

It was also during the Stanford years that the United States escalated the war in Vietnam, through the mid-1960s and well into the 1970s. For those who did not live through this period, it is difficult to convey in brief fashion the sense of dramatic social change, indeed of social and even political revolution, that was discussed and undertaken in the country. And in an era before "social media," the universities served as the nerve centers of both organization and action on behalf of de-escalation of the war and withdrawal from Vietnam. The protest against the war was intensified in reaction to the Selective Service system, or the draft, which was sending hundreds of thousands of young men to war, and ultimately fifty thousand to their deaths. Factor into this the explosions of racial violence in the form of riots throughout the country, but especially in Los Angeles and Detroit; the assassinations of the Kennedys, of Martin Luther King, and of Malcolm X; the upheaval of established religious institutions, including the Catholic Church; the sexual revolution and the simultaneous condemnation of artificial birth control by the Vatican; the political and street uprisings in Paris, Prague, Tokyo, Mexico City, and elsewhere: it was a time of seemingly unprecedented upheaval, if not revolution. And standing as a dark background to all of this, through 1974, was the tragic war in Vietnam.

Brown became highly active in his opposition to the war, giving sermons and public speeches on the moral iniquity of the war, counseling draft resisters, getting arrested in acts of civil disobedience, and traveling to both Washington and Europe with peace commissions. He was often in the company of fellow antiwar activists Daniel Berrigan and William Sloane Coffin.

One of Brown's most audacious moves was to publish an article in the October 31, 1967, issue of *LOOK* magazine, "Because of Vietnam. . . . In Conscience I Must Break the Law." This article drew the ire of many fellow Presbyterians, as well as conservative Stanford alumni, but the Stanford administration stood by him. Perhaps his most prophetic and courageous sermon during this period was delivered at Stanford on Christmas Eve 1972 (published in this book), just as American bombers were engaged in a massive carpet bombing of Hanoi, the capital of North Vietnam.

During the Stanford years, Brown encountered two people who were later to play an important role in his development as a theologian and prophetic Christian leader. The first was Gustavo Gutiérrez, who is sometimes called the "father of liberation theology." Brown knew, upon reading proofs of *A Theology of Liberation*, that he was going to have to rethink his entire approach to theology. Theology could no longer come first, with various possible applications of theory coming second. From now on, as Brown would remind listeners, theology was to become the "second act," the reflective moment. The "first act" would be the experience of human beings afflicted by poverty, marginalization, and oppression—starting from the ground of history, and their efforts to grapple with and overcome these forms of suffering: praxis. Praxis would feed theoretical reflection, and theoretical reflection would in turn inform praxis. Gutiérrez also got Brown to thinking critically about Marx and socialism and, with it, the limitations of capitalism in ways that he had not considered up to that time. Brown was later to become a good friend of Gustavo's and a close follower of religion and politics in Latin America. His book on Gustavo is still a very useful introduction not only to Gustavo's life, but to the main lines of liberation theology as Gutiérrez outlined them.

The second major influence at this time was Elie Wiesel, later to become a Nobel Peace Prize winner, who visited Stanford at Brown's invitation when Brown was serving as interim Dean of Chapel. Wiesel became a close and dear friend and a source of spiritual teachings for Brown, particularly in his evocation of the prophets and of the teachings of the rabbis in addressing the intractable puzzles of evil and suffering, problems that had drawn Brown's attention from an early stage of his pastoral and academic life. Wiesel's literary approach to consideration of the grave challenges to faith in God presented by the Holocaust, and his own movement from a Holocaust survivor who had lost his faith to a human being who could find new ways of questioning God, harmonized not only with Brown's enduring questions, but with his own passion for literature and a "theology of story."

The trajectories set by both of these friendships matured during the three years Bob and Sydney Brown returned to Union, where he had been appointed professor of ecumenics and world Christianity. While this appointment was to prove a temporary waystation on the journey, it gave rise to his works on both liberation theology and the thought of Elie Wiesel, whose literary approach to faith dovetailed with Brown's own literary imagination. Wiesel's friendship also gave a deeply personal context to Brown's decades-long passion for exploring the contours of Jewish-Christian relations in light of the Holocaust.

The Browns returned to California in 1979, where he served as professor of theology and ethics at the Graduate Theological Union, eventually retiring in 1986. It was during these years that the collaboration that Bob and Sydney had long hoped for came closer to fruition. Sydney had not only served as mainstay for the family and for Bob through all the years; she was also

a life-long activist. Born in China in the 1920s to progressive-
minded Presbyterian missionaries, she grew up in Nanking. Her
father taught public health at the university and her mother
taught English. Sydney returned to the United States for college and graduated from Smith, where she had worked with the
American Friends Service Committee, and then earned an M.A.
in sociology from Haverford. Her thesis was on American policy
toward Japanese-Americans in the United States, who had just
recently been interned during World War II. Her activist faith
was put to work during the years of the Freedom Rides and the
war protests, but it was during those same years that she became
interested in socially productive ways to work, especially for
minorities and women. She founded the Bayshore Employment
Service and also New Ways to Work during the 1970s. It was
partly out of this experience that she and Bob co-delivered the
prestigious Earl Lectures at the Pacific School of Religion in
1978 on the theology of work. And she taught several courses of
her own in Berkeley. Later she expanded her palette to include
the environment, founding the Bay Area Toxics Coalition and
become director of the Northern California Interfaith Council
on Economic and Environmental Justice. She was as tireless and
committed as Bob and served as a sounding board and catalyst.
Anyone who knows the story of Bob Brown knows that it is
really the story of Bob and Sydney Brown.

Spirituality and Politics

While Brown wrote a book on spirituality, *Spirituality and Liberation: Overcoming the Great Fallacy* (Westminster, 1988),
virtually all of his works breathe his own brand of prophetic
Christianity. Still, he did not write extensively on the topic of
"spirituality" itself. This is partly due to the fact that Bob was
naturally reticent about talking about himself, and particularly about personal matters involving his God. But, perhaps
more substantively, it also had to do with the fact that his own

Protestant tradition did not concern itself with "spirituality" in the way Catholicism did. It was natural for a Protestant coming from a moderate Calvinist background to explore how God relates to us and to the world and to discover in that exploration the depths of God's love, and then how best to respond to that love responsibly, which is to live in accordance with God's will. But he did not work from a particular tradition or school of spirituality apart from his solid Presbyterian roots and the personal and religious influences already mentioned.

However, he did in some places sketch out what some today might label a "spirituality." In an early sermon on predestination, Brown unpacks that old Calvinist puzzle in two breathtakingly simple moves. First, the doctrine asserts the sovereignty of God in all human affairs and in creation. This means that we must not mistake what is God's with what is our own; we must avoid the substitution of an idol of any kind for God, whether it be personal gain, wealth, or political ideology. An aversion to idolatry in any form—anything that denies the sovereignty of God—appears in countless places among Bob's writings. Second, the doctrine of predestination concerns the free and responsible human response to God's sovereignty. We are not pawns in a game that God has set up in advance. We remain free, and it is God's sovereignty that establishes that freedom. (This we have already noted as a theme in Brunner's theology.) We are therefore responsible for carrying out the divine will in human affairs. And this means that Christian life is fundamentally political, and the political cannot be evaded in the name of faith. We cannot remain neutral, on the sidelines of human life as it is. All of this is informed by a critical reading of the prophetic and gospel traditions, and that reading will lead us in the direction of concern for the poor, the afflicted, the weakest among us, as well as for a reign of peace. We live and work in hope for the establishment of the Kingdom of God on earth, a kingdom that God will establish and, like the people of Israel, that we may

not live to see in its entirety. But we live by faith in hope, and
through a love expressed not only in words, but in deeds. That,
in a nutshell, is Bob Brown's spirituality, a spirituality (or way of
being Christian) that implies that a lived faith in God necessarily
implies political work for justice and peace. Conversely, political
work for justice and peace leads us to the God who loves us so
much as to require that we work with God for the establishment
of the Kingdom.

And so we have in Bob Brown's writings a vivid prophetic
spirituality, where faith and practice, prayer and action, words
and deeds, and religion and politics constitute a circle. Theologically put, theory does not come first; rather theology starts
from the reality of lived human experience, and formal or spec-
ulative theology is Gutiérrez's "second act," necessary but not
sufficient for a life of Christian witness to the prophetic claims
and seemingly impossible demands of the gospel. This is a living and lived spirituality, not a recipe for spiritual comfort. In
Ignatian terms, any "consolation" can be discerned not only
in the light but in both light and dark moments. For Brown,
the "beauty" of God is also disclosed in the darkness of poverty, of humiliation, of suffering, and of tragedy. God is equally
disclosed in the "No" we must declare in the face of injustice
(a Barthian echo), whether it be found within society or the
precincts of the church. Thus, an integral aspect of a prophetic
spirituality is the courage to act on the subversive message of
Jesus, to practice the power of powerlessness, to dissent in the
face of lies, to become a "moral minority," indeed a kind of
heretic in the eyes of the proper. And if this leads to imprisonment and even death, as it did for Bonhoeffer and countless
others, then so be it: this is what the call includes.

A final note on God: This is a spirituality that claims God is
actively concerned with and engaged in human affairs and the
reality of creation. Brown's God is the God of the Old Testament
and rabbinical tales, a God who weeps over the human condition

and who seeks the liberation of the chosen people. This is a God who so aches to see justice accomplished and wrongs righted that God enters the human world in the person of an itinerant Jewish preacher who is rejected by religious and state authorities and strung up to die alone in a garbage dump—a criminal's death. But this is also a God who stirs hope in the hearts of those who wish to share in God's desires for the human family and for the earth and who, through the wind of the Spirit, propels them forward into the world to accomplish God's will. This is not an ethereal, otherworldly God. This is the God of love, of mercy, of justice, and of peace whom Jesus proclaimed. This is a God of both spirituality and politics.

A Personal Word

The compilation of these writings has been a labor of love. I am one of thousands of former students of Robert McAfee Brown who was deeply moved and informed by his words and actions, the integrity of his life, his courage as a Christian, his activism as an academic, and his witness to the gospel of justice and peace. As a Catholic undergraduate at Stanford, I had the privilege of studying with him in a seminar on Dietrich Bonhoeffer and then working with him on my senior essay on Reinhold Niebuhr and Teilhard de Chardin on the problem of evil. I was also witness to the power of his words and actions during the campus mobilizations against the Vietnam War. He was a constant challenge and inspiration, not only intellectually, but through his active faith. Brown opened my Catholic eyes—already awakened to hope as a result of the Second Vatican Council—to the necessity of a Protestant counterpoint in working out a Christian theology and practice for the world. My experience was hardly unique. Bob Brown's former students—Protestant, Catholic, Jewish, humanist, atheist—bear the stamp of his prophetic faith. They are teaching, writing, and laboring in many vineyards today: academic, pastoral, and secular, and their hearts still carry the imprint of Brown's seriousness, humor, and self-deprecating humility.

As the years went on, I saw Bob and Sydney more often. We were reunited during his visiting professorship at Santa Clara University, and then, later, during the years of his illness. I was privileged to become friendly with the Thomson side of the clan during my two years of teaching at Weston Jesuit School of Theology in Cambridge, Massachusetts. It was at the start of that teaching stint, in September 2011, scarcely a week before 9-11, that Bob died. The celebration of his life in the town of Heath, replete with hours of down-home singing, was something I shall never forget.

The summer before Bob's death I had discussed with him the idea of collating his papers for deposit in a library collection one day. He suggested with typical modesty that there wasn't much there, but gave the green light. Two summers after his death, Judy Dunbar and I went through the papers and prepared an inventory. In 2010 Sydney Brown donated them to the Flora Lamson Hewlett Library at the Graduate Theological Union in Berkeley. Sydney donated her own papers in 2012. This book was the suggestion of the director of the Hewlett Library, Robert Benedetto, who helped shepherd the collection to the Hewlett Library.

Why this book now? It is a reasonable question, but the answer for me is simple: I strongly believe that we need to recover for Christian faith the kind of prophetic conviction and voice that Bob Brown offered us not so long ago. Indeed, just after 9-11 and the subsequent scale-up to the Second Gulf War, many of us who knew Bob wished for his voice at such a time—a prophetic voice that would cut through the lies that were being generated by high-level Bush administration officials in order to commence hostilities. Equally, his prophetic voice would have been welcome in recent debates about "religious liberty" coming from conservative sectors of the churches today—an understanding far at odds with the notion of "religious liberty" as expressed by the Second Vatican Council, a teaching that Bob knew better than most Catholic bishops. To put it simply, Catholics today are missing the helpfulness of a classic Protestant counterpoint, and Protestants are missing the voice of an articulate communicator of their own theological tradition.

With only one exception, nothing in this book has been reproduced elsewhere, to my knowledge, although it is almost impossible to make that an infallible claim, as Brown frequently reworked texts for various occasions and then published them. And this book has a limited aim, suited to the distinguished series in which it appears. This is not *The Essential Robert McAfee Brown*. That is a different and much larger project, hopefully to come, drawing on previously published sources, both books and articles. Nor can we cover here every dimension of Brown's life and work, much less all topics on which he discoursed for years (e.g., literature, children's stories, or the theology of story). Thus we are forced to exclude some of the very personal notes, letters, and family sermons on the occasions of baptisms, marriages, and illness that so reveal Brown's soul. What I have included here, then, are some of his spiritual and political writings under different rubrics: his own spiritual and theological foundations, some specific writings on spirituality, his lifelong struggle for human rights, his work in peace activism, and the role that his spirituality plays in his approach to ecumenism and interfaith solidarity. These are not "airtight" categories, as so much of Brown's work is synthetic, drawing upon several of these topics simultaneously. But they are broad organizational topics that will, I hope, guide the reader more deeply into the writings of a prophet.

I have made prudential editorial decisions in preparing these papers for publication. Some references that refer to specific events have been omitted, and all the texts have been edited to a standard style. In cases where Bob himself would have wished for inclusive language, that has been supplied, unless the nature of the text or its context have called for keeping the original language.

I hope as well that this book will acquaint readers who do not know of Robert McAfee Brown's life or work with a period in recent history when there were several outstanding Christian voices in the political sphere who were guided by religious principles that were distinctively prophetic and not culturally conservative. For those who are already acquainted with Brown, my hope is that this volume will offer texts that reveal the spiritual dimension of Bob's life and work. I am sure he would not want us to take all of it *too* seriously, but just seriously enough to get on with the work that remains to be done by us, his fellow travelers.

PAUL CROWLEY, S.J.
Santa Clara University

Robert McAfee Brown:
A Chronology

1920   Born to Rev. George Brown and Ruth McAfee Brown on May 28, 1920, in Carthage, Illinois

1939–43   Amherst College, majoring in philosophy, with a senior thesis on Quaker views of war; meets Sydney Thomson

1943   Enrolls at Union Theological Seminary; becomes protégé of Reinhold Niebuhr and John Bennett

1944   Marries Sydney Thomson Pastoral summer in Higgins, North Carolina

1945   Ordained by New York Presbytery; enlists in Navy as chaplain, serves aboard USS *Bollinger* in the Pacific

1946   Teaching assistant and assistant chaplain, Amherst College, and assistant pastor at First Congregational Church, Amherst

1948   Begins doctoral studies at Columbia

1949–50   Fulbright Fellowship to Mansfield College, Oxford

1950   Teaches at Union Theological Seminary while working on doctorate at Columbia on the theology of P. T. Forsyth

1951–53   Head of Religion Department at Macalester Col-
          lege, St. Paul, Minnesota; works on re-election
          campaign of Eugene McCarthy to Congress and
          preaches against McCarthyism (political investiga-
          tions of Communism conducted by Senator Joseph
          McCarthy of Wisconsin)

1952   Book: *P. T. Forsyth: Prophet for Today* (Westminster)

1953   Returns to Union Theological Seminary as Auburn
          Assistant Professor of Systematic Theology; is pro-
          moted to Full Professor in 1959, followed by sab-
          batical in Scotland

1955   Book: *The Bible Speaks to You*, 2nd ed. (Westmin-
          ster, 1985)

1956   Book: *The Significance of the Church* (Westminster)

1960   John F. Kennedy elected as first Catholic president

          Book: *An American Dialogue: A Protestant Looks at
          Catholicism and a Catholic Looks at Protestantism*,
          with Gustave Weigel, S.J. (Doubleday)

1961   Participates in Freedom Rides; arrested and, after
          appeals, jailed with other Freedom Riders in Talla-
          hassee, Florida, in 1964.

1962   Arrives at Stanford as Professor of Religion; stays
          until 1975.

          Second Vatican Council is convened; adjourns in
          1965

1963   Participates in March on Washington and prepara-
          tions for the Selma to Montgomery March.

          North American representative of the World Alliance
          of Reformed and Presbyterian Churches as observer
          at the second session of the Second Vatican Council.

1963   Assassination of President Kennedy

1964   Passage of Civil Rights Act by Congress

1965   Joins Clergy and Laymen Concerned about Vietnam, an ecumenical group, teaming up with Daniel Berrigan, Abraham Heschel, William Sloane Coffin, and others, commencing years of antiwar activism; by 1967, the FBI begins assembling a file on Brown

       Brown works with Migrant Ministry and César Chávez's United Farm Workers in pursuit of farmworkers' justice

       Watts Riots

1966   Book: *An Observer in Rome* (Doubleday)

       Book: *The Spirit of Protestantism* (Oxford University Press)

       Book: *The Presbyterians* (Paulist)

1967   Book: *The Ecumenical Revolution* (Doubleday)

       Book: *Vietnam: Crisis of Conscience*, with Abraham J. Heschel and Michael Novak (Association Press, Behrman House, and Herder and Herder)

       Detroit Riots

1968   Delegate to World Council of Churches Assembly in Uppsala, Sweden, where he is exposed to third world concerns as well as to the notion of "secular ecumenism," which gave central focus to social justice for the world's oppressed peoples

1968   Tet Offensive, Johnson withdraws from presiden-
        tial race; assassinations of Martin Luther King and
        Robert Kennedy; Chicago Riots; *Humanae Vitae*
        birth control encyclical of Pope Paul VI; CELAM
        Conference in Medellín, Colombia

1970   U.S. invasion of Cambodia, resulting in widespread
        protests, including the shooting deaths of four pro-
        testing students at Kent State University, Ohio

1971   Arrested and jailed with students on Good Friday
        (Passover) for blocking sidewalk in front of Berkeley
        Draft Board

1972   Interim Dean of the Chapel, Stanford, expanding the
        role of interreligious voices on the Stanford campus;
        visits Israel; active in anti-Apartheid campaigns;
        presents daily addresses at the General Assembly of
        the Presbyterian Church of Southern Africa during
        the summer

        Arrested in Congressman Charles Gubser's office as
        part of antiwar delegation to Washington, D.C.; the
        Christmas Eve Sermon

        Book:*The Pseudonyms of God* (Westminster)

1973   "Mission of Desperation" ecumenical group travels
        to England, the Netherlands, Germany, and Italy to
        plead for peace with world leaders

        Book: *Religion and Violence: A Primer for White
        Americans* (Stanford Alumni Association); later pub-
        lished as *Religion and Violence,* 2d ed. (Westminster,
        1987)

        Book: *Frontiers for the Church Today* (Oxford Uni-
        versity Press)

1974   Invites Elie Wiesel to Stanford; a lifelong friendship takes root

Book: *Is Faith Obsolete?* (Westminster)

1975   Attends "Theology of the Americas" conference in Detroit and meets major liberation theologians, including Gustavo Gutiérrez, with whom a friendship develops over the years; later visits Peru

Keynote speaker at World Council of Churches assembly in Nairobi, Kenya

Delegate, Conference of the Fund for Reconstruction and Reconciliation in Indochina (World Council of Churches), Vientiane, Laos

1976   Returns to Union Seminary as professor of ecumenics and world Christianity, establishing contacts with Jewish Theological Seminary and attempting to connect Union with third world theological centers and theologians; Sydney Brown is named co-director of a new program in ecumenics; travels through South and Central America

1977   Brown joins Elie Wiesel and others in lectures on the Holocaust at Northwestern University; interviews Fidel Castro in Cuba

1978   Appointed member of President's Commission on the Holocaust, visiting Holocaust and other sacred Jewish sites with Wiesel; later appointed to the renamed United States Holocaust Memorial Council, which drew up plans for the National Holocaust Memorial Museum in Washington, D.C.; resigns in 1986, protesting Reagan's visit to Bitburg Cemetery, West Germany, where Nazi SS personnel are buried

1978   Participant in WCC Faith and Order meeting in
        Bangalore, India

        Book: *Theology in a New Key* (Westminster)

1979   Brown leaves Union and joins the faculty of Pacific
        School of Religion, a member school of the Gradu-
        ate Theological Union, Berkeley, remaining until
        retirement in 1986.

        CELAM Conference in Puebla, Mexico

        Book: *The Collected Writings of St. Hereticus* (West-
        minster)

        Arrested in nonviolent protests against weapons
        research and Contra war in Nicaragua

1980   Assassination of Archbishop Oscar Romero of San
        Salvador and murder of four U.S. churchwomen in
        El Salvador

        Book: *Creative Dislocation—The Movement of
        Grace* (Abingdon)

        Book: *Gustavo Gutiérrez* (John Knox)

1981   Book: *Making Peace in the Global Village* (Westmin-
        ster)

1983   Brown begins years-long involvement in work
        against U.S. Contra policies in Nicaragua, visiting in
        1985 and 1986 and befriending minister of educa-
        tion, Fr. Fernando Cardenal, S.J.

        Book: *Elie Wiesel: Messenger to All Humanity*
        (Notre Dame)

1984   Becomes active in the "Sanctuary Movement" in the
        U.S., addressing the Commonwealth Club of San
        Francisco in June 1986 on "The Case for Sanctuary"
        and travels to Guatemala and El Salvador

Book: *Unexpected News—Reading the Bible with Third World Eyes* (Westminster)

1985   Retires from Pacific School of Religion; over the years accepts teaching posts at Dartmouth, Carleton, and Santa Clara

1986   Book: *Saying Yes and Saying No: On Rendering to God and Caesar* (Westminster)

Book: *The Essential Reinhold Niebuhr* (Yale)

1988   Participates in the twenty-fifth Anniversary of the National Council of Churches in the Philippines in Manila

Book: *Spirituality and Liberation: Overcoming the Great Fallacy* (Westminster)

1989   Fall of the Berlin Wall; Tiananmen Square massacre in Beijing; Jesuit martyrdoms in El Salvador

1990   Returns to El Salvador to visit the University of Central America where six Jesuits, their housekeeper, and daughter were slain

Book: *Gustavo Gutiérrez: An Introduction to Liberation Theology* (Orbis)

1991   Speaks out against Desert Storm (First Gulf War)

1992   Book: *Persuade Us to Rejoice: The Liberating Power of Fiction* (Westminster)

1990s   Continues to speak out on behalf of social justice and human rights, including LGBT rights in the Presbyterian Church and wider society

1993   Book: *Liberation Theology: An Introductory Guide* (Westminster)

1994   Book: *Reclaiming the Bible: Words for the Nineties* (Westminster John Knox)

1997   Book: *Speaking of Christianity: Practical Compassion, Social Justice and Other Wonders* (Westminster John Knox)

1998   Book: *Dark the Night, Wild the Sea* (a novel) (Westminster John Knox)

2001   Dies on September 3, 2001, Greenfield, Massachusetts

2005   *Reflections over the Long Haul: A Memoir* (Westminster John Knox)

HONORARY DEGREES

Amherst College, 1958
University of San Francisco, 1964
Lewis and Clark College, 1964
Loyola University, 1965
University of Notre Dame, 1965
Boston College, 1965
St. Louis University, 1966
Pacific School of Religion, 1967
St. Mary's College, 1968
Hamilton College, 1969
Kalamazoo College, 1980
Kenyon College, 1981
Hebrew Union College, 1982
Lehigh University, 1988
Carleton College, 1993
Lafayette College, 1993
Santa Clara University, 1993

A Personal Creed

Upon return to California after several years in New York and then working primarily in Berkeley, Brown needed to apply for certification as a Presbyterian minister in the Presbytery of San Jose, within which First Presbyterian Church of Palo Alto is located. The Presbytery asked for a "Vita and Statement of Faith." Brown used the occasion to issue a salutary challenge to more staid formulations of faith.

Vita: ordained 1945, Presbytery of New York City; U.S. Navy chaplaincy, Pacific theater; two years parish ministry; PhD (Columbia); subsequent ministry through teaching theology (Macalester College, Union Seminary, Stanford University, Pacific School of Religion); and an "apostolate of the pen" through writing theology for lay persons.

STATEMENT OF FAITH

I can summarize my faith in two words of the early church, *Kurios Christos* (Christ is Lord), or in ten words of Samuel Crossman, "Love the loveless shown, that they might lovely be." To spell out either affirmation demands many pages, and my instruction to cover no more than "two sides of a single sheet" has been taxing. Within such compass I cannot easily join the two sides of the gospel—personal assurance and social challenge—so I juxtapose two different forms of confession derived from a single source.

PART ONE

I believe that the ultimate disposition of who I am is in the hands of One whose hands are ultimately sustaining and gracious, however sternly they have to deal along the way with recalcitrant cargo as myself.

I believe that I get clues enough and to spare about the nature of reality from ongoing confrontation with the Jesus story and even from occasional confrontation (usually through another person) with Jesus himself.

I believe that such clues are confirmed a hundredfold by who my wife is, who my children are, and who a few incredibly dear friends continue to be.

I believe that I am part of a further circle beyond those just named, who occasionally manage to put others ahead of themselves and God ahead of all, a circle to which I give the name of "church."

I believe that there are tasks to do that give meaning to our lives, and that the degree of our own individual success or failure is of little consequence, since God empowers others to pick up and fulfill whatever we do for good and to transform and redeem whatever we do for ill.

I believe that conversion is not only about changing individual hearts but also about changing social structures, not just cosmetically but radically. This means chipping away at, and perhaps destroying, many things we have taken for granted and building into our own situation what many third world friends have found to be true in theirs, that "to know God is to do justice."

I believe that there are little moments when vast things happen; when bread and wine are shared in certain ways; when brisk walks in the woods are shared with certain persons; when someone else says "thank you" to me, or when I remember to say "thank you" to someone else; when children rise up and bless us simply by who they are; when Beethoven string quartets pierce us with both the joy and woe of our being, the same joy and woe that William Blake assured us were "woven fine, a clothing for the soul divine."

I believe that our lives provide the occasion for flashes of fulfillment, no matter how much they are threatened by surrounding darkness, and that we can even begin by grace to deal with the surrounding darkness, because we have it on high authority that light shines in the darkness and the darkness has not overcome it.

PART TWO

Here I follow the form of the Barmen Declaration,[1] linking affirmations with negations. Although the gospel is finally Yes and not No, a No can make explicit what is only implicit in the Yes.

1. *Scripture.* I say Yes to Scripture as our means of access to the story of God's people; I say No to Scripture as a repository of doctrine.

I say Yes to Scripture as radically "good news to the poor," which can also be good news to the rest of us; I say No to Scripture as consolation apart from its radical social challenge.

2. *Jesus Christ.* I say Yes to Jesus, a Jew from Nazareth, who embodies the present reality of God's Kingdom as *Christos* (God's anointed one); I say No to a deified Jesus whose humanity is thereby negated.

I say Yes to Jesus' life, death, and resurrection not only as sources for our own individual transformation, but as points of decisive confrontation between the power of God and the power of human society that tried to destroy Jesus on the cross. God reversed all expectations by the resurrection, and Jesus' followers became citizens of a totally new order. I say No to interpretations of Jesus that reduce these events to an individualistic meaning.

I say Yes to Jesus as the Jew whose mission to the Gentiles makes possible our inclusion in the promises of God; I say No to attempts to convert Jews to Christianity, since they are already God's covenant people.

3. *God.* I say Yes to the biblical God who shares our plight in suffering love and thereby opens the way for us to love one another; I say No to an all-powerful God who would thereby be responsible for evil, whether the murder of six million Jews or the unjust death of a single child.

I say Yes to the biblical God as the true God in distinction from false gods; I say No to the false gods, believing that continual No-saying to our most dangerous contemporary false god—uncritical nationalism—is a way of saying Yes to the true God. That means saying No when our government invades other countries, breaks international law, deports political refugees to sure death, supports military dictators, and gives priority to the arms race over the needs of the poor.

I say Yes to the ongoing presence and power of God in the Holy Spirit; I say No to our attempts to limit how the Spirit will act.

4. *Human nature.* I say Yes to the image of God in every person, including migrant workers, women, Sandinistas,[2] and homosexuals; I say No to those who deny that image by rewarding the rich at the expense of the poor. I say No to the church that denies full participation to women by *de facto* discrimination in jobs, pay, and use of noninclusive language, and I say no to the church that denies ordination to homosexuals, forcing them to lie if they wish to fulfill God's calling to them.

I say Yes to the presence of sin not only in human hearts but in political and economic structures that exalt competition at the price of destroying others; I say No to those who tell us that sin is the monopoly of our enemies.

I say Yes to the transforming power of divine and human forgiveness; I say No to the proposition that we ever move beyond the need for such forgiveness.

I say Yes to God's concern for every human being and the consequent need for society as a whole to provide basic human necessities for all; I say No to those who leave such tasks to the whim of private charities.

5. *The church.* I say Yes to the church that stresses liberty to the captives; I say No to the church that denies "the cry of the poor" by accepting social structures that violate the poor.

I say Yes to the church that celebrates God's liberating power with bread and wine; I say No to those who do not affirm that accepting food and drink at Christ's table means ensuring food and drink on all other tables.

I say Yes to the need for the church to take sides; I say No to the church when it claims that political or economic neutrality is possible.

I say Yes to the importance of sharing our faith with others; I say No to sharing built on fear or coercion that promises salvation only to those who verbally acknowledge Jesus as Lord.

6. *Eschatology.* I say Yes to a generous view of the power of God's grace to overcome sin and death; I say No to a belief that reliance on grace can exempt us from the ongoing struggle for justice.

I say Yes to the Kingdom of God as a present possibility in this world; I say No to the Kingdom of God as only a future possibility in another world.

I say Yes to the joy of living in a world where "the mercies of God are fresh every morning"; I say No to any ultimate denial of those mercies.

7. *Conclusion.* I say Yes to the ongoing need to restate our faith; I say No to any claim that it can be stated adequately on two sides of a single sheet of paper.

NOTES

1. The Barmen Declaration, issued in 1934 by the Confessing Church and with the full participation of theologian Karl Barth, was a ringing denunciation of nationalist ideology that would subordinate the Word of God to the state, a declaration of the Lordship of Jesus Christ, and a stinging rebuke to Nazi ideology. Brown adopts here the dialectical structure of Barthian theology, evident in such works as *Epistle to the Romans*.

2. The Sandinistas were a revolutionary political party in Nicaragua that overthrew the dictatorship of Anastasio Somoza in 1979 under the leadership of Daniel Ortega. They were the target of U.S. government "contra" warfare, which Brown vigorously protested.

1
Foundations of a Prophetic Soul

The foundations of Brown's prophetic Christianity run like a deep stream in his personal and public life. An accomplished carpenter who could appreciate the beauty of a perfectly crafted joist, he was also a deeply read lover of prose (especially Camus) and poetry (especially Auden), as well as of art (especially Matisse). He was also an accomplished pianist and cellist and a lover of classical music (especially Beethoven). The Protestant singing tradition was strong in his life and that of his family. The other great influence on the development of his prophetic soul was his Scripture, and especially the prophets. It was through the lenses of Isaiah, Jeremiah, Amos, and Hosea, among others, that he framed his understanding of the building blocks of Christian faith: sin and grace, suffering and redemption, faith and hope, as well as love. Another of his favorite texts, often quoted, was Hebrews 11. The following essays reflect these deeper waters, and some of the other sources that flowed through his career, not least Bonhoeffer, Niebuhr, and Wiesel.

BEAUTY ... AND THE HUMILIATED

Brown interlaced many of his sermons with musical references and on occasion coordinated the spoken word with organ melody, hymnody, or choral demonstration. He gave courses on the theology of hymnody in his early days at Union. After learning the cello, he formed an amateur trio at Stanford with two other faculty members, whose recitals were accompanied by whimsical program notes. Music was a source of both joy and inspiration for a soul that found equal footing in the real world. Brown was fond of quoting Bonhoeffer on the "cantus firmus" of faith that stands steady amid so much variation of life and politics.

The following two excerpts demonstrate how Brown used music as a theological source. The first, "Beauty . . . and the Humiliated," was given on November 3, 1978, at the Fiftieth Anniversary of the School of Sacred Music at Union Theological Seminary. (The School of Sacred Music was later transferred to Yale Divinity School.) The second, "Music: The Highest Form of Human Praise," was preached at Stanford Memorial Church on January 25, 1987. Notable is his evocation of some of the influences on his life, both literary and theological, as well as musical: Camus, C. S. Lewis, Bonhoeffer, and Wiesel, as well as Calvin and Daniel Berrigan—all in the service of a message that relates faith to the real world.

Despite my demonstrable amateur status as a musician, my theological writing has always been liberally sprinkled with musical allusions. This is not only my further debt of gratitude to you, but my admission that theological words are inadequate pointers to the reality they are trying to describe, an admission theologians do not usually make (in public), and my recognition that although no pointers are adequate, musical pointers are at least better than verbal ones. A number of years ago in a book on Protestantism I concluded, "Protestantism, when all is said and done, is more adequately represented by its hymns and prayers than by its textbooks." I still stand by that, though I was not prepared for a review that ended, "After having read the 264 pages of this particular textbook, one can only concur."

A sermon should have a text. I'm still enough of a Presbyterian to want to take my texts from Scripture, but today, when many of the hymns are based on biblical texts, a number of which I shall refer to, I have decided to go farther afield and take my text from a so-called "nonbeliever" and if that doesn't make John Calvin turn over in his grave, I don't know what can. My text comes from an early essay by Albert Camus, and it goes: "There is beauty and there are the humiliated. Whatever difficulties the enterprise may present, I would like never to be unfaithful either to the one or the other" (*Lyrical and Critical Essays*).

During the years I worked with many of you, beauty was pointed to by such words as "Sonata," "Great to Swell," "Down Ampney," "Opus 131," "pianissimo." Then for a while the guiding words for me shifted to pointers toward the humiliated—words like "oppression," "human rights," "CIA," "Vietnam," "imperialism," "civil disobedience." These latter words are still crucial for me: I intend for the rest of my life not to retreat one inch, if I can help it, from all that they represent.

But rather recently, and in wonderful ways, the world of beauty has for me been re-entering the world of concern for the humiliated, reminding me that Camus is right, and that however difficult the enterprise, I too—and you too—must try, as he says, "never to be unfaithful either to the one or the other." If concern for beauty alone can lead gradually to insulation and elitism, concern for the humiliated alone can lead swiftly to cynicism and despair. Gustavo Gutiérrez, our leading theologian of liberation and one totally committed to the humiliated, recently said of Ernesto Cardenal, a priest-poet, "We need very badly our poets." I am not trying to justify art merely for the sake of the uses to which it can be put, particularly in the service of a political or even theological cause; we have had enough as art as propaganda. All I am suggesting—and it is a lot—is that beauty, art, music, possessed as they are of an intrinsic value of their own, also sustain and nurture us in concern for the humiliated. I'll return to that a little later.

"There is beauty . . ." Camus reminds us, as though we need reminding. On second thought, perhaps we do. In the world of the humiliated, beauty is usually absent. In our own worlds, beauty is often dulled or distorted or destroyed. I suggest, boldly, that beauty is at the very heart of things. Usually theologians say that love is at the very heart of things, and I suggest that beauty and love cannot be separated. And if beauty is at the heart of things we are (for the purposes of today's service) already talking about music and song.

Let's press that for a moment. In one of his Narnia books, *The Magician's Nephew*, C. S. Lewis so arranges things that the reader is present at the moment of creation. Aslan the Lion, a Christ-figure, is the instrument of creation. How does creation come forth out of sheer nothingness? Aslan sings! Listen:

> In the darkness something was happening at last. A voice had begun to sing. . . . Its lower notes were deep enough to be the voice of the earth itself. There were no words. There was hardly even a tune. But it was, beyond comparison, the most beautiful voice [Digory] had ever heard. It was so beautiful he could hardly bear it. . . .

> Then two wonders happened at the same moment. One was that the voice was suddenly joined by other voices. . . . The second wonder was that the blackness overhead, all at once was blazing with stars. . . . Far away, and down near the horizon, the sky began to turn gray. . . . You could see shapes of hills standing up dark against it. All the time the Voice went on singing. . . . The eastern sky changed from white to pink and from pink to gold. The Voice rose and rose, till all the air was shaking with it. And just as it swelled to the mightiest and most glorious sound it had yet produced, the sun arose. . . .

Valleys, rivers, trees appear, even heather (suggesting to this old form-critic that Lewis must have written the book during a sabbatical in Scotland).

Now I'm not saying that that's a better creation story than the one in Genesis—a claim that would really make Calvin turn over in his grave. But I think Lewis is communicating an incredibly important truth: music and creation are part and parcel of the same thing. They can't be separated. It has been so from the very beginning. Music, beauty, is at the very heart of things. Those who deny it do not deny its truth; they merely affirm that they are spiritually tone deaf.

There are moments, fleeting moments, when we recapitulate that beauty ourselves. We create; or perhaps more accurately, through us something is created; or perhaps most accurately of all, through us God creates something. And it is all of a piece; everything fits, belongs, is clearly and undeniably meant to be just the way it is. The melody of the hymn we will sing as soon as I stop talking is to me an example of this. Listen: (*Organist plays the melody of 52 in* Ecumenical Praise, *"All Poor Men (Folk) and Humble"*).

That melody, unknown to me until I began to prepare for this service, has been in my life a gift of pure grace. Before hearing it, I was a little annoyed that the words "All Poor Folk and Humble," which I know and love to the Welsh tune *Olwen*, has been given another setting. And yet, the melody you have just heard seems to me to offer an almost perfect matching of words and music—communicating a sense of wonder, awe, wistfulness, simplicity, tenderness, love. Hearing it, I hear again that song of creating, Aslan's song, not now at the beginning of time, but repeated in a later moment of time, coming to me as creating itself first came to all of us—as a gift, undeserved, unexpected, and yet renewing and rekindling the human spirit by an infusion from the Divine Spirit. Once we know the words and music, we almost don't need the words anymore. The music says it all—a further reminder that Aslan's creation song had no words.

But I am not about to surrender words to oblivion. We will sing another hymn in a few moments, "My Song Is Love Unknown, A Savior's Love to Me." Here also is beauty, not only the beauty of John Ireland's melody that now and then moved in unexpected fashion, as though reminding us of the unexpected-ness of the story it celebrates—the story of "love unknown"—but also the beauty of words that communicate in a few lines what it takes theologians many volumes to communicate.

If I were told that I could have only the length of a ten-word telegram to communicate the gospel, to include everything that was crucial, to omit nothing that was essential, and to tell it in an unforgettable image, I would be in despair. "It can't be done," I would say or scream. And yet, back in the seventeenth cen-tury, old Samuel Crossman did it. For the two lines that imme-diately follow the title lines of the hymn do say it all. What is it we Christians sing about, what is our message? Ten words are enough: "Love to the loveless shown, that they might lovely be."

Notice how that message builds up. What is the center of the message? "Love." What kind of love? Love that loves just good people? Love that demands that we be worthy in order to receive it? No, it is "Love to the loveless": those without love, love to the unlovely, love to those who do not necessarily return it, love that does not demand that we be worthy in order to receive it, love to us.

How do we know that? Do we read a treatise about love? Does somebody tell us that such love is around? No, it is "Love to the loveless shown . . ." It is enacted love, demonstrated love, embodied love, "shown" love.

Why is love shown to the loveless? To make them feel guilty? To make them throw in the towel and grovel? To annihilate them in love's burning light? No, it is "Love to the loveless shown that they might lovely be." We who in the first line are described as "the loveless," those without love, can now, because of this amazing gift, be transformed into "the lovely," those who are love, to whom love is not only a possibility but a reality.

Now if you need some doctrines—conversion, justification, sanctification, grace, Christology, or whatever—it's all there in those ten words: "Love to the loveless shown that they might lovely be." Unbelievable. No wonder Crossman goes on, "Oh who am I, that for my sake, my Lord shall take frail flesh and die?" Who indeed? One who was "loveless" and is now empowered by the gift of God to be "lovely." If you want good news, good news that was launched from a stable, that is hard to beat.

So come, accept the invitation to our next hymn: "All poor folk and humble, all lame folk who stumble, come haste ye, nor feel ye afraid. For Jesus our treasure, with love past all measure, in lowly poor manger was laid." (*The sermon continued after a second group of hymns was sung.*)

"There is beauty," Camus said, "and there are the humiliated," he also said. We have looked at his first assertion briefly, let us now look even more briefly at his second assertion. How do we join the two together? How do we relate the incredible beauty that music represents, to the pain and suffering and anguish—to the humiliation—that is the experience of most people most of the time? We do not have to figure out the answer to that question on our own: the answer has already been given to us by God. We have sung about how "all poor folk and humble"—the humiliated of the earth—are invited to the stable. The carol continues, "And Jesus in beauty, accepted their duty." Yes, the act of God in sending Jesus into the world is an act of creative beauty, the supreme act of love, but it was love that from the very first endured humiliation. The scene was a stable, not an inn or a villa or a penthouse. It is a humiliated love, this beauteous love of which we sing. Beauty and the humiliated come together in the Jesus story. We will sing about it in a moment: "O love, How Deep, How Broad, How High." "How Beautiful," we might also say, if the meter only allowed it. But listen to what happens to that love: "For us to wicked men betrayed; scourged, mocked in purple robe arrayed; he bore the shameful cross and death, For us gave up his dying breath." Our God is a God whose beauty is expressed in the midst of humiliation.

For Camus, the question is: how can beauty and the humiliated be understood together? For the Christian the question is: how could they possibly be understood separately?

Recall the hymn we sang, "By Gracious Powers." It too, conjoins beauty and the humiliated. After affirming joyfully that "God is with us night and morning, and never fails to greet us each new day," the hymn goes on to acknowledge that our hearts are "tormented," that "civil days bring burdens hard to bear," that the cup we are given is often "filled to the brimming with bitter suffering." Even so, "we take it thankfully and without trembling out of so good and beloved a hand." This makes possible a new "brightness"—since the suffering path we walk is a suffering path along which God has walked with us, and helped us to conquer. But the recovery of joy is not lightly received; no, even at the end, "We shall remember all the days we lived through," the good and the bad, "and our whole life shall then be yours alone." Our whole life, not just the joy and the beauty, not just the pain and the humiliation, but all of it together with something that can be affirmed with gratitude.

Does that sound a little too neat, a little too schematic, a little too removed from life? Then look again at who wrote those words. Their author was Dietrich Bonhoeffer, who, as you know, spent a year at Union in 1931 and then returned to Union in 1939 on the eve of World War II, only to realize that he couldn't stay here but had to return to Germany and throw in his lot with those resisting Hitler—a decision that led, as he knew it would, to his death. The words we sang were written by him in prison as he awaited execution. He was able in the prison cell, in the midst of the humiliation, to affirm the beauty and the joy. He found that in both beauty and humiliation, God was present for him; the Jesus story brought together for him many things that otherwise would have remained apart.

That particular hymn brings together still other things that might otherwise remain apart, and this is a further grace that music sometimes gives to us. The writer of the words, Bonhoeffer, is German; the writer of the music, Père Gélineau,[1] is French. The writer of the words is a Lutheran; the writer of the music is a Roman Catholic, and a Jesuit at that. They would have been "enemies" in World War II, cut off from one another, separated. But in this hymn the separation is overcome. The gifts of German and French culture, of Protestant and Catholic tradition, are co-mingled here for us, and by their co-mingling lend further credibility to the affirmation that beauty and humiliation are likewise co-mingled.

This drawing together of so many things in one comprehensive unity, the wedding of words and music, of diverse cultures, of beauty and the humiliated, of things that might seem to be local and yet turn out to be universal, is imaged for us in many other hymns. We who work in the U.S.A. have sung about a Palestinian, "Christ the Worker," and the music for our singing comes from Ghana. First world, third world, Middle East! We, who are predominantly white, have sung "Rise an' Shine," and we are dependent on the black culture, which we have historically so opposed and devastated, for both the words and the music. That hymn not only sings of giving God glory, but tells us to do so "in the year of Jubilee," which we know from our own Old Testament was to be the year when social, economic, and political ills were set right, when slaves were to be freed, debts would be forgiven, a fresh start made possibly for everyone. God and politics—not two separate entities but interconnected realities neither of which we can ignore.

In a moment we will sing a hymn, "God in His Love"; the name of the tune is *Ecology*, and that is what it is about. We worship God on high and yet that same God has set us in the midst of the world and bade us take care of it. Yes, the earth is the Lord's, as the fifth verse reminds us, but also "It is ours to enjoy it," as well as take care of it. Updating the concerns of other centuries, the hymn ends with the petition, "Now from pollution, disease, and damnation, Good Lord deliver us, world without end."

So none of the concern for beauty is finally a moral copout. It plunks us firmly down in the midst of where we are. Where this is beauty apparent, we are to enjoy it; where there is beauty hidden, we are to unveil it; where there is beauty defaced, we are to restore it; where there is no beauty at all, we are to create it—all of which places us in the arena where humiliation occurs, where the humiliated congregate, and where we are called to struggle with them. We won't be on the mountaintops; we'll be back in the midst of the site about which Erik Routley's[2] hymn, "All Who Love and Serve Your City," speaks so well. In that city there are those who "curse," there is "loss and sorrow," there is "helpless strife." But there are those who "bless" as well as those who curse; there are those who "love and serve." The city need not be "the city of despair." Why not? Why is the city not only the arena of humiliation but also the arena of the potential and beauty? The final words of the hymn tell us why: because (in words Dr. Routley takes from the vision at the end of the book Ezekiel) the name of the city can be "The Lord is there." Jesus wept over the city of Jerusalem, but he also entered into it, went through his deep and bitter humiliation within it, and through that humiliation brought us beauty—Jeru-shalom—shalom, the peace, the beauty, that in the presence of the most threatening humiliation is our constant challenge and our deepest hope.

Prayer at the End of Service

O God, whose creative power is imaged for us in the music you bring to birth in our spirits so that our music, is finally your music; we give you thanks that you have given us voices to praise you in song, hands to praise you on instruments you give us the skill to make and play, and hearts to praise you through all that we do. We now offer you these gifts you have given us, so that through our praise others may be brought to praise you too, both so that you may be praised for your own sake and so that beauty, enlisted in your service, may also enlist us in the service of the humiliated, and all things conspire to make this world a world of song—so that in the end it may be as it was in the beginning.

These things we ask through Jesus Christ our Lord, your song to us, sung in ways we can understand, in whom your beauty shone forth in one who was humiliated, and whom you raised up from humiliation to live and reign with you, so that his song and your song could also be our song. Praise and thanks to you, forever and ever.

MUSIC: THE HIGHEST FORM OF HUMAN PRAISE

Elie Wiesel, the 1986 Nobel Peace Prize winner, writes about the deepest things of the human spirit and we respond. And yet Wiesel insists that his whole venture is ultimately a failure. He is trying to communicate what cannot be communicated—the reality of Hitler's death camps. It can't be done, he insists on the one hand, because there is nothing with which to compare the Holocaust. There are no words, no similes, no metaphors that will work. It can't be done, and yet, he insists on the other hand, it must be done. One must attempt to communicate, however inadequately, something of the horror of Auschwitz, because if one does not do so, it could all happen again.

That is a kind of negative pointer to the problem of trying to speak about God. To do so, as we attempt to do when we gather here for worship, is also doomed to failure, and for the same reason. There is no one with whom to compare God. To attempt to use finite words to communicate something of the reality of the Infinite can't be done, and yet it must be done. If the story of the Holocaust must be told again and again so that it will not be repeated and destroy life, the story of God must be told again and again so that it will be repeated and ennoble life.

Different subject matter but the same problem: how to communicate what cannot be communicated and yet must be communicated.

So, faced with an impossible task, people try all sorts of positive ways of pointing to the divine—sculpture, painting, architecture (of which this building [Stanford Memorial Church] is an exceedingly aggressive example, what Daniel Berrigan,[3] speaking once from this pulpit, called "the Celestial Fun House").

I personally believe that music is the highest form of human praise. Our words can sometimes take wings and soar into poetry, and our poetry can sometimes take wings and soar into song. Beethoven found out, in composing the Ninth Symphony, that when he wanted to communicate the reality of joy, he had to move beyond instrumentalism and introduce the human voice, an unprecedentedly bold maneuver on which all the critical evidence is not yet in. Even John Calvin (for whom, in the typical undergraduate lexicon, the adjective "joyful" is not likely to be associated) recognized that the verbal austerity of the classical creeds could be transformed in worship by having them sung so that even the creeds could be acts of praise and not just litmus paper tests of orthodoxy.

In fact it was one of the finest accomplishments of the Protestant Reformation that singing was restored to the congregation. Medieval polyphony had become so complex that only professional singers could master it, and so Luther introduced the tune, employing a simple melodic line that everyone could learn. Here is an example of one such melody: (organist plays melody of *"Von Himmel Hoch"*—*From Heaven Above*). That, you will notice, is little more than an exercise up and down the scale, and the last line is simply a descending octave with one tiny twist: (organist plays last line). Everybody could learn to sing such a melody. And listen to what it could become when harmonized (organist plays one verse of the chorale harmonized).

Music opens up channels of communication that words alone cannot provide. Consider that article of Christian faith that is most difficult to communicate with words—the doctrine of the Holy Spirit. I can guarantee that if I were now to give a short lecture on the Holy Spirit you would be more confused at its completion than you probably are now. There is a reason for this: the Holy Spirit points to precisely that dimension of the divine that cannot be caught in time or space or words or formulas—that which breaks all bounds and becomes more mysterious the more we think we understand. The doctrine of the Spirit points to God's hovering, brooding, invisible presence, the holy or the "other" that nevertheless can permeate our lives. Words limp and fall in the face of such a reality. A moment ago I appeared to slight medieval music: let me now atone for that by inviting you to hear from the choir a brief invocation of the Holy Spirit from medieval time, which communicates much more profoundly what I have been trying, without success, to put into words: (choir sings "*Veni Creator Spiritus*"—Come, Creator Spirit).

But we are not yet done with the Holy Spirit. For in the Bible the activity of the Spirit is not only one of a brooding presence, but one of intense activity, power, challenge, transformation. The verbal images most frequently invoked are earthquake, wind, and fire. When the Holy Spirit descended on the first disciples at Pentecost, as described in the Scripture lesson of the morning, they thought the house was falling apart. The imagery was whirlwind and fire—and whirlwind and fire are very volatile companions. This transforming power so filled the disciples themselves that onlookers thought they were drunk. (Peter, you remember, had to respond, "Drunk? Don't be silly. It's only nine o'clock in the morning.") Mere words simply can't communicate such power and energy. But music can. Listen to a portion of one of Bach's chorales, "*Komm, Heileger Geist*" (Come, Holy Spirit) which captures that sense of power and energy beyond what any words of mine can do (organist plays beginning and ending). Remember, you heard it here first: Johann Sebastian Bach is the greatest theologian of them all.

SIN AND REPENTANCE IN
CONTEMPORARY CHRISTIAN THOUGHT

Brown offered this undated paper at an unidentified Jewish-Christian symposium. In his own words: "What follows is not a paper for subsequent publication so much as an attempt to share certain problems as a basis for further discussion...." It reflects the strong influences upon his thinking and spiritual life of both Reinhold Niebuhr and liberation theology.

Where do we begin a discussion of sin, repentance, and atonement? Any systematic starting point is finally arbitrary; it is surely the experience of all of us that we are in a "theological circle" (whatever we call it), which means that any starting point already presupposes all the other points in the circle, including the conclusions, and until we have been fully around the circle we have hardly begun. Much Christian theology has begun with a doctrine of God, in the light of which sin is understood as defiance of God's will. Only in the light of which sin is forgiven can we understand how desperate was the plight from which we needed to be rescued. But other analyses start with the nature of the human condition, in its finitude, misery, and estrangement, and (once having established that we cannot save ourselves) the good news is that the gift of salvation for new beginnings has been provided by God. Wherever we start, if the good news presupposes the bad news, the bad news also presupposes the good news.

In this methodological dilemma, I propose that we take our cue from what is happening in a great deal of the contemporary Christian theology and begin where we are, in the midst of things, rather than with some timeless truths that have been previously validated by revelation and are then "applied" to our contemporary situation. Theology, in our day, must begin "where the pain is," since that is the location of the great majority of the human family. Only a tiny percentage of comfortable people can assume that their situation is normative, and that leisure to reflect abstractly about issues of metaphysical truth is widely available.

If this decision to begin *in medias res*, in the midst of suffering and oppression, is characteristic of much "contemporary Christian thought," especially in the third world, this suggests an appropriate approach to the particular cluster of issues for contemporary Christian thought that focus around sin, repentance and atonement. (We might revise our catechisms to begin: *Question*: What must one do to be forgiven? *Answer*: Sin.)

Sin

So let us begin with sin, a starting point where many contemporary Christians will feel quite at home. "Sin" is certainly a grand old Christian, or at least Protestant, word. Our own generation was the recipient of its rediscovery by Reinhold Niebuhr and attendant witnesses. The "liberal theology" that preceded Niebuhr had tended to de-emphasize sin as a gloomy hangover from Calvinist or Lutheran days, which from modern life and modern culture had mercifully delivered us; things were getting better, and education, enlightenment, and modern science would emancipate us from the need for such a negative and archaic assessment of the human venture. But as Niebuhr pointed out, "Contemporary history has refuted contemporary culture," and he was able to demonstrate with considerable acuteness that pride—spiritual, national, radical, ecclesiastical—was a dominant reality in human nature, and that a creative human destiny could be forged only through the overcoming of sin by the power of divine atonement and forgiveness.

So much is very familiar. Niebuhr swayed an entire generation and even more, and while his star is not at the moment in the ascendancy, it would be hard to discount the probing and acerbic treatment he gave to our individual and collective pretensions.

It is the latter—our collective reality—on which I want to focus as a new emphasis in "contemporary Christian thought." For what is now coming to the fore in recent theology is a new stress on the pervasiveness of *social sin* and its fruit or exemplification in what is often called *systemic evil*. The dilemma that thus faces Christians on the theological front is that while alleviation of the pangs of individual sin may be possible by many traditional devices or formulas (as we will see in the next section), such resolution by no means transfers easily to dealing with the consequences of social sin or systemic evil. To be sure, the latter notions are not a new discovery; early in his career, after all, Niebuhr wrote a book called *Moral Man and Immoral Society*, though he later felt it should have been called *Immoral Man and Terribly Immoral Society*. But I think this recognition of systemic evil will assume a much more central place in Christian reflection on sin today than it has occupied in the recent past.

By social sin I mean the degree to which relatively decent people may find themselves caught ("trapped" might be a better word) in structures that, despite all individual intentions of good will, persist in doing things that actually work against the common good. People find themselves beholden to social structures that are engines of evil, systems of organizing life and experience that hurt rather than heal—hence "systemic" evil. These structures can be of all sorts. Critics on the left will see well-intentioned members of boards of directors in giant corporations forced, in the name of securing great profits for their stockholders, to engage in exploitive practices against workers, such as looking for new plant locations where unionization will not be a "problem." In the name of their mandated task, doing good for their own constituencies, the stockholders, they will be forced to do evil to other constituencies, marginated peoples in Taiwan or El Salvador or the Dominican Republic. Critics on the right will see well-intentioned "liberals" becoming, as they feel, the pawns (intentional or unintentional) of those who manipulate them in the name of more and more collectivized patterns of human life that will finally destroy human initiative and make us all subject to the whims of a few who run the local or regional politburo. (It is interesting that in both cases, the analysis suggests that too much power is being concentrated in too few people, whether of a multinational corporation or a small political oligarchy.)

That is one dimension of the reality of social sin and systemic evil: that we can find ourselves working with good intentions inside of systems that actually produce evil results—economic enslavement or political enslavement.

I see two glaring examples of this with which contemporary Christian thought has got to come to terms. One of these is located for us by the cry that comes to us from Christian theologians in the third world, who tell us that the social structures that are benefiting people like ourselves, giving us relative comfort and security, are working destructively on them, increasing their dependency on us, reducing their ability to forge their own destinies, and leaving them increasingly destitute—a scheme of things in which the rich are growing richer while the poor grow poorer. (Many of these theologians would add that they see a cause-effect relationship between those facts.) What makes this analysis difficult for many of us to confront is that it seems to suggest that people we know are sitting around in boardrooms scheming for ways to make third world children starve to death. That, of course, is not the case. But the fact that it is not the case only adds to the poignancy of the problem. For our friends, with good intentions to help humankind, are caught up in structures that seem to third world analysts to have malevolent consequences. The evil, the sin, is not so much in our hearts as in the system within which we live and operate—a combination of political, social, economic, and national outlooks that dominate who we are and how we act.

The other example of systemic evil that I cannot escape is the Holocaust, though here the cast of characters is not so innocent at any level; evil is apparent throughout. Nobody now calls Nazis good or leaders within Nazism "well intentioned." Taking us beyond the question of evil and the diabolical cunning of top Nazi officials and the way in which that evil seeped down into the lower echelons of power, we are still faced with the undeniable fact that many of those who carried out the Nazis' "final solution" were ordinary people, people like many of us, people who simply "obeyed orders"—drove the trains, pushed the papers, stoked the fires—people who in themselves were not demonic, but whose collective compliance led to the efficient carrying out of demonic ends. There are all sorts of degrees of guilt to be assigned along a wide spectrum, but it took the whole spectrum, including those who remained rather unthinking instruments of well thought-out orders, to achieve the desired ends of the top officials. The evil was imbedded in the system, in this case the Nazi system.

These examples, and particularly the second one, suggest an important aspect of the notion of social sin that Christian thought has underplayed. Christians have always been strong on the strong sins—pride, aggression, exploitation, and the like— and have failed to see that perhaps the worst sin of our time is not perversity but *indifference*. In confronting this, I must say that I have been most helped (if that is the word) by the writings of Elie Wiesel. As he examines the various stances that we can take toward monstrous moral evil—victim, executioner, madness, self-destruction, and so forth—the one that turns out to be the worst of all, for him at least, is the stance of the spectator, the one who by indifference and passivity becomes complicit in the evil that is being done by others. Indifference is the sin of presumed neutrality; the adjective is important, because, according to this view, there is no neutrality possible. As Wiesel has put it, "He who is not with the victims is with the executioners." The spectator seeks to opt out of the moral struggle but actually throws his or her weight by default on the side of those in power.

And if those in power are evil, every spectator compounds the power of that evil. The spectator in *The Town beyond the Wall* remains passively removed when the deportation of Jews from the town square is going on; but that is not neutrality. It is an act of support for the Germans. Such a person, Wiesel asserts, is not properly an object of hatred, since hatred is possible only toward that which is human; such a person is an object of contempt, an attitude reserved for that which is less than human. Indifference de-humanizes us ourselves.

It seems to me that contemporary Christian thought has to take this powerful reality of the sin of indifference, so manifest in the time of the Holocaust, much more seriously than it has. The concern is reinforced by the fact that the same note is struck by third world Christian theologians, who remind us that those Christians living in countries that have the power, as long as they remain indifferent to the uses to which that power is being put, become complicit in the evil that is being done by the engines of power.

Repentance

That is not a comfortable reminder. According to it we are complicit both in what we *do* with our good intentions (since the system manages to turn them to ill) and in what we *fail to do* (since evil consequences follow more easily when we remain on the sidelines). It is the social dimension of all this that adds complicating factors to traditional ways of dealing with sin.

Now Christianity has long had ways of dealing with the dimension of individual sin. We are invited as individuals to confess our sin (to a priest, to an assembly, to God), to repent (to "turn about" and begin again),[4] to recognize that we can do this only by the grace of God (we are "justified by grace through faith"), and to produce fruits worthy of repentance (to lead a new life, amended and empowered by the presence of God working through us). Resources for keeping this experience alive and well are offered through the sacraments, the sustaining power of the community, the example of others, and repeated exposure to the healing power of the Word of God.

That is not to be put down. It has led to a lot of new beginnings for a lot of individual Christians for two millennia. It has led to a few new beginnings even for me as one untimely born. But my current difficulty with it is that (by itself at least) it does not get to the heart of the social dimension of sin. One can do all of these things and still manage to live untroubled within the same structures of systemic evil whose ability to tear apart and destroy human life continues unhindered and unchallenged. We know that people who torture political prisoners in Argentina and arrange for the annihilation of the "disappeared" go to confession and Mass with clear consciences, and, what is more, are recognized as pillars of their society. We know that there were Lutherans who manned the gas chambers in Birkenau and Treblinka and then went home at night to play with their children, listen to the music of Mozart, and make love to their wives. We know that there are people in our own society who make their individual "peace with God" and still supervise the construction of antipersonnel weapons. The mechanisms for repentance and forgiveness in relation to individual sin do not necessarily impact the ongoing pervasiveness of social sin. The evidence simply does not support the notion that transforming individuals will lead to the transformation of the society in which those individuals live. It may, in fact, bolster the ongoing presence of systemic evil, by persuading those who live within it that the requisite steps for transformation have already take place through the piecemeal conversion of individuals. So the question with which contemporary Christian thought must deal more frontally is how repentance works in this larger social context.

Individuals can repent. That is a patently true proposition. Can a society repent? That is a quite different proposition. It would seem at the very least that societies do not do so with alacrity; it is not part of human history that many nations repent very openly for past misdeeds. Indeed, the very concept of social or national repentance almost seems artificial: what would constitute such repentance? a statement by the president? an act of Congress? a national day of bell-ringing? some deeds of reparation?

Some deeds of reparation. Perhaps this latter notion provides a clue. On a social level, repentance for social sin is unlikely to be verbal; if it exists at all it will be defined by deeds more than words. If repentance means to "turn about," to begin again, then the proof of its reality will be in the change of posture rather than in statements that precede or accompany the change of posture. Possible example: it seems clear that a majority of our citizens now feel that our military presence in Vietnam was wrong. As that mood was growing, we did not trumpet the fact in any collective way, and one attempt later on to have a national day of repentance was a disaster by default. But we did, in fact, remove our military presence from Vietnam far short of military victory. We "turned about," rather literally, and started going in the opposite direction, away from Hanoi rather than toward it. We ceased using napalm; we stopped deploying troops. Our social posture was rather dramatically transformed. Perhaps this is an analogy of social repentance, achieved without benefit of clergy.

Now I do not personally think such actions constitute an adequate expression of repentance (which would have to include reparations for the damage we did, help in rebuilding, and so forth), but they do at least suggest that "turning about" can happen on a social scale and that its consequences are far from negligible. To be sure, there has been no public confession of sin, no acknowledgment that we are dependent on the grace of God, no affirmation of the necessity of sacramental means of grace, none of the devices that usually accompany individual repentance. But there has been a change in the situation. From a strict theological (or at least Protestant) perspective, such an example may seem to trivialize a great theological truth, somehow making repentance the fruit of human effort (shades of Pelagius), rather than the sheer gift of God's grace, but it might be argued in rebuttal that mighty nations do not change policies to which they have been awesomely committed, save (at the very least) by the "hidden" grace of God.

A second characteristic of social repentance would be (whether stated explicitly or only assumed implicitly) a corporate recognition that the sins of the past are not to be repeated in the future. Or, to make a more realistic proposal, there is the hope that by reflecting on the lessons of the past we may make their future repetition less likely. It is a characteristic of our recent national history that we have rather consistently supported military dictatorships that were anticommunist, proposing that it is *our* way of life that should be the model for other nations. With whatever good this has produced (in terms of "stemming communist aggression" and so forth) it has also made us complicit in the internal repression and oppression of those dictatorships, including the denial of human rights, the torturing of political prisoners, etc. Are we beginning to learn from this baleful history so that the errors (sins) of the past will be less likely to be repeated in the future? What we do in places like Nicaragua will be an interesting case-study.[5]

A third component of social repentance, implicit in the first two, would be an increasingly clear commitment to social change. To "turn about" is to turn one's back on what was there before, to change one's perspective, to look in new directions, and to do so from a new standpoint. There is not a lot of evidence to suggest that this is happening to us as a society, and there is a lot of evidence to suggest that this is not happening, but if a large social unit such as a nation, decides, in however small or tentative ways, that it will no longer seek to be "policeman of the world," that represents a recognition that social change is coming.

These may seem to some pretty thin (or even far-fetched) reeds on which to build a social counterpart to personal repentance. So let us try to deepen the discussion by referring once again to the Holocaust. Here is a social sin, systemic evil, with a vengeance. In the light of that dark and unique history of evil, what would it mean to talk about repentance, either individual or social? Is such a concept even conceivable? No amount of repentance—individual, social, national, or global—can undo the consequences to the six million or to their families. There is an irredeemable, irreversible fact and reality never to be expunged. In what sense, then, could we talk about a collective "turning about," repentance on a social scale for a social evil of unparalleled magnitude? Here it would seem to me that the most that could be offered, as an instance of trying to "turn about" would be the collective resolve that it shall not happen again. Such a resolve contains a double focus—a recognition of our past complicity (we are responsible for what happened then), and a recognition of our future obligation (we are responsible to see that it is never repeated).

The first of these two assertions, I have found, often draws storms of protest ("What do you mean, *we* are responsible for what happened then? We weren't even there!"). And yet, even in the midst of such discussion, after the first wave of indignation has passed, one or another sensitive person will begin to reflect, "If we *had* been there, would we have acted any differently?" And gradually the acknowledgment begins to come forth (from the *goyim*) that *we* could have been SS guards, *we* could have been the minor functionaries who obeyed orders without asking questions because to do otherwise would have gotten us into trouble, *we* could have carefully avoided asking the questions to which we did not want answers. And all of that is an important step on the road to assuming responsibility for the future. Only out of the confession of the likelihood of past complicity can we seriously face the likelihood of present complicity. Thus part of corporate repentance is the corporate telling, hearing, and responding to the Holocaust story. Only in seeing the step-by-step episodes back then, initially so small, that became cumulatively so devastating, will we be sensitized to the discerning of counterparts today that could produce repetitions tomorrow. (One of the reasons, I am convinced, for the incredible revisionist history now being produced to show that the Holocaust never really happened is not only to provide a new vehicle for anti-Semitism, but to fill a need many people have to discredit the Holocaust so that we can think better of ourselves and don't have to dwell on such unpleasant demands as repentance.)

In 1945, a few leaders of the German church issued the "Stuttgart Declaration," in which they confessed their complicity in what had happened in Nazi Germany—they did not fight hard enough against the currents of the time, they did not love enough, trust enough, and were thus themselves engulfed by the currents of fear. And only now, thirty-five years later, is the German church beginning to face honestly the consequences of all this in its relationship to the Jews.

But the discussion thus far still begs a fundamental question. It is so awesome for me that I can do little more than raise it. If repentance involves a plea for forgiveness, to whom would such a plea be addressed, particularly in the case of the Holocaust? Those who were wronged, the dead Jews, are hardly in a position to hear such a plea, let alone respond to it. Living Jews would scarcely feel it appropriate for them to absolve in the name of the dead. Can the plea be addressed to God? Is God the one who was ultimately wronged? But would not such a decision trivialize the anguish of the six million who were the immediate recipients of the demonic actions needing forgiveness? Beyond all that (and this is the worst and newest question with which I must wrestle) are there some sins of such magnitude that forgiveness is not possible? Can one who burned babies, no matter how penitent in retrospect, be guaranteed, or even offered, the promise of forgiveness? And once again, who could grant it? (Simon Wiesenthal's *The Sunflower* is a powerful and probing exploration of such issues.)

Christians are told that there is a sin against the Holy Spirit that is unforgivable, but no theologians have ever been helpful in deciding which sin it is. Perhaps only in our era can we answer that question; perhaps we have seen that the perpetrator of absolute evil against innocent children is beyond the pale of forgiveness. These are hard considerations for Christians, for whom the central message is always focused on forgiveness. But the magnitude of social evil may not have been measured with sufficient seriousness until such questions are clearly faced. Christians are always in danger of resorting to what Dietrich Bonhoeffer called "cheap grace," the reality to which W. H. Auden referred in "For the Time Being," when he put into the mouth of Herod the words, "Every corner boy will say, I like committing sins, God likes forgiving them, really the world is admirably arranged."

But these comments have already led us into our final area.

Atonement

Clearly sin, whether individual or social, is sin against someone. And repentance, whether individual or social, is directed toward someone. And both imply, indeed demand, response, reciprocity. If sin has been committed, the victim of the sinful acts has been harmed, and justice (and even love) calls for some kind of reparation. If repentance has been verbalized or enacted, that too is set in relation to one who is felt able to set things straight, grant the assurance of pardon, promise new beginnings, or whatever. In every case, a distance has emerged, a chasm has been created, and there is a need for at-one-ment, the drawing back together of what has been sundered or severed, the restoration of a broken relationship. Traditional Christian thought has had some clear, if rather mysterious, ways of dealing with this. The ultimate gulf is between God and ourselves, we have created it by our sin, God is the one who, nevertheless, out of his love and grace, bridges the distance between us, reaches across the chasm that divides us, coming to us in human form in the person of Jesus of Nazareth in order to restore relationship and, taking the consequences of our wrongdoing upon himself, atones for, expiates, the sins we have committed, sets the record clean and makes a fresh start possible. The punishment for sin that should be visited on us, God bears Godself in his Son, and thus creates a new situation. Redemption has occurred. We live in a redeemed world and can consequently live redeemed lives.

In some such telling of it, that has been the Christian story, and it has worked a healing power in many Christian lives. It bristles with difficulties for non-Christians (and, I might add, for some Christians as well, myself latterly included among them). The difficulty I face is the difficulty of reaffirming the triumphant cry of the New Testament church that the principalities and powers, the forces of evil, have indeed been conquered, that the redemption of the world has already taken place. There is just one trouble with this—the redeemed world does not look very redeemed. Can one make such an assertion without either flying naively in the face of the facts, or (much worse) demeaning the anguish and suffering of those who live in that supposedly redeemed world and feel only its unredeemedness? To revert to our former examples, how can this message really speak to the woman in Chile or Uruguay whose husband is a political prisoner and whose children are starving to death, and how can it speak to the Jewish parents in Auschwitz who have just seen their child burned alive because that is a more "efficient" way of disposing of Jewish children than sending them into the crematorium into which their parents will shortly go? Christians are told by Jesus to "be of good cheer; I have overcome the world." It's not easy. And what makes it so hard is that it seems so callous. Even when I recall that things weren't exactly easy for

Christians in the first century, I have also to recall that nineteen intervening centuries have hardly added impressive evidence to substantiate the victory cry.

As we reflect further on this dilemma of the reconciling and atoning God, offered as the answer to these perplexities, we confront the age-old tension between divine love and divine power. Christians have tried for two millennia to reconcile them. I no longer think it can be very satisfactorily done, and if I have to choose between the two, in the light of what I see in the world, the choice is not hard. I relinquish a belief in the divine power; I want no part of a divine power that condemns Chilean children to starvation and Jewish children to burning. But what about divine love? I see it at work in those who intercede on behalf of Chilean children, or those who took the part of Jewish children in the noble if futile interventions against the SS guards, as occasionally happened. I see it in Jesus' identification throughout his life with the poor and the oppressed, ranging himself with the outcasts instead of with the Herods and Pilates of his day (as do many of his contemporary followers), and I see it imaged in the Suffering Servant passages in Second Isaiah.

This may not seem like much to start with, but (if the choice remained only that) still better to affirm a defeated love than a conquering power, in the light of the kind of world where those options appear to have been played out. At the end of Elie Wiesel's *Ani Maamin*, when the patriarchs have told God what is really happening on earth and the only response from the throne of God is silence, Wiesel tells us that the patriarchs give up; they will go back down and tell the people that God knows and can do nothing or that God knows and doesn't care. But as they leave, each tells the story of a Jew who continued to believe in spite of all the evidence to the contrary. And the narrator tells us that finally, in the face of such stories, God weeps, and that when Abraham, Isaac, and Jacob leave the divine presence to return to the misery of earth, God leaves the divine throne and, unknown to the patriarchs, accompanies them back down to earth to share their lot.

That ending draws a great variety of responses. Some feel it is weak. A weeping, crying impotent God? Who needs him? So he finally makes it down to earth? Too late! Six million lives too late. I feel the force of these arguments. But I also feel the force of the assertion that whatever else we may say about God and God's struggle with evil, such a conclusion tells us that God is at least not aloof and uncaring, but seeks from the divine side to bridge the abyss. Issues of God's power are still not resolved: Why was all this evil permitted to happen? Why did it take so long for God to become concerned? Why is the divine presence still hidden? Perhaps God is still answerable for many things. But at least the charge of indifference has been removed, along with the charge of malevolence.

When I transpose all this to Christian terms, I am called upon to see the Jesus story as the way Christians must try to grapple with atonement in their own community. Where is the God Christians proclaim to be found? Where must such a God be sought? Clearly, once again, among the poor, the dispossessed, the defeated of this world—among the criminals. And if one is going to seek to repent and hope to have a cry of penitence heard or an act of penitence acknowledged, it will be in some kind of new identification today with those among whom Jesus was present, that any such assurances will come. In terms of social sin and social repentance, this will say something about social engagement in concern to transform structures so that they do not perpetuate sin and injustice and entail the likelihood that entering into such a struggle may have modern counterparts to crucifixion, suffering at the hands of the modern Herods and Pilates who remain unwilling to let Jesus' love be anything but an apparently defeated love.

That is rather easy to talk about, as long as someone else is being described. And the only thing that can keep all this from being "cheap grace" is an acknowledgment that any such identification must be voluntarily assumed. No Christian has a right to tell Jews to suffer; no Christian has a right to decide that another Christian shall become a martyr; nobody, in other words, can assign the suffering servant role to anybody else. That would be the worst sort of chicanery. But when, or if, it is voluntarily assumed, then perhaps, some new forces begin to be unleashed. The apparently defeated love of God in history begins to have some allies, and new beginnings become possible, as people seek God in the places God is already present seeking them. Perhaps suffering love is the source from which power finally comes. But only those who voluntarily assume it—not those who thrust it on others—would finally be entitled to say so.

THE NEED FOR A TRAGIC SENSE OF LIFE

In this undated sermon given while Brown was teaching at Macalester College in 1952–53, Brown strikes a Niebuhrian tone in addressing undergraduates. The text is John 16:33, "In the world you have tribulation, but be of good cheer; I have overcome the world." It was during this period that Brown became involved with the campaign to reelect Eugene McCarthy in an era of rising McCarthyism. His courage in rising to Eugene McCarthy's defense and his strong denunciations of the ideology of Senator Joseph McCarthy of Wisconsin were stunning in their boldness for that time. His work with Eugene McCarthy was also his first practical experience working alongside Roman Catholics, and Brown attributes to that experience the dawning of his later ecumenical interests. Here he addresses the younger college generation, calling them to an active sense of the reality swirling around them in the early 1950s.

I would like to direct your attention toward an area of Christian concern that seems to be absent from the thinking of most

Macalester students. I propose that we have a Christian obligation to develop a tragic sense of life. And although I do not want
to end on that note, I want to begin with it and linger over it for
a few minutes.

YOU WILL NOTICE THAT in Jesus' statement, "In the world
you have tribulation, but be of good cheer, I have overcome
the world," there are two foci, two points between which the
thought oscillates. On the one hand tribulation; on the other
hand cheer. Mature Christian faith always has these two elements woven together. You can call it the tension between sin
and salvation. The tension between despair and hope. Between
pessimism and optimism. Between understanding the human
being as a sinner and the human being as a child of God. When
one of the foci disappears, or one is stressed to the virtual exclusion of the other, you get a distorted Christian faith. Thus on the
one hand, you get people who are bleakly pessimistic, who feel
that the world is going to hell, that people are nothing but selfish
depraved brutes and that the skies are completely black. Or, on
the other hand, you get people who feel that life is a wonderful
game from start to finish, "bouncy Christians" who are always
smiling and assuring you that things are all right really, and isn't
it a lovely morning. Now it is my feeling that Macalester students are much closer to the second attitude than the first, that
there is a kind of sunny optimism among the campus Christians
that is liable to be shallow and naive and that may be riding for
a terrible fall. And since, as I said, Christian faith seems to me to
involve seeing pessimism and optimism in proper relationship, I
would like first to try to stress to that group of people the need
for, and the provisional value (at least), of a tragic sense of life.

LET US, THEN, look for a moment at this. My first contention is
that the Christian has the moral obligation to see the depth of
the human problem as clearly and as honestly as one can, to see

the side of the truth affirmed by the statement, "In the world you have tribulation." No Christian has the right to look at life through rose-colored glasses.

I do not intend to give you one of those dreary catalogues of the predicament of the modern person, which seems to be part of the standard equipment of the visiting firemen who come to a college campus. I shall not need to remind you that we live in a critical time (and all the rest of the clichés) when it is up to you, O youth, to go out and build the brave new world. The present critical time is only a sort of magnified example of the perennial crisis in human life. And that perennial crisis has a lot of elements of tragedy in it. We live in a world where a young child can be reduced to a gibbering idiot because of incessant fearful night bombings, as happened in Hamburg and London; in a world where decent and highly educated people will kill each other for a piece of bread, as happens in Seoul; in a world where a mother who has four children knows that three of them will starve to death within a year, as happens in certain parts of India; in a world where a person is denied the privilege of living where he wants to live because of the color of his skin, as happens in the Twin Cities; in a world where a person may give himself totally and unreservedly to another person in marriage and then discover that the other person is unfaithful, as happens everywhere. This is simply a fractional recital of quite commonplace and ordinary events in twentieth-century human life. Unless you have an understanding of life that makes room for these tragic elements, you have, I submit, failed to look at life as clearly as you should.

But why dwell on these things, you may ask? Why get so morbid? Why not concentrate on the happy things of life and emphasize "progress" and Going Onward and Upward? Let me suggest briefly a few reasons why you must dwell on these things:

First of all, because they are there. Because they are an undeniable part of the stuff of human life. Because you are simply closing your eyes and hearts naively if you try to blot them out. You are being dishonest with yourself.

Second, you must see the tragedy of life, now, as a guard against premature disillusionment. To leave college, thinking, as I am afraid many students do, that the world is just your oyster, is to let yourself in for a shocking disillusionment. And there is nothing more bitter, more pitiful, than the disillusioned idealist, the starry-eyed dreamer who wakes up with a thud to find that life has a sordid, ugly, and despicable side.

Third, you must see these things because to see the tragedy as well as the beauty can be a check against complacency. Nobody has the right to feel comfortable and at ease in a tragic world. To be aware of evil in the world is at least one step toward realizing that you must try to combat these evils. If you do not know that they exist you will hardly be concerned to obliterate them. The Christian is one who must live with an "uneasy conscience."

My first point then, is that the Christian has the moral duty to see as clearly and as honestly as one can the element of tragedy that runs through human life.

But this point needs to be simplified and expanded in the following way. The one who would be a mature Christian must do this, because it is only as you see the depth of the problem of human life that the Christian resolution of the problem makes any sense. If you are quite convinced that you are a specimen of splendid health for example, you are not likely to take seriously a doctor's suggestion that radical surgery is needed to save you. If you dismiss the notion of "sin," let us say, as an outworn and incredible term, then you are not likely to concern yourself about being "saved" from sin. If you don't sometimes feel a sense of despair about your life, you are unlikely to be reaching around very vigorously for some sort of deliverance from despair. My point is either irrelevant or utter nonsense to you, so long as you are convinced that everything is just swell, there is nothing wrong really, and that with a little manipulation of your glands or of the social order, utopia will have arrived. "The Kingdom of God," James Denney once said, "is not for the complacent, but for the desperate."

Consequently, unless you are willing to accept in some form or other the Christian diagnosis of the [human] plight, you are quite unlikely to accept the Christian "cure." And the Christian diagnosis faces squarely this tragic element in human life. If anything, it heightens the tragic element. For Christianity does not tell us that the fault in the human situation is due only to ignorance, that we just don't know enough to solve our problems intelligently, and that a few imperfections in our social system can be adjusted neatly and easily and life made perfect. Nor is it some gigantic ineluctable fate that has us trapped in a situation from which there is no exit possible whatsoever. Christian faith says that the root of the problem lies within our hearts. That our wills have gotten distorted. That even when we know the good we do not necessarily do it. That there is something radically wrong inside. It is something of this sort that I take it Christianity means by the word "sin." The "word" sin has very little to do with specific actions and prohibitions of notions such as don't smoke, don't drink, don't swear. Those miss the point rather spectacularly. You can call sin worshiping the creature rather than the creator, playing the part of God yourself rather than acknowledging God's sovereignty over your life, refusing to surrender the center of the universe to anyone else but yourself; you can call it all sorts of things. The point is that Christian faith says that this is at the heart of our trouble: the perverse glorification of myself at the expense of yourself, and both of us at the expense of God. This is what needs to be cured.

Now the question is not so much whether you like this analysis or not, but whether the analysis is fundamentally true. After resisting it for a long time, I can only offer my testimony that I finally came to the conclusion that it was, that this was a more

profound understanding of the human situation then the humanists or the secularists or the religious legalists or the communists
had come up with, that it made sense of the human situation and
that it was an accurate description of my own heart.

And it is only as we see this dimension of human life that we
can fully see how relevant the Christian "solution" is. I shall
not offer a detailed spelling out of that solution, since one of
the greatest dangers is that we will arrive at it prematurely and
accept it simply on the say-so of someone else, in which case it
is merely a secondhand faith. But I will try very briefly to suggest some of the ways in which the relevance of the solution can
come home to you if you have truly seen the tragic sense of life.

I submit that to one who is desperately seeking but not finding
God, it makes sense to believe that God has sought us, that God
has taken the initiative in approaching us, since we cannot find
God by ourselves. That is what Christianity affirms about Christ.

I submit that one who is desperately trying to live life as it
ought to be lived, trying to fulfill the high demands we feel laid
upon us and yet failing all the time, it makes sense to believe
that God is undergirding and sustaining these efforts, even our
failures, and that to the degree to which we surrender to him,
God will empower us to do God's will. That is what Christianity
affirms about the Holy Spirit.

I submit that to one who is desperately conscious of one's
own shortcomings and failings and who sees no way out of that
terrible impasse of "The good that I would I do not, and the evil
that I would not, that I do," to such a person it makes sense to
believe that God takes up our failures, bears the burden of them
in suffering love, relieves us of the intolerable burden of sin and
guilt and enables us to start again afresh. That is what Christianity affirms about God's forgiveness and grace.

I submit that to us who are desperately concerned about the
lack of community and human fellowship in the world, who feel
compelled to enter into the struggle for it even when the odds

are against us, and realize that we will die without achieving our purposes, it makes sense to say that God is likewise concerned about what happens in human history. It makes sense to say that God too is working through all the avenues of modern life—politics, economics, social institutions—to establish God's reign and rule eternally, beyond the bounds of time and space, as well as partially within the bounds of time and space. That is what Christianity affirms about the Kingdom of God and the life everlasting.

And so one could go on through every element of Christian faith and practice. To those who are really concerned, to those who measure the depth of the problem, there is in Christian faith an assurance that God has the resources for meeting the problem. And only those who see the depth of the problem will ever be convinced that Christianity has anything meaningful to say.

That then is my second main point. That it is only as we see the depth of the human problem, in all of its tragic dimensions, that we can see that the Christian resolution of the problem makes sense.

BUT A THIRD THING must be said, and it is an important thing. Christian faith is not essentially a tragic and pessimistic faith. It may have to be provisionally tragic and pessimistic in order to make people face up realistically to their situation. But the final word is not tragedy but hope, not despair but promise, not only the statement "In the world you have tribulation," but also the concluding part of the text, "Be of good cheer, I have overcome the world." Let the third thing, then, be this: Christian faith, rather than refusing to face tragedy, looks it squarely in the face and claims to be able to transform it. Christian faith does not try to ignore tragedy. Nor does it succumb to tragedy. In the words from the title for one of Reinhold Niebuhr's books, it goes *Beyond Tragedy*. And my point is simply that you cannot go beyond tragedy, or transform it, by ignoring it, pretending it isn't there, refusing to face up to it resolutely and squarely. "A tragic sense of life" is no place to end, but it is a very important place to begin. All the emphasis in Christian faith upon sin, for example, is because Christian faith claims to have a way of conquering sin. All the emphasis upon mortality and death is because Christian faith claims to have a way of consoling mortality and death. All the emphasis on human insufficiency is because Christian faith claims that the all-suffering God meets and conquers the insufficiency of human life lived by itself.

Let me offer one illustration of this central claim of Christian faith. The place where this transformation of tragedy is most apparent is at the heart of the most apparent tragedy of Christian faith, the cross. I think that many non-Christians would concur in the judgment that the crucifixion of Jesus is the most supremely evil event in human history. Here is the place where the very best is absolutely at the mercy of the very worst. Here is where complete and outgoing life is repudiated, spat upon, hung up to die. Here is the place where good is thoroughly conquered by evil. It is mere unmitigated tragedy.

And yet from the standpoint of Christian faith it is not tragedy. For the tragedy of Calvary is transformed into the triumph of God's love in the total event of Crucifixion-Resurrection. To our mighty NO to God, God had an almighty YES to us. Out of this worst evil, God did God's very best, which was to make out of that cross the event of the restoration of God and humankind in fellowship. Where we hated, God loved. Where we rejected, God accepted. Out of death, God brought resurrection. Out of despair, God brought hope. Out of destruction, God brought new life. So that the cross is not for the Christian a symbol of tragedy; it is a symbol of triumph, and the cross, an empty cross, is the emblem of hope of the Christian faith. It is empty, because the Christ hung there is no longer there; Christ has been raised by God. But it is still a cross, a symbol of execution and degradation, because it was through the tragedy that God brought triumph. The cross was not bypassed. It was accepted and transformed.

I AM TOLD THAT there is a type of pine tree called the knob cone pine. It does not grow new seedlings in the ordinary way. The seeds are encased in the tough little ends of the pinecones. The only thing sufficient to break the cones and cause the seeds to fall to the ground and sprout, is a forest fire. As long as things go along serenely the knob cone pine does not reproduce itself in the forest. But when a forest fire comes, and the world of the knob cone pine is destroyed, then the seeds are released by the heat and a new forest begins to grow from the ashes. That is a parable of our situation. We are living, if you will, in a world on fire. It is only by seeing the tragedy of that world, and through that experience seeing squarely the relevance of our Christian faith and then discovering that that faith transforms tragedy, that we will be fit citizens for this day and age in which we are called by God to live.

OUT OF DESTRUCTION,
"... A FUTURE AND A HOPE ..."

The following is a portion of the keynote address given by Brown at the National Liturgical Week held in Milwaukee in August 1969. The emphasis is on hope and how we can find hope in the midst of so much in the world of both religion and politics that might lead even the most stalwart to discouragement.

If there is anyone to whom we can properly go to learn about hope emerging out of destruction, it is to the German Lutheran Dietrich Bonhoeffer, who was killed by the Gestapo after two years in prison for his part in the plot against Hitler's life. Actually, it is not so much *to* Bonhoeffer we go as *through* Bonhoeffer to another individual who also lived in troubled times and who, in the midst of the destruction of all he saw around him, was nevertheless able to hope. It is because he could hope that Bonhoeffer was able to hope, and it is because Bonhoeffer was able to hope that perhaps we can also. This lonely individual was the prophet Jeremiah. The portion of Scripture to which Bonhoeffer refers most frequently in his *Letters and Papers from Prison* and the one from which he drew most sustenance is Jeremiah 45.

Typical of his use of this passage is the following excerpt written in 1944, a passage that could surely have been penned in America [later on]:

> We have learned that it is impossible to plan even for one day ahead, that all our work may be destroyed overnight, and that our life, compared with our parents, has become formless and fragmentary. Despite everything, however, I can only say that I should not have chosen to live in any other age than our own . . . regardless of our external fortunes. Never have we realized, as we do today, how the world lies under the wrath and grace of God. [And then, after quoting Jeremiah 45, he continues:] If the Creator destroys his own handiwork, what right have we to lament over the destruction of ours? (*Letters and Papers from Prison*)

1. "*Woe is me. . .*" The context of Jeremiah 45 is familiar. Jeremiah has been in hot water for some time, and Baruch, his secretary or helper, has just about had it. Things were not easy for prophets in those times (nor are they ever), and Baruch was naturally disturbed when attempts were made on the life of Jeremiah, and when they were both subjected to whatever was the Old Testament equivalent of being ridden out of town on a rail. Finally, Baruch has had all he can take, and he lets go with the words that form the first step of a very significant sequence: "Woe is me! For the Lord has added sorrow to my pain: I am weary with my groaning, and I find no rest" (45:3).

Who of us, if he is honest, can deny that this is the mood in which we live most of the time these days? If we are going to talk about hope in other than sentimental terms, we had better let our starting point, if not our finishing point, be somewhere in Baruch's neighborhood. If hope is a word for our day, it must be a word that senses the depths of the discouragement, if not the despair, that are the hallmark of our common experience.

But even at this low point we must note that it always seems to be in the context of a low point that hope is born. Jürgen Molt-mann reminds us, "The believer is not set at the high noon of life, but at the dawn of a new day, at the point where night and day, things passing and things to come, grapple with each other" (*Theology of Hope*). And St. Paul prefaces one of his most triumphant and hopeful passages, the beginning of 2 Corinthians, with a description of the grave affliction he experiences in Asia: "I was so utterly, unbearably crushed," he writes, "that I despaired of life itself. Why, I felt that I had received the sentence of death" (2 Cor. 1:8). Herman Schleier comments on that passage: "Precisely in the situation of extreme helplessness and of not knowing where to turn, hope springs up" (*The Relevance of the New Testament*).

2. *"What I have built up I am breaking down. . ."* How does "hope spring up" for Baruch and Jeremiah? Not in any very obvious way, particularly at first. Having addressed his complaint to Yahweh, Baruch not unnaturally expects some sort of response. Baruch gets his response, all right, and it comes in a sequence of responses that is surprising, then discouraging, and finally hopeful.

The *surprising* response had a very special meaning for Bonhoeffer and can have a similar meaning for us. For in response to Baruch's complaint that things are tough, Yahweh replies, "Behold what I have built up I am breaking down, and what I have planted I am plucking up—that is, the whole land" (45:4). The surprising word Baruch gets through Jeremiah is that Yahweh himself is going through a time of tribulation, that his own plans for his earth are having to be drastically altered, that

humans have so despoiled creation, have let it get so out of hand
and so far astray from its original purposes, that it must be broken down before it can be lifted up again.

Early in the book, Jeremiah describes what Yahweh is doing
as follows: "To pluck up, and to break down, and to destroy,
and to overthrow, to build and to plant." We must note that
only after the plucking up, breaking down, destroying, and overthrowing, can there be thought of building and planting.

Clearly it grieves Yahweh that it has come to this. To Baruch,
therefore, he can only say in effect, "You are having a hard time
seeing your dreams die? Well so am I. I had a different dream for
my world and my children. But that dream cannot, for the moment,
be realized. So just as your plans are being destroyed, so are mine.
Before they can be resumed, there must be breaking down."

Those were the terms in which Bonhoeffer saw what was happening in Europe in the 1940s. Evil had become so rampant and the
hopes and plans of God for God's children so distorted that before
there could be further creativity, there had to be destruction. God
was having to participate in it, and Bonhoeffer, to do the bidding
of God, must share in that time of destructiveness, namely, help to
bring about the end of Hitler. His was not a time of consolidation
and upbuilding; it was a time of challenge and destroying.

Are we entitled to put any other reading on our own era?
The more I reflect upon the times through which we are living,
the more I am convinced that Jeremiah's time and Bonhoeffer's
time and our own time are remarkably similar. We are in a time
of upheaval, of breaking down, and no wishful nostalgia for an
earlier time that was "simpler" is going to restore that earlier
time. It is our lot to be cast in a particularly painful period of
world history, painful to God as well as to us, and through it all
God is striving to work out God's purposes, weaving into the
design the terrible mistakes we make.

So Baruch makes the important discovery that he is not alone
in his tribulation. God enters into it and shares it. As Martin
Buber puts it, borrowing another image from Jeremiah:

[God] stands over the wheel, and presses the misshapen
vessels into a lump of clay—but He shares in the trouble of this rebellious human clay which, on the potter's
wheel of world history, takes shape and loses it again
through its own fault. (*The Prophetic Faith*)

It will not do for the Christian to try to read New Testament
imagery into the Hebrew Scriptures, but we see in this passage
something of what Christian imagery has tried to evoke in the
picture of the crucifixion; namely, that God identifies with all
that is most devastating in God's own creation, that God is not
exempted from the suffering that is the lot of God's children,
that as Buber puts it, "He shares in the trouble of this rebellious human clay," that God too experiences the pain of dreams
deferred and rudely challenged. From all of which Bonhoeffer
draws a strange but powerful kind of consolation: "If the Creator destroys his own handiwork, what right have we to lament
over the destruction of ours?"

3. *"Do you seek great things for yourself? Seek them not . . ."*
After that surprising word, Yahweh speaks a further word to
Baruch, and this time it is a *discouraging* word. Having reminded
Baruch that he, Yahweh, experiences weariness and pain, he then
goes on, "And do you seek great things for yourself? Seek them
not; for, behold, I am bringing evil upon all flesh" (45:5a).

Talk about a letdown! Yahweh answers Baruch's plea for a
respite with the words, "You think things are tough now? Just
wait. They will get worse. The time of plucking up, breaking
down, of destroying and overthrowing, is not yet over. So don't
look for easy times ahead; gird yourself for worse." [*Brown here
alludes to racial tensions in Milwaukee, and cautions: Wait till
you confront the third world.*]

Now to be told, in our present weariness, that worse is in
store for us, seems like no more than an invitation to throw in
the towel. However, whether it consoles us or not, we had better
take account of the fact that such a projection is very likely to

be the truth. At least we cannot accuse Yahweh (or Jeremiah) of a lack of realism.

There are times in human history when people are entitled to hear another word than this, when we need to be reminded that our warfare is accomplished, that our iniquity is pardoned, that we have already received from the Lord's hand double for all our sins, and that the crooked places are being made smooth and the rough places plain. But I do not believe that that is the word for our era, and particularly I do not believe that it is the word for Americans in our era. Rather, the word for us is just this word of Yahweh to Baruch—that we are not at the end of the tunnel, that a release from our troubles is not just around the corner, and that tough times will continue but get tougher.

Far better that we approach the future with the realism Baruch has offered here. "Do you seek great things for yourself? Seek them not." Whether we like it or not, this is not the time of upbuilding but of tearing down, and the process is not yet complete. Tearing down racist mentalities; uprooting notions of white supremacy in international affairs; tearing down exploitive economic systems; uprooting the notion of business as usual; tearing down antiquated ecclesiastical structures; uprooting national priorities that insist that the dust of the moon is more important than the people of the ghetto. This kind of attitude describes the need in Jeremiah's Palestine, Bonhoeffer's Europe, our America.

This is what we are in the midst of, and the end is not yet.

4. *"I will give you your life . . ."* There is some difficulty with the translation of this verse, but at least Baruch is being told that whatever happens to him, or wherever he is sent, his life will be spared. The "prize of war" imagery apparently refers to the booty a soldier might get after battle. As John Bright says in his commentary on Jeremiah in the Anchor Bible:

> One suspects that it originated in the army. Victorious
> soldiers customarily brought home the booty they had

seized; one can imagine that a soldier, returning after a defeat from which he had barely escaped alive, might, when asked where his share of the booty was, have replied ironically that his life was all the "booty" that he could bring away. As the expression passed into general parlance, it came to mean: barely to escape with one's life. But one cannot be sure about this.

Perhaps that sounds like "cold comfort," as Bright, indeed, goes on to remark. But one cannot overestimate its importance to Bonhoeffer, and the passage is crucial to understanding how he maintained hope in the midst of the despair of prison life. Throughout most of his letters, Bonhoeffer expresses hope and confidence that he will soon be released, that his life will be spared, and that what was true for Baruch will also be true for him, namely, that God will give him his life as a prize of war in all places to which he might go.

One has to point out, immediately, that Bonhoeffer was wrong; his life was not spared. But it is important to point out, also immediately, that for the later portion of his imprisonment Bonhoeffer realized that he would not be released; as soon as his part in the plot against Hitler's life was uncovered, he knew that it was only a matter of time until he would be killed. But his genuine serenity was never greater than on the day after the plot failed, and he knew that the jig was up. He wrote on that day, July 21, 1944:

> It is by living completely in this world that one learns to have faith. One must completely abandon any attempt to make something of oneself. . . By this-worldliness I mean living unreservedly in life's duties, problems, successes and failures, experiences and perplexities. In so doing we throw ourselves completely into the arms of God, taking seriously, not our own sufferings, but those of God in the world—watching with Christ in Gethsemane. That, I think, is faith, that is *metanoia*: and that

is how one becomes a man and a Christian. How can success make us arrogant, or failure lead us astray, when we share in God's sufferings through a life of this kind? (*Letters and Papers from Prison*)

What is being said to us through Yahweh's promise to Baruch and through Bonhoeffer's own appropriation of that promise is something very simple and very profound at the same time: *You have a future.* You can bank on that. Things are going to get tougher, yes, but you can be there to respond to whatever happens. You are not left by yourself in that tough future, because what you are going through God, too, is going through, and God is there also. Bonhoeffer hit the theological nail precisely on the head: "How can success make us arrogant or failure lead us astray, when we share God's sufferings through a life of this kind?" The final word is not bleakness but promise.

5. "... *a future and a hope* ..." Thus far, Jeremiah 45. Elsewhere, he took a further step, and we can take it too by calling attention to one other episode in his life. When things finally did go to pieces and the Jews were deported to Babylon, where they had no reason to hope for anything at all, Jeremiah wrote a remarkable letter, preserved now in Chapter 29. My own awareness of the poignancy and relevance of this letter came to me when I spent a week in East Berlin, behind the Iron Curtain, in 1960, just before the [Berlin] wall went up. I was at a conference of East German Christians who were consigned to live under an anti-Christian regime and for whom at that time there were always reasonable possibilities of escape into West Germany through Berlin. But the ones we were meeting with had decided to stay, in the midst of a situation at least as bleak as that of the Jews in Babylon. As I tried to discover why they did, I found them referring again and again to Jeremiah 29. What could the Jews do in a hostile environment thousands of miles from home? Jeremiah writes to them:

Build houses and live in them; plant gardens and eat their produce; take wives and have sons and daughters. . . . Seek the welfare of the city where I have sent you into exile, and pray to the LORD on its behalf, for in its welfare you will find your welfare. (29:6–8)

Grim words to a Jew in Babylon—or to a Christian in East Germany. And yet, strangely hopeful words as well, to us as well as to them. For they say that we can affirm, even during a destructive time. We can—we must—not only cry, but also laugh; not only be long-faced but also joyful; not only take grimly realistic glances at the future but also celebrate the present; not only fear, but also love—even in a time of tearing down. Jeremiah made his own symbolic gesture: just at the time when the future was bleakest and his own life was in jeopardy, he bought a piece of real estate in his old home town. By that act he was affirming that there was a future, that one is never entitled simply to throw in the sponge, but must continue to plan and build.

In the letter we are considering, Jeremiah goes on to promise the exiles that in seventy years Yahweh will visit them. And although seventy years is considerably longer than the remaining life-expectancy of those to whom the letter was addressed, they are to live in the light of that promise. He concludes with the words, "For I know the plans I have for you, says the LORD, plans for welfare and not for evil, to give you a future and a hope" (29:11).

And that, I believe is the ultimate word that emerges for us. It would be curiously sentimental hope if it were not heard against the backdrop for hope that Jeremiah has already sketched. As we live through the destruction that is a part of our own life-times, whether of our nation, or our church, or our own projected futures, we can do so believing that out of it all will come what Jeremiah calls "a future and a hope," and we can align ourselves with those movements and tendencies most indicative, even now, of the direction of that future and that hope.

2

Living the Gospel of Justice

For Brown there was no sharp distinction between the life of faith and the life to which we are called as political agents. Spirituality feeds the political dimension of our human lives, and the political dimension vivifies the life of the spirit. This was a major theme of his life, writing, and voice from the earliest days, found even in the senior sermon he delivered at Amherst. It would guide all of his actions in every arena: politics, civil rights, race relations, economic and social justice, antiwar activism, the pursuit of human rights, and every dimension of Christian faith. In this chapter we find various instances of this principle come to life, including its foundation for him in the life and inspiration of Dietrich Bonhoeffer. It was a principle that would be both challenged and explored at Stanford and elsewhere during the years of the Vietnam War. But he would deliver that message to Catholic nuns, as well as to the World Council of Churches. And he would find it reflected in the courageous witness of Archbishop Oscar Romero and the martyrs of El Salvador.

DIETRICH BONHOEFFER

The following sermon was given on April 10, 1972, at St. Ann's Chapel in Palo Alto, the home of the Catholic Newman Center, while Brown was teaching at Stanford. During those years of ecumenical flowering, pulpit exchange between St. Ann's and nearby First Presbyterian, Brown's home parish, were frequent.

Bonhoeffer was for Brown an exemplar of the consequences of choosing Christ over nation or any form of nationalistic or racist idolatry, and his example of courage and martyrdom deeply inspired Brown's own life. Union Seminary had a special chapel devoted to the memory of Bonhoeffer, who had briefly been a guest there. Brown offered courses on Bonhoeffer throughout his teaching career. We include here the conclusion to the sermon, which captures the essence of Bonhoeffer as inspiration for Brown's life and work.

Now that's a long introduction to a person. I should probably go on to describe the famous *Letters and Papers from Prison* that were smuggled out and published after his death that have given Bonhoeffer major stature as a theologian in our era. But instead of doing that, I want merely to concentrate briefly on a couple of things that the events of his life show us today. But I will do so out of the major question with which he was wrestling in the prison correspondence: As he put it in a letter to his friend Eberhard Bethge: "What is bothering me incessantly is the question of what Christianity really is, or indeed who Christ really is, for us today." Bonhoeffer launched into a long polemic against "religion," a pejorative term for him, which he interpreted to mean trying to find God off in some other world or realm removed from the here and now, or else, within the solitude of my own private existence. He decried the notion that God is either only out there, somewhere else, or "in here," locked within my own personal, private, individual self. So, for Bonhoeffer, God is "in the midst" of life, as he put it—not just at the edges, but in the very center, in the day-to-day engagements in which all of us are thrown together and have to work out our destiny together. This is what the Christ event meant to him. Where is God? God is found in the midst of a political trial, exchanging words with Pontius Pilate, on the secular place of a dump heap outside Jerusalem, where human beings are crucified, instead of confined within the religious place of a temple inside Jerusalem.

That is the first thing, I think, that Bonhoeffer's life and death say to us. God is "in the midst," not somewhere else. You may want to withdraw sometimes to get perspective, and Bonhoeffer did that too, but what you find is that God is calling you back into the midst of life, with all of its frustration, compromise, and ambiguity, because that is where God truly is.

Secondly, Bonhoeffer's life and death show us the unlikely stuff out of which martyrs are made. Let's not over-sensationalize that word "martyr." It is from the Greek word meaning "witness," and it becomes associated with death because the true witness has to risk the possibility that that witness will be unacceptable to those in power. To the degree that we take our faith with any seriousness, we have to realize it may make unexpected demands on us, of a sort that nothing has prepared us for. The first letters to Bonhoeffer in prison from his family are full of their confusion over the fact that someone of their social status should have a son in prison. The German church, after World War II, could not get used to the idea that a Lutheran pastor would have engaged in the kind of political activity that the resistance represented. They still wanted to keep religion and politics in two separate watertight compartments, even after Bonhoeffer's valiant attempt to break down that division. We never know into what roles we may be cast or how we may be misunderstood. Nothing in Bonhoeffer's upbringing or vocational training had prepared him for the role he felt he had to play. God has an unexpected way of casting us in the roles God chooses for us rather than the ones we choose. We must always remain open to that uncomfortable but rather exciting possibility.

TAKE PRAYER

At the height of the Vietnam War, Stanford was the site of major antiwar protests. Brown's high-profile role in antiwar protests and draft counseling for conscientious objectors was joined by other religious leaders at Stanford, including the dean of the

chapel, B. Davie Napier. The Arena, *a conservative student publication, had issued an attack against Napier. Brown's sermon at
Stanford Memorial Church is a rebuttal of the premise that politics and religion cannot mix. The texts are Amos 2:6–8, 5:21–24,
and Matthew 25:31–36.*

Take prayer. There is a good, safe "spiritual" subject. Prayer
obviously belongs in what the editorial refers to as the "House
of God," even if Watts and Vietnam don't. All right, what shall
we pray about? We can pray for those we love, and for faith
and for forgiveness, but then there's that pesky little bit about "I
say to you, love your enemies and pray for those who persecute
you." We are called upon to pray for our enemies. If we pray
for our boys in Vietnam, apparently we have to pray for the
Viet Cong also. And if we are praying for such people, it isn't
very long before we have to consider what our relationship is to
them, how that relationship has fallen apart, what must be done
about that relationship, which soon becomes, "how can we end
the war in Vietnam?" The line from prayer to politics isn't a very
lengthy one, and the minute you start praying, you are getting
dangerously close to the edge of political action if you want to
take a serious part in implementing the concerns of the prayers
you offer here in worship.

What about worship itself? Here in church we engage in
liturgy, and we often speak of liturgy, and perform liturgy, as
though it were at a fully safe remove from the world outside. But
this is the worst possible missing of the point, for we have scan-
dalously narrowed and constricted the meaning of this word
and the meaning of these deeds. The word itself is simply a con-
flation of the two words *laos* and *ergos*, Greek for "people" and
"work." Liturgy is simply "the people's work," the work they
do wherever they are. It originally had nothing in particular to
do with a church. Your liturgy was keeping house, or working
in a precinct office, or checking footnotes, or making love, or

writing Congressional representatives, or singing praise, or playing center field, or giving a lecture. And it was an impoverish-
ment of the word when we began to constrict it to mean not
what-the-people-do-wherever-they-are, but what-the-people-do-
when-they-are-in-church. The point is that what goes on inside
is related to what goes on outside and vice versa. We simply miss
the point if we think that we can talk about liturgy and circum-
scribe it to mean only "spiritual" things inside a church building.

A convenient way to illustrate the inextricable connection
between inside and outside is in the high point of the liturgy that
takes place inside. For virtually all Christian bodies, this it the
Eucharist, or the Lord's Supper. It means many things, of course,
to many Christians and many confessional bodies of Christians.
But whatever else it means it also means this: that the vehicle
through which Christians are made most aware of the living
presence of Christ in their midst is not something "spiritual" or
ethereal or unrelated to the rest of their life. On the contrary, the
vehicle is bread, and the action appropriate to the reception of
the presence of Christ is not a spiritual ethereal act, but the very
ordinary mundane act of eating, munching, chewing, and swal-
lowing. The bread represents Christ—but since it is bread it also
represents many other things: it represents the acts of sowing,
harvesting, threshing, baking, and distributing. It represents the
economic process by which [people] finance these operations.
It represents the political process by which people see to it that
when others do not have enough bread they get enough bread. It
is all wrapped up with the most earthy, political down-to-earth
dimensions of human existence of which we can conceive. And
Vietnam is partly a struggle over bread, that is to say, over how
political and economic and social processes shall be organized
so that people do not starve, do not become desperate, do not
need to kill in order to get bread. By demonstrating concern for
Christ you also demonstrate concern for bread and whether or
not people have it. The two cannot be separated.

Let me now turn to illustrate the theme in one other way. The editorial writer in *Arena* says that Christianity and not Vietnam is the proper subject for attention in the house of God. We should be talking about God. Let's try that on for size too. What are some of the things to say about God? Can we really talk about God and remain nonpolitical?

Some of you have been exposed to the prophet Amos, who has a few rather definite things to say about God, one of them being that God is a God of justice. Very theological, very orthodox. A proper subject surely for Memorial Church even by *Arena*'s standards. But what does it mean to say that God is a God of justice? It is to say that God demands that God's children live justly. Amos insisted that that was a tall order, because everywhere he looked around in Bethel he saw nothing but injustice. The judges were corrupt. The rich were idle and soft, while the poor starved at their gate. The priests were fat. The services of worship in the house of God ignored all this injustice at their gates, and Yahweh says through Amos that the worship that does not come to grips with injustice is an abomination to the just God, that God hates and despises it. Let's not leave it in paraphrase. Yahweh says:

> I hate, I despise your feasts, and I take no delight in your solemn assemblies. Take away from me the noise of your songs; to the melody of your harps I will not listen. But let justice roll down like waters, and righteousness like an ever-flowing stream. (Amos 5:21–22)

The social order has become corrupt and when religion does not seek to transform that social order, it not only condones, it perpetuates the corruption. The social order must be reconstituted or utter doom will follow.

If you take seriously that God is a God of justice, that our society must be based on justice, and that in fact it is incredibly unjust, you must seek to change that social order. If you believe that God is just and that destroying hundreds of civilian villages

in South Vietnam with napalm and bulldozers is unjust, then
you have to act, and God and Vietnam can be separate no longer.

God has placed us in this world. It is a beautiful world and
a terrifying world. It is a world of fantastically creative potentialities, and even more fantastically destructive potentialities.
Whatever else it is it is also a political world, a material world, a
worldly world. And it is God's. I grant you it is often very hard
to know just where God is in this world, and I don't have any
inside track on God's whereabouts or any spiritual radar that
can locate God with pinpoint accuracy. But wherever else God
is in this world today, I'm willing to stake my all on the fact that
God is in the midst of what is going on in Vietnam, suffering
with the agonized peasants whose homes we destroy, bleeding
with the dying, binding up the wounds with the medics. God's
love is lacerated by antipersonnel weapons, and God's might and
power and goodness are challenged every day in the enflamed
and charred bodies of victims of napalm. At least if the cross is
a picture in time of what is always true for God, then we can be
sure of that, and can appreciate in a new way what Pascal meant
when he wrote, "Christ is crucified to the world's end." To talk
about a Christian God who is not also a loving God is impossible, and to talk about a loving God who is not also suffering with
those God loves is to cheapen love to the point of blasphemy. So
if God is a proper subject for Memorial Church, O ye readers of
Arena—so is Vietnam, and so is Watts, and so is East Palo Alto.
There is no way we can properly or honestly separate them.

SPIRITUALITY AND POLITICS:
THE NATURE OF THE MIX

*The following address was given on May 10, 1990, at a con-
ference marking the opening of the United States Holocaust
Memorial Museum in Washington, D.C., a project on which
Brown had worked with Elie Wiesel. The venue was the State
Department.*

For two thousand years the Christian church has had an off-again, on-again, attitude toward the interweaving of so-called spirituality and so-called politics. It has sometimes affirmed their unity but more often, perhaps, has insisted that they be kept separate. My sympathies lie totally with the former option, and I have spent a large part of my professional life arguing against the latter option.

I am not really suggesting that there are two entities, spirituality and politics, and that our task is somehow to mix them together. What I am really affirming is rather that each word, when truly understood, includes the other. Which is to say that if you are committed to a life of spirituality, part of the spiritual life is that you will be actively engaged in the political arena; and that when you are committed to a life of political involvement you will be exemplifying the life of the spirit. And I don't mind if the latter word is spelled with a capital "S."

Now this is one of those theological proposals that partakes of the problem of most theological proposals, namely, that it is much easier to understand what is being denied than it is to understand what is being affirmed. What I am denying is that we can divide life into two separate compartments—a position known historically as dualism—and that attempts to do so sell the Christian faith short (not to mention Judaism, which has a much better track record than Christianity on this matter). Judaism affirms that the God of the Hebrew Scriptures is not exclusively ensconced in some remote heaven but is right in the midst of all that is going on among the chosen people, and a lot of not-so-chosen people as well. As Abraham Heschel[6] points out, the Hebrew word for "earth" appears five times as often in the Bible as the Hebrew word for "heaven." Christians affirm that for them God is not mainly found in exclusion or apartness, or deserts or mountaintops, but right in the midst of messy human life, and in one particular human life that itself got pretty messy before people were finished trying to snuff it out. That the Word, the creative power of God, was made flesh, as the Fourth

Gospel says quite starkly, is an astonishing and initially shocking assertion. For if that is true, then what happens in that same
world of the flesh—poverty, war, suffering, economics—has got
to be a paramount concern of those who acknowledge Jesus as
the focal point of their lives. And that means that we are already
talking politics.

And rather than argue that out in theoretical fashion, let
me illustrate it by referring to the events that Christians have
been remembering in recent liturgical celebrations—Jesus' entry
into Jerusalem and the other events of Holy Week. I shall argue
that these events are almost paradigms of the inseparability of
spirituality and politics, because they were themselves political
events up to the hilt in which Jesus was centrally involved up to
the hilt himself. For Jews, the same point is made in relation to
Passover, which, as we shall see, comprises the recalling of one of
the most intensely political events in Israel's history.

Consider the context of Holy Week (which for our purposes
might also be called Spirituality-and-Politics Week). Jesus had
been leading a small and not terribly effective movement in the
north of Palestine for a couple of years. Having started with
the grassroots, the Jesus movement seemed mired there. So the
group retired to the far north, Caesarea Philippi, to take stock
of the situation, and for whatever reasons, a decision was made
to move south, clear to the other end of the country, go to the
capital city, and, so to speak, confront Caesar in his lair, in the
persons of Herod and Pilate. Jesus' entry into the center of political power has ever since been called "the triumphal entry," and
the acclaim he got on that occasion must have struck initial terror in the hearts of the governing authorities. To be sure, he did
not enter on a white charger, as the standard-bearer of a direct
political insurrection, and his choice of a donkey, hardly a symbol of political pizzazz in those days, may have defused some
of the anxiety in high places. But as the week went on, there
was confrontation after confrontation, and by Thursday night
the fair-weather friends of Sunday afternoon had muted their

huzzahs and disposed of their palm branches, and even Jesus' closest friends were saying to servant girls (also not exactly symbols of political power that one might need to fear): "Jesus? Never heard of him."

Whatever Jesus' intentions were—and it is highly doubtful that he came to Jerusalem to lead a political rebellion—he was perceived by the politicians as a political danger, and when they strung him up on that first-century equivalent of an electric chair, the placard identifying him as "King of the Jews" was really no more than a series of first-century code words for "subversive."

Earlier in the week we recall, Jesus had made the enigmatic pronouncement, "Render to God what belongs to God and to Caesar what belongs to Caesar," which has had the exegetes working overtime ever since, but which, whatever else it means, stated quite clearly that there were certainly a lot of things that didn't belong to Caesar and therefore could not be rendered unto him, whether Caesar felt that he was entitled to them or not. And that, of course, whether it is couched in political language or not, is the thing that Caesars, heads of government, prime ministers, shahs, and presidents, cannot abide: namely, that somebody else might be defining what is their turf and what is not.

But that's only part of the story. Adding fuel to the fire of the tensions in Jerusalem that week, was the fact that it was the season of Passover, and Jews from all over the empire were gathering in Jerusalem for services. The Passover was the enacted memory of the first really big encounter between spirituality and politics, back in Egypt, centuries earlier. Here, too, a religious leader whose initial credentials didn't seem any more imposing than Jesus' credentials, got locked into a battle royal with the then-Caesar, who in those days was called a Pharaoh.

How anyone can read the story of the Passover and ensuing exodus of the Jews from Egypt and claim that "religion and politics don't mix" defies any rule of logic to which I have access. This was perhaps the religion-politics encounter par excellence, not only in its own right, but because the Jews seized on the event as the central memory of their corporate life, the one that they most assiduously remember and re-enact every year—the event in which the power of their God and the power of the number one political leader met eyeball to eyeball. And it was the number one political leader who blinked. The Passover also represents a milestone among those human events in which spirituality and politics were all entangled with one another, and in which it was seen as perfectly proper, and indeed mandatory, for those with so-called spiritual interests to rally around charges that the political interests were engaging in manifest injustice—such as owning slaves, beating them, denying them dignity, oppressing them economically and politically and in every other way, sexual abuse not excluded. But to the slaves, that wasn't just a political issue, it was a religious issue as well—indeed there was no way to draw a line between them. God cared about what was happening to them.

[*Here Brown turns to a contemporary application of the principle that religion and politics mix: the sanctuary movement that was then in high gear during the civil war in El Salvador*].

WINDOWS ON THE WORLD

The following excerpts are from an address, one of two given by Brown to the Twelfth General Chapter of the Sisters of Mercy, held in Baltimore July 22–27, 1986. His comments contributed to the development of a core constitution that helped to bring about the unification of Mercy congregations in 1991 as the Sisters of Mercy of the Americas. Brown had been asked to comment on the proposed constitution in light of the theology of liberation. This address reflects not only the trust placed in him by Catholic religious women, but also his own remarkable familiarity with the situation of religious women in the Roman Catholic Church. It still resonates as a call to encouragement, courage, and faith in pursuing the paths these women took in

*the wake of the Second Vatican Council, with which Brown was
also intimately familiar.*

The starting point of your constitution is a wonderful example
of liberation thought. You define yourselves as those "responding to a call to serve the needy of our time . . . to serve the poor,
sick, and ignorant . . . to respond to the cry of the poor."

Your inspiration comes from a recognition of the poor and the
needy in the world. You do not say, "Let us develop a theology
of poverty and then look around for some places to apply it."
No, you are struck not so much by the reality of the "poverty"
as by the reality of the "poor people"—and you recognize that
there is all the difference in the world between an intellectual
formulation and an individual in need. There is plenty of room
for intellect and reflection, but it is commitment to persons, not
to ideas, that must be a starting point.

The phrase you use, "the cry of the poor," is central in the
life of the church in the third world today. In the Exodus story,
you will remember that it is God who says, " I have heard the
cry of my people," and who then follows it up with two crucial
affirmations. God says, "I have come down to deliver them," but
God also says to Moses, "I will send you to Pharaoh, that you
may bring forth my people." God is in the midst of the struggle,
and that is our final hope; but that does not exempt *us* from
being in the midst of the struggle as well. Our role is not to
watch God establish justice. The fact that God is in the midst of
the struggle is what can free us to get into the midst of the struggle also, confident not only that we are on God's side if we side
with the poor, but also that it is through us that God chooses to
bring about the justice so sadly lacking in Egypt back then, or in
Baltimore and Scranton and Nicaragua and South Africa today.

Leonardo Boff[7] (whom it is once again okay to quote in Catholic circles now that his silencing has been lifted) has a book
on the Lord's Prayer, which he subtitles "The Prayer of Integral Liberation." This word also refers to what is necessary for

wholeness, completeness, the sense of parts forming a whole. Boff insists that the Lord's Prayer gives no support to a "spiritual" liberation divorced from the world of poverty and hunger. All sides of life must be brought together, integrally, and this is done, he claims, in Jesus' prayer, which undercuts reductionism, whether as "theologism," on the one hand, or "secularism" on the other. "Prayer," Boff writes, "is not the first thing a person does. Before praying, one experiences an existential shock." So every phrase of the Lord's Prayer has a dual focus—toward God and toward us. They cannot be separated.

Conclusion: there can be no dividing the world into "sacred" and "profane" arenas, no assigning of Christian tasks so that some are "doing" while others are "praying," no dichotomy between spiritual and material. There is not a special realm we have to seek in order to "find" God. The more we look in the one realm we all inhabit, the more likely we are to discover that God has been there all the time. Word and deed, as your constitution puts it, have an "integrity," a wholeness; they are not separate parts of life.

I plead with you to keep this emphasis central. Those outside your group will urge you to stick to "spiritual" things and not get messed up in politics or economic analysis. (Even bishops have been known to make this plea.) Your constitution asserts that you refuse to divide the world so artificially, and you have mandated to keep "integration" and "integrity" central to all that you do. Prayer is not only what you do in the chapel; it is what you do in the world. Work is not only what you do in the world; it is what you do in the chapel. It is all of a piece. And when they challenge you, simply remind them that this is not heresy or "horizontalism," or reductionism; it is simply incarnational Christianity. Jesus did not become an idea, or a principle, or an otherworldly type. He was "made flesh," right in the midst of politics and economics and disease, and he got tired and hungry and discouraged just like the rest of us. Christians find God not elsewhere, but right in the midst of the nitty-gritty. In your words, we have *integral* faith.

Probably the most important single Christian task is to keep mercy and justice together. Mercy without justice is sentimental; justice without mercy is harsh. Both are needed. You could spend a lifetime trying to embody that commitment, and I am sure you would go down to your graves justified. But no, you had to make it even harder for yourselves, which is to your eternal credit and, I hope, will make you rise from your graves sanctified, for you have not been content to leave matters in the arena of a theological dialectic. As a way to model mercy and justice, you promise "to promote systemic change." How easy it would have been to leave that off, settle for saying, "If we just work within our lives to combine mercy and justice, we'll change individual human lives enough so that society will gradually be changed as well." That is the biggest booby-trap on the theological battlefield today, and I'm glad you avoided it. For the problem is not just a few evil individuals who want to run the world their way; the problem is a lot of good individuals absolutely trapped in a system that won't let them do the good they want. The reality is not that evil boards of directors are sitting around saying, "Let's find a way of increasing profits so that children will starve." It is rather that boards of directors, whose job by definition is to increase profits, sometimes have to act in ways that (quite unintentionally as far as they are concerned) have the practical consequence that the economy of a region is destroyed and children *do* starve. The fault is partly individual, of course, but it is also the fault of the system as a whole, which puts profits above persons.

In the face of that, you have indicated that you see "systemic change" as part of the gospel mandate. I fully agree. But we are in a very intimate minority as far as the world and even the church are concerned! So I hope you will finely hone this one, work on it, discuss it, find ways to begin to implement it, and never, never forsake it. (Indeed, if I were to have my druthers, I would suggest that you inflect this paragraph to read that you "endeavor to model mercy and justice *by promoting* systemic change.")

Another example you offer of the need for a kind of balance is harder to attain. You write on the one hand of "the spirit of obedience" (which has a long history with which you are more familiar than I), and a few lines later you promise to "respect freedom of conscience." It is the perennial struggle of all Christians, and not just women religious, to keep these two things in creative tension. You are aware of the problem in community life—one need only invoke the names of Agnes Mary Mansour and Teresa Kane and Margaret Farley[8] to know how hard this can be—and you know that there are never two cases alike when we have to adjudicate the proper boundaries of "freedom of conscience" in relation to "the spirit of obedience." Catholic sisters have had a painful struggle over this.[9] I think it is only a preview of the conflicts that will arise for those of you who take seriously the need to work for "systemic justice."

You state that we are not just to affirm our corporate world; we are to "celebrate" it, and we are to do so with "the courage of a deep faith and interior joy." Those words—"celebrate," "faith," "joy"—are the crux of the matter. The times in which we live are not times for long-faced Christians who are afraid to "celebrate," either because they don't know what to celebrate or because they are afraid that celebration will appear to make them unresponsive to human misery. H. L. Mencken's definition of Puritanism is a constant challenge to me: "the awful fear," as he put it," that somewhere, somehow, someone might be happy." I'm sure such Puritanism has its Catholic counterparts as well. Perhaps your invoking "celebration" and "joy" can help us keep the good news good.

This too, is a strong liberation theme. Gustavo Gutiérrez, commenting on North American visitors to Peru, says:

> People come down here and they say, "Oh, how terrible, so much suffering, so much poverty, so much oppression." And they are right; there is much suffering and poverty and oppression, and things may well get worse. But in addition to those things, we now have, for the first time in our history, a sense of hope. We know that it need not remain the way it has always been. It can be better; if not for us, at least for our children. And that is enough for which to live and die joyfully.

Gutiérrez talks about "the joy of the poor." I, as a nonpoor person, can attest that such qualities as joy and hope and celebration—and courage (another word in the passage we are looking at)—are real and deep and authentic. They are saying in their context what you are saying in yours when you introduce another great verb: "We rejoice. . . ." So, in the midst of all that looks bleak and discouraging, I am refreshed and empowered by your words, and I remind you that you can continually be refreshed and empowered by them as well.

Some comments on two resources to which your constitution points—the Holy Spirit and Mary.

You propose to receive God's word as Mary did "and to act upon it," making your own her rhythm of contemplation and action. May a Protestant urge you to make Mary more and more your model? Let her (if the image doesn't seem frivolous) assume top billing in your lives. In earlier Catholic history and devotion, Mary seems to be a model for distanced passivity—the demure maiden always dressed in expensive, unsoiled and perfectly ironed blue garments, high above the world (on the moon, no less, in the holy pictures), the hallmark of whose virtue was to accept a role she had no part in choosing, and to allow her will to be overridden by divine and angelic forces who would not have responded kindly to a refusal on her part. But while there may be virtue in that posture, the Mary we are rediscovering today, largely thanks to our Latin American sisters and brothers (who have forced us to read the Magnificat not only in English but in its entirety) is very different. And if you want someone who will become, as you put it, "our model of faith," then it is Mary the liberator, Mary the mother of the liberator, Mary who asserts that the mighty will be brought low and the poor lifted up, Mary the revolutionary—who provides the exciting model. Make no mistake about it: to affirm the Mary of the Magnificat is to affirm a commitment to social justice, to "a preferential option for the poor," to the need for "systemic change," and all the other challenging emphases that have made their way into your constitution. As Catholic women, you have a model not dependent on patriarchal images or macho world-views or masculine presuppositions. If it is still true that "one can never say too much about Mary," let it be the case that you say the new things.

The other resource I want to highlight is the passing reference to the Holy Spirit. It is the very nature of the case that the Spirit defies categorization, and doesn't "fit" into our tidy schemes, our systematic theologies, or even our brand new constitutions. It might be the case that one of the neatest divine tricks that will ever be played on you is that your one-liner about the holy Spirit, "We rely on the Holy Spirit to lead us," will turn out to be the inner power of the entire constitution. For it is a very subversive thought. Didn't anyone tell you that it is exceedingly dangerous "to rely on the Holy Spirit," if you want to keep things safe and tame and wish to remain on good terms with hierarchical power? We can accept as axiomatic that any claim that the Spirit blows where it wills is going to make hierarchical types very, very nervous. The whole experience of the Latin American *comunidades de base* attests to the fact that Spirit-filled communities can arise and function without episcopal supervision and even without priestly guidance. And if women religious, who are neither bishops nor priests—at least not yet—are going to start invoking the leading of the Spirit, who knows what may happen? To say that you will "rely on the Holy Spirit" is to unlock previously closed doors, to let lots of life and fresh air into the church (as Pope John XXIII said so well), without any final control over what happens. A fantastic prospect!

It is possible, of course, to invoke the spirit in perfunctory fashion, and Christians have done that very well for many centuries. I choose to believe that your own invocation is *not* perfunctory, that you know exactly what you are doing, and that you are prepared to take the consequences. If I'm wrong, watch out. The Spirit might decide to overrule us both.

Let me, to conclude, be a bit hortatory, and urge some things upon you for that future. Your vows, whatever their hardships, provide you with a marvelous gift for the future—the ability *to travel light.* In a world so encumbered with things and so enamored of possessions, you give communal support to one another in refusing to succumb to those temptations. You give up much—marriage, motherhood, close family ties—but you do gain the possibility of knowing many men without complications, the privilege of seeing all children as your own, of claiming humankind as your family, and you gain *mobility.*

The greatest asset on the journey of the pilgrim people of God is the ability to travel light. Abraham and Sarah had it, putting their lands and their wealth behind them; the prophets had it; Jesus and the disciples had it, being instructed to take only what was needed for a single day; Francis and his followers had it, and most third world Christians have it. I think it is evil to justify the lack of possessions of others, who have not chosen that way but had it imposed on them. However, if the decision to travel light is voluntarily assumed, as it has been by all of you, then it can be not only a grace but an empowerment. So I urge you, nay, I exhort you, to make the best possible use of your mobility—spiritual, physical, psychic—and claim it as an asset rather than as the price you have to pay for being a sister. A phrase from one of the New Delhi documents of the World Council of Churches strikes the right note: Christians are those who are "glad to dwell in the tent of perpetual adaptation."

That base of traveling light frees you to be radical, in the true meaning of the word, getting to the *radix*, the root, of things—not just alleviating the present reality of poverty, but exploring the root causes of why there are poor people, which, as we have seen, has to do not only with sinful human hearts but with sinful human structures as well. In such a world, this is not a time for halfway measures, for making peace with the world, for accommodation to principalities and powers, who would like nothing better than to have religious folks, by staying on the sidelines or remaining quiet, give their tacit approval to the monstrous things that are being done every day in our name.

In Thoreau's image, you—and I—are called to march to the beat of a different drummer; your constitution affirms the theme if not the image. During an interview with those under indictment in the Sanctuary trial in Tucson, Arizona, a reporter asked, "Who is the real 'leader' of the Sanctuary movement?" And it was a Jewish lawyer who replied, "The leader of the Sanctuary movement, as I have learned from the defendants, will always be one step beyond the jurisdiction of any Federal court." You know who your leader is, and you know that he is answerable to no court, no curial official, no government, no contemporary fad or way of life. And you know what that means for you and me. It means that we are called upon to be living embodiments of the claim by Cardinal Suhard, archbishop of Paris during World War II, that "[To be a witness] means living in such a way that your life would be inexplicable if God did not exist."

WHO IS THIS JESUS CHRIST
WHO FREES AND UNITES?

Brown's keynote address at the Fifth Assembly of the World Council of Churches, held in Nairobi, Kenya, in November 1975, is one of the most important speeches of his career. By this time in his life he had not only engaged in activities for peace, but had also undergone a conversion through his introduction to the world of liberation theology. The focus here is on the person of Jesus. While some of the specific historical references have been removed from the present version, its reference to the tensions generated by the situation of a postcolonial world remain germane to the development of an ecumenical Christian spirituality that will lead to mutual understanding and solidarity.

> Now when Jesus came to the district of Caesarea Philippi, he asked his disciples, "Who do people say that the Son of Man is?" They answered, "Some say John the Baptist, others Elijah, and still others Jeremiah or one of the prophets." "And you," Jesus asked, "who do you say that I am?" Simon Peter answered: "You are the Messiah, the Son of the living God." And Jesus answered him, "Blessed are you, Simon son of Jonah! For flesh and blood has not revealed this to you, but my heavenly father. . . . From that time on, Jesus began to show his disciples that he must go to Jerusalem and undergo great suffering at the hands of the elders, chief priests and lawyers, and be killed, and on the third day be raised. And Peter took him aside and began to rebuke him, saying, "God forbid it, Lord! This must never happen to you." Then Jesus turned and said to Peter, "Away with you, Satan! You are a stumbling block to me. You think as people think, not as God thinks." (Matt. 16:13–17, 21–23)

Peter's Problem and Ours

Who is this Jesus Christ who frees and unites? Let us put ourselves in Peter's shoes. Peter's role in the episode is astonishing. First he is the hero—the one who gives the right answer to the question, "Who do you say that I am?" But a moment later he is the villain; the spokesperson for God has become the spokesperson for Satan. Peter knew the right words but he didn't know what they meant.

So as we deal with the question, "Who is this Jesus Christ who frees and unites?" Let us listen particularly to those answers that initially threaten us the most, rather than reassuring ourselves with the answers with which we are already comfortable. If your present answer focuses on Jesus the personal savior, then be willing to confront Jesus the liberator whose social message threatens all the human securities you take for granted. If Jesus the revolutionary is the one who now gives you hope, then hear also the Jesus who reminds you that evil is embodied not only in oppressive structures but also in every human heart—not only in the heart of the evil oppressor but in your own heart as well.

Three Claims

Among the many claims made about Jesus Christ, on which shall we focus our attention? Our assembly theme gives us some direction. The Evanston assembly described Jesus as "The Hope of the World," New Delhi described him as "The Light of the World," and Uppsala described him as "The One Who Makes All Things New."[10] Nairobi describes Jesus as the one who "Frees and Unites—Jesus the Liberator, Jesus the Unifier." As I shall suggest later, I believe that we cannot truly put those claims together unless we insert between them a claim that Jesus is also the Divider. As Jesus liberates us, we are required to face the potential divisions that liberation brings so that we can move toward a truer unity than would otherwise be possible. Let us explore these three claims.

Jesus the Liberator

To call Jesus the Liberator narrows our field of inquiry, but it is still immensely broad. *From* what does Jesus free us, and *for* what does he free us? I need not elaborate some of the answers on which we could dwell. It has been the Christian experience that Jesus frees us *from* many things: the wrath of God, the law, sin, death, fear, ideology, racism, oppression, hunger, wealth. And it has been the Christian experience that he frees us *for* many things as well: love, caring, suffering, joy, courage, the neighbor, the enemy, a new society, the fruits of the Spirit.

We cannot talk about all of these. Some arbitrary choices must be made, and I shall make them. I shall assume that we can take for granted the liberation that Jesus brings in the area of our personal lives; we already know something of that or we would not be here. I shall also assume that we recognize that the false division between a gospel for the individual and a gospel for society is seen to be just that—false. There are further things, then, about Jesus the Liberator:

1. Negatively, he frees us from false securities by which we try to make our lives secure. He makes an uncomfortably exclusive claim upon us. We are to give primary allegiance to him, and that means that we can give only secondary allegiance to anyone or anything else. Those other loyalties that have heretofore claimed us turn out to be inadequate and therefore false. They do not free; they destroy, particularly when we build them into the structures of our society.

Take the forms of oppression in our society mentioned a moment ago—racism, sexism, classism, imperialism. These do not free; they enslave. They enslave not only those on whom they are imposed; they enslave those who do the imposing. If I seek security in my whiteness, I discover that Jesus does not love us according to our skin color, and that skin color confers no special privileges in God's sight. If I seek security in my maleness, telling myself that "this is a man's world" and that men must make the decisions, I discover that in Christ there is "neither male nor female," and that sexist domination has no place. If I seek security in my class situation, attempting to hold on to the benefits of being relatively affluent, I discover that Jesus' message is addressed centrally to the poor, and that my attempt at class privilege impedes, rather than furthers, the doing of his will. If I seek security in my United States citizenship, I discover that it is the nations whom Christ has called to judgment (Matt.

25:32) and that by his tests—have we fed the hungry? clothed the naked? visited the sick?—not only my nation but all nations are tried and found wanting. Negatively, then, allegiance to Jesus the Liberator can free *from* allegiance to those false centers of security.

2. Positively, he frees us for the possibility of seeing the world through eyes other than our own. I offer that phrase as a "non-theological" equivalent for the theological word "conversion." He leads us to a fundamental change of direction, so that the concern of the "other" can become our own concern.

In the midst of much that remains unclear to us, one thing at least becomes increasingly clear: there is a convergence today between the biblical view of Jesus the Liberator and the cry of oppressed peoples for liberation. For our own day, to "see the world through eyes other than our own" has simply got to mean seeing it through the eyes of the poor and dispossessed. When the story of Jesus and the story of human oppression are put side by side, they fit. They are simply different versions of the same story. The cry of the hungry is overwhelming. The cry of the politically and economically exploited is overwhelming. The cry of those in prison and under torture is overwhelming. The cry of parents who know that their children are doomed to stunted and warped lives is overwhelming. We cannot meet in Africa, indeed we cannot meet anywhere, and shut our ears to that human cry. There may have been other emphases needed at other points in Christian history than talking about Jesus as Liberator, but I am persuaded that for this time and this place, the claim of Jesus to bring freedom and the cry of oppressed peoples for freedom converge and cannot be separated.

People today are in chains—not only the chains of personal guilt and inadequacy and individual shame, but also the chains forged by those who have too much power and have abused it, the chains forged by those who deny freedom to all but them-selves, the chains forged by those who use political and economic systems for their own gain and destroy whole peoples and continents in the process.

Gustavo Gutiérrez has underlined the point unforgettably. He acknowledges that there is an important form of Christian witness that reaches out to the nonbeliever, the one for whom belief in God has become difficult if not impossible in "a world come of age."[11] But he insists that the problem for Christians in the third world is not how to reach out to the nonbeliever, but how to reach out to the nonperson—to the one whom the world ignores, or uses and crushes and then discards, the one who is "marginalized," whose cry not only for food but for meaning is simply not heard, whose personhood the rest of us simply deny. We cannot talk about the lordship of Jesus Christ, or the reconciling love of God, or the meaning of the cross, or Jesus as Liberator, unless the cry of those we treat as nonpersons is the central thing we hear, unless the vision of a world so structured as to take them into account is the central thing we see, unless we can come to see the world through their eyes.

Where is the gospel imperative for that? Take only one part of the cry, the cry for food, acknowledging that that cry must be heard in relation to agriculture, economics, population control, the use of energy resources, and all the rest. Remember, in the midst of all that complexity, that while Jesus said that we do "not live by bread alone," he never pretended that we can live without it. Not only are his stories about the Kingdom of God replete with images of meals, feasts, and banquets for the poor and dispossessed, but on a number of occasions he acted in quite scandalous fashion to make sure his followers had bread. He let them break the law of the Sabbath by plucking up grain from the field. When he spoke to a large crowd and it got to be supper time, he did not tell them that food for their souls was enough; he went to extraordinary lengths to see that they had food for their bodies as well—bread and fish, you will recall. And when he wanted to leave his followers his clearest possible reminder of his ongoing presence, what did he leave us? He left us a meal, telling us that to be aware of his presence we should eat and drink. And I have come to believe that the modern equivalent of the Pauline warning about abusing that meal by "eating and drinking judgment upon ourselves" (1 Cor. 11:27–29) is for us to share that meal with Jesus and at the same time deny meals to millions of his children, or even one of his children.

He frees us to see the world through eyes other than our own, and in our time that means striving to see the world from the perspective of the poor, the starving, the dispossessed.

3. But it is not enough to "see" something; we must also act upon what we see. And so that means a third thing: Jesus not only frees us from false allegiances, so that we can begin to see the world through eyes other than our own; he also frees us for struggle with and on behalf of those "others" who are the poor and dispossessed.

Let me try to suggest some of the things this would have to mean for me; only you can determine what it might mean for you. Since the gospel makes clear that we cannot settle for a world dominated by the white minority and helps me to see the world through the eyes of nonwhites, I can be freed to struggle for a world in which the white minority will no longer have power out of proportion to what is due to it. Since the gospel makes clear that we cannot settle for a world dominated by males and helps me to see what male domination has done to women (and also to men), I can be freed to struggle for a world in which my maleness will no longer guarantee certain jobs, income, or privileges denied to women. Since the gospel makes clear that we cannot settle for a world dominated by the affluent and helps me to see the destructive consequences of a system in which 6 percent of the world's population consumes 40 percent of the world's resources, I can be freed to struggle for a world in which my own standard of living will have to be significantly lowered as we work toward a more equitable distribution of the world's resources through a restructuring of our political and economic systems. Since the gospel makes clear that we cannot settle for a world dominated by the United States (or any other nation) and helps me to see how brutal are the attempts of one nation to control the destinies of other nations, I can be freed to struggle for a world in which my nation will no longer be Number One, a world in which an exploited Chilean worker will count for more than the profits of an American corporation, a world in which napalm is no longer an instrument of diplomatic pressure.

I won't do these things very well. It is far easier to speak such words on a podium in Nairobi, Kenya, than to act upon them in California, U.S.A. But part of the liberation they struggle to describe is the liberation that comes from being part of the supportive community that is the church and the exhilarating discovery that we are not alone in such efforts. We must support and challenge and prod each other in our common allegiance to the smiting and healing Word of God, embodied in Jesus, who promises to free us not only from inner attitudes but from oppressive outer structures as well.

Jesus the Divider

And that of course means that Jesus Christ not only liberates. He also divides. That is initially surprising. "Surely," we respond, "it is Satan who divides, not Jesus." Division for the sake of division must indeed be the devil's work. But let us not evade too quickly the reality that in different ways Jesus also is the divider. Consider:

Commitment to Jesus Christ divides Christians from the majority of the human family who make no such commitment. He divides us from the secular colleagues with whom we work, from our Jewish friends with whom we otherwise share so much, from Hindus, Muslims, Buddhists, Marxists, and humanists. That is simply a fact of human experience.

But the fact that Jesus divides is not just a sociologically descriptive fact. It has been a reality of the gospel from the very beginning. Remember some of those verses we usually forget: "I have come to set fire to the earth. . . . Do you suppose I came to establish peace on earth? No indeed, I have come to bring division" (Luke 12:49, 51). In the parallel passage the metaphor is even stronger: "I have not come to bring peace, but a sword" (Matt. 10:34). Jesus tells us that because of him a man will be set against his father, a daughter against her mother, that our enemies will be found within our own households (Matt. 10:35–36). He makes divisions between wise and foolish maidens, sheep and goats, lost and found.

Such divisions continue among his followers. What I have said about Jesus as Liberator has already divided me from those of you who feel that I have betrayed the gospel and made Jesus too political. And yet, persons sitting across the aisle from you may feel that I have not made Jesus political enough, and that I am too conditioned by bourgeois categories to understand the full thrust of liberation.

There is still another way in which Jesus is Divider, for, as we see in Jesus' sermon at Nazareth (Luke 4:16–30),[12] the good news he brings to one group is (initially at least) bad news to another group. If Jesus' liberating message is good news to the poor, it means that the rich stand to lose something. If slaves are freed, slave owners are threatened. If those in captivity are liberated, those who have kept them in captivity had better beware.

Let us press the point: Christians in Latin America often proclaim the message of liberation in the framework of the Exodus story: if the good news is that God freed the oppressed Israelites from the power of the ancient Pharaohs, then God must be able to free the oppressed today from the power of the modern Pharaohs. And that can hardly be good news to the modern Pharaohs!

Who are these modern Pharaohs? They are the local oligarchies, the tiny minorities who have betrayed their people. But they are also those who have supported the local oligarchies with money, guns, intellectual rationalizations of injustice, and sophisticated torture techniques. Much of that kind of support comes, of course, from the United States and other wealthy nations. So if it is good news to Latin Americans that God promises to free them from the modern Pharaohs, it can only be bad news to North Americans to discover that according to the Exodus scenario a lot of us are serving in Pharaoh's court and that Pharaoh is doomed.

Position yourself where you will in such a scenario. I know that it divides me from many of my Latin American sisters and brothers who see me as the oppressor who must be conquered. It divides me from most of my North American sisters and brothers, who reject such an analysis emphatically and are outraged that it should be offered as an exposition of the gospel. And it divides me from God and Jesus Christ—for if the analysis is correct, I am, whether I like it or not, on the wrong side in a struggle in which God has clearly taken sides with the oppressed, the poor, the downtrodden. Jesus is the Divider.

Jesus the Unifier

Finally, however, he is the Unifier. Jesus did not come "that all may be divided"; he came "that all may be one" (John 17:21). But this must be said last (as it is now being said) rather than first. For if it is said too quickly, it will underestimate the reality of division, and the unity it proclaims will be superficial. During the civil rights struggle in the United States, for example, we discovered that "Black and White Together" had to give way for a while to "Black Power" and an insistence by blacks that they work with blacks alone. Similarly, many women have discovered that they need to meet for a while without men in order to learn from one another how to work for their own liberation.

But such postures can never be accepted within the Christian community as more than provisional, transitional postures. For the meaning of Jesus Christ is that he finally frees us from such postures. If he is provisionally the Divider, he is not finally the Divider. He is the Unifier.

The world around us exhibits deeper divisions than ever before, perhaps in human history. Nation lifts up sword against nation, earth's resources and earth's people are alike exploited, ploughshares are turned into swords, the "haves" grab from the "have nots"—on and on the dreary litany goes. And we Christians have added to those divisions some further ones of our own—the divisions between Catholic and Protestant, Orthodox and Pentecostal, Anglican and Quaker, Calvinist and Lutheran.

But let us stress now the divisions that are of central concern to the entire human family: the divisions between black and white, north and south, rich and poor, left and right, male and female, oppressor and oppressed. What task do these realities lay upon us, meeting in a world whose divisions are also our divisions, and yet meeting in the name of Jesus Christ, who not only frees and divides, but also unites?

I think the task is clear. We have to demonstrate that we have been sufficiently freed to go beyond our divisions and begin to embody the unity to which Jesus the Unifier beckons us.

That is easy to say and difficult to accomplish. But because of who Jesus Christ is, it is something we can dare to attempt. In the Matthew passage with which we began, Jesus tells his disciples that he must go to Jerusalem to suffer and die. He does exactly that, exposing himself to the ultimate division and separation, residing in the powers of sin and death. He bears the full brunt of their attack and they destroy him. But it is our faith that the story does not end there and that in facing those enemies he has overcome them, for, even as was promised, on the third day God raised him from the dead. Here is our promise: that if we too face division and separation, we will find that beyond the division and separation is healing and unity, for Jesus draws us into oneness with him and therefore with one another, just as he is drawn into oneness with his Father.

How do we, here and now, begin to move beyond our divisions toward that kind of unity? There is only one way, and we know what is involved. It involves confession and repentance, before God and to one another. In the days ahead this will involve reaching out toward one another at risk, officially and unofficially, individually and corporately, hoping to be heard and accepted but willing if necessary to endure rebuff patiently, believing that sooner or later the healing power of the risen Christ can reach out across the awesome division by which we are presently scarred.

It is not my task to tell you what sins you should confess. But is my task to suggest that along the path we walk, mutual confession and forgiveness will be important ways in which we respond to Jesus the Unifier. For out of common repentance can come the beginnings of a new common obedience, in which we mutually pledge to struggle together to destroy both the inner attitudes and the outer structures that perpetuate the evils we must eradicate. By such steps toward one another we could begin to embody a little more fully the unity we so easily talk about.

This would be important not only for those of us at Nairobi, but also for those not at Nairobi. When Jesus prayed "that all may be one," he continued "that the world may believe." Imagine what it would mean if it could be said once again of us, as it was said of the early church, "See how these Christians love one another!" So I have a dream for this Assembly. It is that we could be sufficiently freed by Jesus Christ to recognize our divisions and work through them, with whatever conflict and threat is necessary, toward a new degree of unity with one another, so that we could be, however imperfectly, a microcosm of what the human family in its totality is meant to be, demonstrating such things as the following: that although I am a citizen of the United States, and you are a citizen of Vietnam, nevertheless both of us are first of all citizens of the Kingdom of God; that although I am a member of the white race and you are a member of the black race, nevertheless both of us are first of all members of the human race, God's all-inclusive family; that although I am male and you are female, both of us are first of all made in God's image, part of a creation God saw as "very good."

To point to such realities is not to lessen the imperative for basic change in the structures of our life that nurture and sustain division. It is in fact to heighten that imperative, for it reminds us that we need not be bound or defined by those structures and that therefore they are malleable to our needs. We are never permitted to forget that the gospel asserts clearly that no matter how deep our divisions, God's healing grace can reach across them.

So the final note of the gospel is not division or ambiguity or tension or condemnation. It is joy. It is not a joy procured by ignoring what we clearly see going on in this bent and bleeding world, but a joy received by recognizing that in addition to what we clearly see going on, some other things are going on as well. As we look at the world, it seems to be only the shattered world of the cross—love defeated. For most people, as Ignazio Silone[13] has put it, "In the sacred history of humanity on earth, it is still, alas, Good Friday" ("Preface," *And He Did Hide Himself*).

For most people, but not for all. For Christians, to see Good Friday at its worst is to begin also to see it at its best. For it is our faith that the seeming defeat is turned into a victory, that out of the very worst God can bring the very best, that God is working in our midst—patiently and impatiently, painfully and power-fully, judgmentally and healingly—to fulfill the divine purpose for us. In an astonishing phrase, we are told that Jesus, "for the joy that was set before him, endured the cross" (Heb. 12:2). It is in the light of the resurrection faith that we can affirm that joy and thereby continue to cope with the world that seems to be only the world of the cross, perplexed, to be sure, but not unto despair (2 Cor. 4:8). Ours is an Easter faith that frees us to respond to God's call to join in the divine struggle, so that as God's children are set free, we too may be set free and thereby united with God and with one another.

FIRST ANNIVERSARY OF
THE UCA MARTYRS

On November 16, 1989, six Jesuit priests, their housekeeper, and her daughter were brutally murdered by U.S.-trained Salvadoran military personnel on the campus of the University of Central America in San Salvador. One year later, Brown offered this reflection to students and faculty at the Jesuit School of Theology in Berkeley, California, now a school of Santa Clara University. Brown was at the time visiting professor in the Religious Studies Department at Santa Clara. Archbishop Romero of San Salvador had been slain by government agents on March 24, 1980, and Brown's prayer for the archbishop is placed here after his remarks on the martyrs. Theirs were lives, like Bonhoeffer's, where faith was lived for others in the pursuit of justice.

This is a solemn occasion. All of us know exactly where we were at the time of the earthquake just over a year ago at 5:05 p.m.[14]

All of us who are older know exactly where we were when we heard that JFK had been assassinated in Dallas.

All of you who are Jesuits know exactly where you were one year ago today, when you heard the six fellow Jesuits, their housekeeper, and her daughter, had been murdered in San Salvador.

Today the rest of us want to occupy that latter space with our Jesuit friends and colleagues and to share their loss (which is also our loss) and to reflect together on ways to extract some good from such massive evil.

I am going to propose four perspectives from which to look at the event of the killings and how we have to respond—four handles, if you will, to enable us to do something with the event so as to lessen the likelihood that it, and events like it, can be repeated in the future. These perspectives will be the political, the ecclesial, the personal, and the theological. For each I have a text.

The first perspective is the political, and to indicate the nature of the adversary with whom we have to deal, my text is a quotation from a recent position of the U.S. State Department: "The Salvadoran army has become increasingly professional and submits to civilian control."

Now we know that's a lie, and the fact that it is a lie, masquerading as the truth, tells us more than we want to know about the reliability of our State Department and the appropriateness of its policies in Central America. When we further examine the track record of the State Department and the White House in Central America, we learn even more about the nature of the adversary—not only that for ten years the policy toward El Salvador has been one of lies and deceptions, but that in addition it has been politically naïve, humanly destructive, economically counterproductive and morally bankrupt. I do not think that on this occasion and to this group it is necessary to spell out those charges. They are self-evident to those who know even a smattering of the history.

Against whatever further evidence anyone wants to mount, there are two bottom line political-economic realities we cannot escape, given the ten years in which we have provided $3.4 billion to El Salvador. (1) The great bulk of that money has been military aid, whether direct or indirect, and (2) within the same period of our giving, seventy-five thousand Salvadoran civilians have been killed by death squads financed out of our economic largesse. That's not seventy-five thousand military casualties in combat, but seventy-five thousand civilians—men, women, children, the elderly, educators, heads of co-ops, sisters, campesinos, political leaders, housekeepers, priests, catechists, day laborers—and all the other human beings whose nefarious activities clearly marked them as communists and subversives and who were therefore worthy of torture and death. And this has been done at the cost of gutting the Salvadoran economy and maximizing the people's despair and sense of helplessness.

Within that seventy-five thousand total are Elba Ramos and Celina Ramos, who were killed because they were sleeping in a house too close to the murdered Jesuits to be allowed to survive. So their crime, deserving of death, was "occupying inappropriate domicile." We honor the Jesuits and mourn their loss, but the six of them would be the first to say that they should not be honored apart from Elba and Celina, and the eight of *them* would insist that they must be seen as part of the seventy-five thousand nameless dead. The USA is the chief architect of all those deaths, and we as taxpayers in the USA are complicit in those deaths.

Those are political-economic realities, resulting from evil policies. How do we deal with that? There is only one way: we change the policy. That has begun, thanks, in grim fashion, to the deaths of your friends. But we must not pause too long in self-congratulation. The word must be: keep the pressure on. That is a mode of response around which everyone—Jesuit or no, Salvadoran or no, Christian or no, U.S. citizen or no—can unite. So much is patently clear, and needs no further development: keep the pressure on.

A second perspective is relevant particularly to those of us here today. This is the ecclesial perspective. We are united with the eight who died a year ago today, not only as members of the human family, but even more deeply as members of the Christian family. No matter what things may separate us institutionally, we all claim membership in the one, holy, catholic, and apostolic church, in which, when one member suffers, all suffer. How, as the church, do we begin to deal with that? Here the text is from Jon Sobrino,[15] writing about the church from Santa Clara less than two weeks after the death of his Jesuit family: "More can be seen from below than from above."

That's not so hard to see and believe in Central America, where the vitality and the courage and the true embodiment of "church" are coming not from the top down (from the bishops) but from the bottom up (from the people). To try to live out the gospel in that situation is to give license to someone else to issue a death warrant. As Archbishop Romero said with utter descriptive accuracy, "They kill those who get in the way." That is the Salvadoran reality, empirically verified over seventy-five thousand times.

Archbishop Romero has said another thing about the church in his country that initially sounds shocking and even callous, but is one of those hard truths of the gospel to which we have to listen, words that (as Jon Sobrino has commented) "make us shiver to this day." Romero said:

> I am glad, brothers and sisters, that they have murdered priests in this country, because it would be very sad if in a country where they are murdering the people so horrifically, there were no priests among the victims. [Their murder] is a sign that the church has become truly incarnate in the problems of the people.

We know that it is that kind of commitment and driving force that has stamped with authenticity the life of the Salvadoran church—or, even more accurately—the lives, deaths, and resurrections of the members of the Salvadoran church. And it continues to be a possible outcome, lurking around every corner, for all from the North who work in the South, including Jesuits who have been trained in this institution.

But when we seek to relate that stark reality of the Salvadoran church to our own situation, we have to be equally realistic and acknowledge that the nature of the risks *we* take are infinitesimal by comparison to the great risks taken by the Salvadoran church. When we take stands, we may sometimes undergo a little inconvenience, a little name calling, possibly a command appearance at the chancery office, maybe less assurance of getting on the tenure track, and so on. In some ways, temptations to fudge on the gospel are more widespread for us in our situation, because the expressions of temptation are so subtle, and so often clothed with smooth rhetoric, such as "for the good of the church, don't rock the boat," or, "After all, we have to take the long view," coupled with references to "in God's good time."

A footnote (to telegraph that this going to be an academic point): Let us, in none of this, disparage the life of the mind. Sometimes we get impatient with "learning" and its seeming irrelevance to the bent and broken world out there. Elie Wiesel has a pertinent insight here: "Words can sometimes, in moments of grace, attain the quality of deeds." Let us remember that the six Jesuits were shot not as revolutionaries, not as members of underground terrorist units, not as part of the ruling structure of the FMLN; they were shot because they were educators. They were teachers. They were thinkers. They did research. They wrote monographs. They were . . . professors! So let us remember that those are honorable callings, even in times and places of revolution, and that the six of them were killed not in spite of, but precisely because of, the fact that they were educators. They were killed because the ideas they dealt with were dangerous. They were killed because if you let people think too much, they may become dissatisfied with the present order of things. They were killed because if you have knowledge, and share it, you let loose in the world an instrument of incalculable power. It is grimly appropriate that they were all shot through the head, brains splayed out, in a mute message to all who saw them: thinking is dangerous. Don't think, if you want to avoid the fate of these six men. Revolutionary stuff.

So the question to us is: Do we ever think thoughts dangerous enough to get us in trouble? Does our learning relate clearly enough to the world around us to make the principalities and powers uneasy and thrown off balance?

I am already moving from the ecclesial perspective into my third perspective, which is the personal—a fitting sequence, reminding us that it is in community that our true individual personhood is molded, rather than the other way around. And here our text comes, appropriately, not from the church fathers, or the professional theologians, but from a Salvadoran woman who said, in a memorial service I attended at the UCA, only yards from the site where the murders took place, "Do not mourn their deaths; imitate their lives." That's not a total either/ or, of course, for the best way we can mourn their deaths is, indeed, to imitate their lives. Whenever that happens, mourning comes very close to being celebration.

How we "imitate the lives" of the martyred Christians we are remembering this day is, of course, a question that has as many answers as there are persons in this room. Perhaps there is only one common denominator—a negative one: We are not to seek suffering or, in occasional moments of misplaced bravado, seek martyrdom. As Alan Paton said, who had reason to know: "To seek suffering is not Christian, it is merely sick. But to act on the basis of what we know is right, acknowledging that suffering might be one of the consequences—that is something else altogether."

Nor are we, at the opposite end of the spectrum, to be permitted to pass by on the other side. "We are," the Central Americans have told us, in their document *Kairos Central America*,[16] "the wounded man lying on the side of the road on the way from Jerusalem to Jericho." We have to bind the wounds of the injured, but also (to go beyond the boundaries of the gospel story) to create conditions such that brigands and death squads will no longer be able to inflict any wounds at all. And that means examining issues of systemic evil, the reasons why all people can get off the hook by blaming it on someone else or on the "system," and so on.

What I am searching for, in terms of our personal responsibility, is a new kind of logic to describe our role in making personal witness. The old logic of motivation, I believe, often goes something like this, if we are honest: "The Jesuits have been shot for speaking out. Therefore, I must not speak out or I will be shot too." That won't do any longer. The new logic of motivation has to be something like this: "The Jesuits have been shot for speaking out. Therefore, I must speak out or their message will not be heard."

A FINAL PERSPECTIVE is theological. I consider it a triumph of my humanity over any professional self-interest as a theologian that I place it last rather than first. But I do so also in an attempt to be faithful to the methodology that has grown up in Central America and other third world countries, where theology comes *after* an analysis of the situation and is defined as "critical reflection on praxis in the light of the Word of God." This time I shall not invoke a text—or rather, I shall offer two *living texts*, two episodes concerning which you may create your own commentary.

The first text was enacted at Santa Clara University last November, less than two weeks after the murders. There was a memorial service in the Mission Church in which I was privileged to participate along with Jon Sobrino and several other speakers. But at the conclusion of the service, the students took charge. Instead of offering more speeches, they offered a symbolic action that said more than most speeches. During the service, there had been a plywood outline of the country of El Salvador, perhaps four feet wide. After the service, the students carried it outside, as we gathered around the huge cross that is planted in the earth in front of the church. And then, by an arrangement of ropes and pulleys, the students hoisted the map of El Salvador up the cross until it hung at the cross-piece. And they made a vow that it would stay there until the war in El Salvador was over.

It was a powerful reminder of Pascal's dictum that "Christ (*El Salvador*, the Savior) is crucified until the world's end," that evil continues to pierce the heart of God today just as it did two thousand years ago, and the Savior, *El Salvador*, still hangs on the cross. And we see that ongoing crucifixion today in the lives of God's children, those who endure their own grim Calvaries with nothing going for them save the realization that they are not alone, that in their moments of deepest distress, Christ is there, sharing that distress, and that they and he are both part of what it means in the world today to affirm faith. I go past that cross several times a week. I note with gratitude that the students have kept their pledge. El Salvador is still on the cross. And every passerby is reminded that God is not isolated in some painless antiseptic heaven, but is participating in the suffering of God's children on a pain-filled earth and that it will be right with neither God nor God's children until the slaughter of God's children has ceased. That is a theological image to which to cling.

The other text was enacted on another university campus, this one in San Salvador. I was there, a few weeks after the shootings, and for the first time in my life I knew, beyond any shadow of a doubt, that I stood on holy ground. I have been to other shrines, the sites of other martyrdoms that commemorate events hundreds of years ago. But in San Salvador, the blood of the martyrs was still visible where it had saturated the earth. The blood in the pock-marked walls had dried but not peeled off. The windows were smashed, the doors were buckled, the rooms were a shambles, just as they had been when the murders took place.

And having had much time with Jon Sobrino just days before this trip, it was suddenly very important for me to see his room, the room in which he had not slept that night, since he was in Thailand, but the room in which one of the other Jesuits had slept, and from which he had been ruthlessly dragged out of bed, taken outside and shot, and then dragged back into the room. One of the Jesuits there recounted for me that, as the murderers dragged the corpse back into the room, they hit the edge of Jon Sobrino's bookcase, and a book fell to the floor, mingled with the martyr's blood. That book was Jürgen Moltmann's *The Crucified God*.

I'm still pondering the meaning of that powerful juxtaposition, and I think I will be pondering until the day I die. But I think its message complements the message on the Santa Clara University cross. It is the message that no matter where we are, no matter how awesome and awful are our circumstances, God is never closer than at just those moments. Indeed, God is already there when we arrive, already sharing the pain, the agony, the blood—blood shed very directly and very clearly for others. And it means further that crucifixion is never the final word, however strong a word it may be along the way. For just as we know that Jesus is risen, we know that Archbishop Romero has risen in the hearts of the Salvadoran people; that the seventy-five thousand nameless are risen, that Ita Ford, Maura Clarke, Dorothy Kazel, and Jean Donovan[17] are not dead but risen; and that we too, from within our own petty deaths are risen likewise; and that in company with the risen Lord we can all make fresh dedication of ourselves, to see that the things that bring about any death, any crucifixion, are enemies for whose defeat we must work, imploring God's grace and power to help us.

Amen.

PRAYER FOR OSCAR ROMERO

Oh, God, you who are the Lord of life, we thank you for the life of this humble servant of yours, Oscar Arnulfo Romero, one who lived without pretension or pride and saw his life as an opportunity to serve. We thank you for the courage with which he broke out of a conventional way of viewing the world, and began to see it from the standpoint of the victims. We thank you for the clarity of his thought and the simplicity with which he could speak to people in his homilies, his masses, his radio broadcasts. We thank you for the courage with which he took increasingly unpopular stands, arousing the anger of his government because of his refusal to remain silent in the face of manifest injustice. We thank you for the way his words and deeds were one, so that he did not speak one way and act in another, but achieved a consistency and harmony in his inner and his outer life, giving to all who knew him an example of authenticity and honesty. We thank you for the increasingly burning passion with which he voiced and lived his concerns, calling for his government to bring an end to the killing and calling upon our government to make an end to exporting the instruments of death and destruction. In the light of his piercing words to us, we confess with shame that the instruments of death have continued to go from our country to El Salvador and that we have become complicit in the ongoing deaths of those he sought to save.

O God, you are also the Lord of death, and we thank you that in the midst of so much death, the death of Oscar Arnulfo Romero and tens of thousands of his country's citizens, we can still believe that not even death can ultimately defeat your purposes. We are grateful that even in death the signs of your presence are with us. We thank you that Oscar Arnulfo Romero died as he lived, witnessing to the Lord of his life and the Lord of all our lives. We thank you for the signs of his fidelity to you and to the Salvadoran people, unflinchingly maintained even when his own death was clearly imminent. We thank you that just as Christ died on behalf of all people, so Archbishop Romero died on behalf of all people and especially the poor, the afflicted, the oppressed. We thank you that the moment of his death was the moment of his highest witness to your power, the moment of the Mass when we believe you are present in our midst in special and unique ways. We give thanks for the sure sign he gave us by his death that even in death you are present and that your own identification with us is found not only in life but in death as well.

O God, you are not only the Lord of life and the Lord of death; you are also the Lord of new life, the Lord of resurrected life, and we give you thanks that in Oscar Arnulfo Romero you have shown how your power is greater than the power of death and comes alive beyond death to continue the reality of all that you wish and hope for your children. We believe, O God, that Oscar Arnulfo Romero, although killed, is alive and raised up in the lives of the Salvadoran people and that there is now no way that any junta, any death squad, any evil force or power can touch or harm him. We give you thanks that he has been liberated to be in all places with those who need his presence, as an ongoing reminder of your presence in places of terror or despair or urgency.

And so, O God, we your people, gathered to remember the life and death and rising again of your Son Jesus Christ and also your son Oscar Arnulfo Romero, ask that you empower us with some of their courage, that you remind us that they are in our midst and that there are tasks for us to do. Empower us to continue the struggle against injustice; empower us to work on behalf of refugees; empower us to stop the evil ways of our own government in seeking to control the destinies of other lands and other peoples; empower us to engage in "the preferential option for the poor" that was also his option; empower us to reach out to all in need and help those without power to speak and work and act on their own behalf.

> *Tu eres nuestro Señor; nosotros somos tu pueblo*
> *Te pedimos por todas las otras víctimas,*
> *por la causa de los pobres*
> *Te pedimos por la lucha en favor de la justicia y de la paz*
> *Te pedimos por la causa de tu Hijo,*
> *nuestro compañero y Señor Jesucristo.*
> *Amen.*

> You are our Lord; we are your people.
> We pray for all the other victims,
> for the cause of the poor.
> We pray for the struggle for justice and peace.
> We pray for the cause of your Son
> and our companion and Lord, Jesus Christ.
> Amen.

3

The Struggle for Human Rights

Brown's concern for human rights may have had its roots in the Social Gospel principles he received from his family. But they were honed as he witnessed prejudice in everyday life in America as well as in the military. He made frequent references to the injustices of racism and anti-Semitism in his early sermons. It was therefore a natural risk for him to participate in the Freedom Rides of 1961. This and similar actions were built on a well-developed theology for promotion of human rights, as well as an attraction to the principles of nonviolence taught by Gandhi and Martin Luther King Jr. He carried this concern for human rights to other political issues, such as ballot measures in California designed to codify discrimination. And he included in his prophetic challenges the rights of LGBT people both within the Presbyterian Church and in wider society. We have here but a sampling of some of his thinking on these topics.

WHY I MADE THIS TRIP

From the earliest of his sermons and in his pastoral work in the Navy, Brown had called for racial justice. His early concerns reached into deep involvement in the civil rights movement of the late 1950s and 1960s, working alongside other Protestant pastors, rabbis, and, later on, Catholics. He was a participant in the Freedom Rides of the early 1960s, which tested the implementation of federal laws mandating integration of public facilities, and he was also present at the organizing events leading up to the Selma march in 1963. Later, he was to become a strong supportive voice of the efforts of César Chavez in the farm workers movement in California. The following is a brief reflection on the reasons for his involvement in a Freedom Ride in 1961, which landed him in a Tallahassee jail. It was while serving time in that jail that he received a letter of appointment as professor of religion at Stanford.

As a Christian, I believe that all men are created in God's image. Indignity or injustice to any man is not only a defilement of my brother but of God as well.

As an American, I believe in liberty and justice for *all*. When liberty and justice are denied to any in a democracy, it is no longer a true democracy.

The pattern of segregation seems to me a denial of both of these fundamental assumptions. It works indignity on many created in God's image, and it makes impossible liberty and justice for all. Therefore wherever segregation exists, it is morally wrong and must be opposed.

The only creative means for opposing segregation seem to me to be nonviolence. The alternative to this will not be "cooling off" periods, but the threat and possibility of violence beyond anything we have yet known.

These overall considerations have led me to an increasing concern about ways of challenging the patterns of segregation wherever they exist. They form the background for the specific reasons for which I agreed to participate in this particular Freedom Ride when asked to do so. These specific reasons are as follows:

1. I felt that a Freedom Ride composed of ministers and rabbis, both white and colored, could be a demonstration of the fact that men of different backgrounds and convictions could work together in the solving of common problems.

2. I felt that this Freedom Ride could be a symbol of the concern and involvement of the church in the righting of racial wrongs. Too often, churchmen have spoken but not acted; here was a chance to act. I felt furthermore that such a Freedom Ride, composed of ministers and rabbis, could help to belie the frequent charge that the rides are conducted by "communists" and "atheists."

3. I felt that this Freedom Ride could demonstrate our solidarity with our beleaguered Negro brethren of the South in their lonely battle for rights due them under law and that we could at least demonstrate to them that some of us care enough to stand with them. Similarly I felt that white Southerners who share our concerns might welcome our participation with them in a struggle which for them, too, is a matter of conscience.

4. I felt that the pledge of nonviolence required of all Freedom Riders was an integral part of any attempt to cope with the race problem in the south. I am more and more sure that this must be part of any movement for Negro emancipation, and I was led to identify myself with it in this open way.

5. I was persuaded of the value of a trip with certain limited and discernible objectives. We were not making this trip to advocate the integration of hotels or the joining together of separate universities; we were making the trip simply to test travel facilities for interstate passengers. This seems to me a clear-cut issue, defensible both on moral and legal grounds.

6. I became persuaded that the problem of segregation was not a sectional problem. This is not a Southern problem; it is not a Northern problem; it is a human problem. It is found everywhere. Therefore it must be opposed wherever it is found by anyone who feels it is wrong. One is not exempted from concern for it because he does or does not come from a particular part of the country. On the contrary, everyone is called upon to involve himself in getting rid of segregation wherever and however it manifests itself.

All of these factors, then, entered into my decision to participate in the Interfaith Freedom Ride with a group of Negro and white ministers and rabbis. I can do no more now than offer up what we have to God, trusting that he can use whatever may happen to us his servants for the further fulfillment of his purposes.

THEOLOGICAL AND BIBLICAL FOUNDATIONS: CHRISTIAN RESPONSIBILITY IN HUMAN RIGHTS

The following address was given at the Human Rights Day Observance at the Interchurch Center in New York City on December 9, 1977, shortly after Brown's return to Union from Stanford. In light of recent American involvement in torture, his fifth point, toward the end of the talk, may sound an ironic tone to the contemporary reader.

Had I been giving this speech three or four years ago, my task would have been simpler: I would have set forth some "theological principles" as part of a common and unchanging Christian heritage, and I would have derived from those principles certain conclusions about human rights that I would have offered as special and possibly unique Christian insights. There are two things that militate against my doing it that way anymore.

One is that such "troublers of my (theological) peace" as Gustavo Gutiérrez have made it clear that truth, and especially the truth of the gospel, does not consist in abstract or disembodied concepts; it is forged out of engagement and struggle in specific situations, because it is dynamic rather than static. We do not arrive at truths and then "apply" them. We commit ourselves to

struggle and carve out our appropriation of truth in that situation, from being "in the midst"—which is where, after all, the
Bible tells us God is to be found.

My second reason for not deducing conclusions about human
rights exclusively from previously established theological norms
is that I have discovered that such an enterprise involves intellectual cheating. Concern for human rights is not an exclusive pre-
rogative of Christians; we may not claim that only in the light
of theological or biblical insights can people have a responsible
position on this matter. We need a little theological modesty at
this point. Many who have never heard the gospel preached have
a commitment to human rights that puts our own to shame.

So LET ME BEGIN with some observations about human rights
that all sorts of people share. I believe that such an approach is
faithful to the title of "theological and biblical foundations," for
it represents a theology characteristic, for example, of *Gaudium
et Spes*[18] of Vatican II, with its consistent theme that "we must
hear the voice of God in the voice of the times" and the biblical
recognition that, as Isaiah 10 reminds us, God can work through
the pagan Assyrian to proclaim and exhibit the divine will while
the self-denominated "people of God" harden their hearts or
stuff their ears with theological wax.

Concern for human rights is thus pretheological, or at least
paratheological. One need not be a theologian, a biblicist, a
Christian, or even, in the conventional meaning of the word, a
"religious" person to be passionately concerned about human
rights. Rather than being threatened by this fact, I think we
ought to rejoice in it, grateful that we can join hands with others
far beyond our enfeebled and often dispirited Christian band.
The United Nations Declaration on Human Rights, whose anniversary we celebrate on this occasion, is an example of this. It
is not a "Christian" nor an avowedly "religious" document; it
rather self-consciously seeks to avoid such adjectival charges.

But we must certainly affirm with it that the rights it enunciates are to be guaranteed to all—life, liberty, and security; protection from slavery and torture; equality before the law; protection from arbitrary arrest, detention, or exile; the right to freedom of movement, to marry, to own property; the right to freedom of thought, conscience, and religion; freedom to hold opinions; freedom of peaceful assembly; freedom to vote in secret; freedom to social security; freedom to work, to equal pay for equal work; freedom to join a union; the right to rest and leisure, to education, to live in a supportive social and international order, and so on.

The World Council of Churches conference on human rights at St. Pölten, Austria, in 1974 itemized six rights: the right to life, which included protection from unjust political and economic systems; the right to a cultural identity; the right to participate in the decision-making process of one's community; the right to dissent; the right to personal dignity; the right freely to choose a faith and a religion.

With different nuances, other declarations would affirm similar agendas. There are clearly some things on which most rational people are agreed, though different contexts may produce different emphases—a matter that is important enough for brief examination.

In our Western, democratic, capitalist countries, for example, we have put particular stress on individual human rights—the right of protest, of dissent, freedom of speech, of movement, and so on, and these have been and remain a precious part of our heritage. In other situations, more stress is put on social human rights for all—the right to food, clothing, shelter, education, and medical care, for example. These are the rights that we need to take more seriously in our own context today. Our culture has de facto tended to say that such things were not rights but privileges, available only to those who could afford to pay for them. A society tends to stress one of these sets of concerns and to slight the other—if we in the "West" have championed individual human rights above social human rights, it can be argued that elsewhere, when social human rights are championed, individual human rights may be in danger of being subordinated. At worst, neither is taken seriously—a reality that can obtain under both rightist and leftist regimes. Part of our own task is to get over the often frenetic fear that concern for social human rights is "socialistic" in the pejorative meaning of that word, i.e., un-American.

Some of you may be getting restless because theological and biblical bases have not yet been indicated. But I have been trying so far to press the point that Christians have no corner on this issue. Furthermore, we have burned our share of witches, heretics, and other deviants whose human rights were denied, and whose tortures were arranged, in the name of the Bible by God-fearing men (one time when I think the sexist language is probably appropriate).

LET US GO ON, however, in the light of what we observe about the human scene today, that this is a time of gross violation of human rights and also a time when many people are rallying around the need to defend human rights, often at great cost. Let us go on to reflect on these realities, biblically and theologically. What kinds of things could we affirm that would bring some important further emphases into the discussion and the action? Let me indicate some of the reinforcing emphases that come out of the gospel.

1. Surely one of the most important things we can affirm theologically and biblically for an understanding of human rights is the conviction that every person is made in God's image. This says many things. It says that each person is unique and precious, and the one who is unique and precious may not be tortured, starved, left without shelter, or denied a chance to develop the fullest capabilities. It says further that what is a right for anyone must be a right for everyone. It says once again that to reflect the divine image is also to share, in ways appropriate to the creature, in the creative properties of the Creator. If God is creator, and we are molded in God's image, then being co-creators is part of the definition of who we are, called to bring the divine intention to fulfillment rather than to thwart it. And if that divine intention is love, then whatever thwarts love is to be condemned, and whatever fosters love is to be affirmed and enacted. It should not be hard to draw some conclusions about what that means in the area of human rights.

2. It has sometimes been said that the one empirically verifiable Christian doctrine is the doctrine of sin. Particularly when we reflect on violations of human rights, we are made aware of the pervasiveness of human sin. Human behavior may shock us, but there is an important sense in which it ought never to surprise us. We should always be aware that human beings can stoop to unprecedented depths of depravity, and that when we see such activity in another we must acknowledge that it mirrors possibilities to which we ourselves could stoop. The reality of sin can keep us alert to anticipate possible abuses of human rights in even the best-run human societies (such as, presumably, our own) and to seek ways to forestall the ease with which violators of human rights can get away with it. This is part of the corruption of the best in us, not simply an italicizing of the worst. We are wrong to call torturers "bestial." As Dostoevsky pointed out long ago, that is an insult to the beasts. So if we reflect on the interrelationship between our world and our faith, we will recognize that there will always need to be social structures that will deny to individuals the chance to abuse their power. If a belief in the *imago dei* means that everyone must be invested with infinite worth, a belief in sin means that nobody can be invested with infinite trust.

3. It is always a danger to concentrate the biblical message in one concept or emphasis, but at different times in Christian history different themes have properly been stressed: grace and nature in the Middle Ages, justification by faith at the time of the Reformation, sin in the 1940s. Today the rallying theme that has emerged is liberation: Jesus came to bring liberation to the captives and freedom to the oppressed. It is hard to fault that as a central biblical concern. So let us take it seriously. If liberation is meant for one it is meant for all. To be free, to be liberated, means more in the biblical understanding than just to be liberated from personal guilt and sin. It must also mean to be liberated from structures of oppression, bondage, and evil—what the Bible calls "the yoke of the oppressor." It is not the full message of the gospel, that one has "found Christ" if one's child is still starving; even more, if someone else's child is still starving. So let us recognize that a stress on liberation is the theological side of the coin that says on the reverse side, "human rights," but human rights defined in ways that get to the heart of the social, corporate dimensions of human existence, and challenge the structures—whether political, economic, sociological, or ecclesiological—that deny full humanity to anyone. We forget very easily that in the parable of the last judgment, it is the nations that are held accountable for failing to feed the hungry, clothe the naked, and minister to the sick. Biblical faith will not give us the luxury of retreating into the private arena of individual rights for the relatively privileged; it will demand social rights for the poor.

4. To talk about God today is difficult for many people. Let us observe that the arena in which human rights are talked about—oppressed peoples, demeaned individuals, the wretched of the earth—is also the only arena in which the biblical God can be talked about or observed or responded to or known. It is clear, however little we like to admit it, that there is a bias in the Bible toward the poor, as those among whom God dwells in a special way. It is with the victims that God is working, whether Israelites in Egypt or Babylon or Palestine.

When God becomes flesh it is as one of *am-ha'aretz,* the poor of the land. The God of whom we speak and to whom we pray is a God who has identified with those who suffer. So as I look at the world today, I have no difficulty affirming that the God of the Bible is with the tortured rather than the torturer; with the one who is in jail for political reasons rather than the one who did the jailing; with those who are hungry rather than with those who are stuffed. So let us realize that our understanding of God, our commitment to God, will be nurtured not by aloofness from partisan struggle, not by disengagement, but by partisanship, by involvement, since God is partisan and involved. To affirm torture, or to be indifferent to world hunger, is "practical atheism," a denial of the God of the Bible.

5. The other areas of biblical and theological concern could be adduced: a belief in the church as the recipient of grace and as the community of those trying to embody the Jesus story themselves, that this church must be a servant church, a remnant church identified with the needful, a protagonist of human rights. The sacraments, which show forth a broken body and shed blood, must be seen as stern reminders that those nourished thereby must commit themselves to see that no more bodies are broken and no more blood is shed, either in prison cells or through the "silent genocide" fostered by indifference to the "least of these" God's children.

INSTEAD OF EXTENDING that exercise, however, let me conclude by trying to do something very briefly with what has been said so far. I am not willing to distinguish "principles" from "application." I think they intermingle and mutually affect each other. So having started with our situation and moved to a biblical perspective, let me now in the light of that biblical perspective move back to our situation. Here are a few things that I have to begin to take seriously in a new way:

1. I think we need to develop a fresh capacity for anger. I am not talking about hatred, but anger, outrage, of the sort that characterized Amos, Jeremiah, Isaiah, and Jesus in the face of injustice. We have been outraged in a new way in the last few days, not only by the details of the Steve Biko[19] murder. Let us remain outraged by the further reality that for every Steve Biko we know about there are hundreds, thousands, in South Africa and elsewhere that we do not even know about. Paul's injunction, "Be ye angry, and sin not!" (Eph. 4:26) is clearly a biblical word for our time.

2. Let us take sufficient account of a new dimension in the human rights struggle—the rights of unborn generations—who have the right to inherit an earth not contaminated by atomic wastes or polluted streams or exhausted resources for heat and food. The ecological issue must not be counterpoised to the human rights issue as though one had to choose between them. If "the earth is the Lord's," so are "those that dwell therein," and vice versa.

3. We must see more clearly how our economic structures often lead to denial rather than protection of human rights. A competitive economy breeds an attitude that renders the life of the competitor expendable; work life based solely on profit justifies dehumanizing those who threaten profit; an economy based on corporations accountable to no one beyond themselves means that human rights will not be taken seriously if they interfere with corporation goals; social systems designed for pocketbooks rather than persons will end up destroying persons for the sake of pocketbooks.

4. In concern for the victims of human rights violations, let us remember that while it is important to be the voice of the voiceless, that is not enough; what must be done is to find ways to help the voiceless gain a voice of their own; put another way, our task is not to do things for the poor, but to empower the poor to do things for themselves. Otherwise we end up with a paternalism that demeans those whom we mean to help; they are manipulated, objectified, denied the chance to become full and responsible persons who can create their own destinies rather than being recipients of a destiny decided on by someone else, which is a clear denial of human rights.

5. Let us rethink the prohibition against "interfering in the affairs of another nation." Granted that it can be self-righteous always to be looking at others rather than ourselves for violations of human rights, granted that we are not to tell Switzerland what its tariff policy should be or demand that Britain change its driving rules; there nevertheless comes a point at which human concerns override national autonomy—what is now beginning to be called "the Hitlerian exception." The torture of political prisoners is clearly one of those exceptions. But perhaps the list of clear exceptions should be further extended: if children are dying of slow starvation because economic or political policies dictate that their parents shall not be granted a living wage, that too is torture. Worse than that, it is murder, the "silent genocide" that condemns millions to die annually as long as we stay on the sidelines. Perhaps more aggressiveness is needed from us in these areas; inaction may be a worse sin than moving over-zealously.

6. Finally, let us remember that there is a connection between rights and duties. It is a duty to intervene on behalf of the rights of another if those rights are being violated. Indeed, it is a duty to act ahead of time in such a way that the violation is rendered less likely by our attempt to create a just society in which people will not need to torture in order to stay in power, nor foster unjust economic systems so that others will be unable to gain power. Maybe then justice could "roll down like waters, and righteousness like a mighty stream" (Amos 5:24). That would produce a beneficent flood, requiring no ark.

CHRISTIAN RESPONSIBILITY
IN THE HUMAN RIGHTS STRUGGLE

*Brown offered the following comments at an interfaith confer-
ence on human rights held in Dallas on May 23, 1988.*

1. First of all, precisely because people like us are at some
remove from the immediacy of human rights violations, we have
to give others the proxy for our vision. We are not entitled to
extrapolate from our immediate situations to describe the rest
of the world. We have to try to see the world through the eyes of
others and extrapolate from their immediate situations to a new
understanding of our own situation. We are not given the luxury
of thinking, "The world is really a pretty nifty place, but unfortunately there are some exceptions to that rule with which, of
course, we must concern ourselves." No, we are forced to reverse
that procedure and begin by saying, "There are terrible things
going on in our world. The great majority of the human family
lives in fear, fear of the midnight knock, fear of the unexplained
disappearances of loved ones, fear of the possibility of torture,
fear of arrest without charges, fear of being forgotten in prison.
Those events are so much more common than our own experience would lead us to believe, that we have got to give them a
place of priority in understanding the world we live in."

So when individuals or peoples say, "We are hurting," the
initial presumption has got to be that they are right. Whether
the persons are Palestinians or Chileans or Filipinos or Jews or
blacks or lesbians, their stories must be believed. And if they go
on to say, "We are hurting and your involvement in our hurting,
or your indifference to our hurting, is making the pain worse,"
we have an added obligation to respond.

2. This means that if we personally are at some distance from
the instances of violations of human rights, it does not mean that
we are distanced from a high measure of responsibility for those

violations. Not all violations of human rights take place far from us, however. There are violations of human rights within our own borders. We deport Salvadorans from our country to their death; we deny full personhood to Asian Americans, Native Americans, Chicanos, gays and lesbians, women in the work force, and so on. And part of the moral suasion we can exert in relation to dramatic violations of human rights elsewhere will depend on the degree of our commitment to stop less dramatic violations here at home. (And need I add, that the phrase "less dramatic" is a terribly relativistic term—for never is violation of human rights not seriously dramatic to the victim.)

3. I want to highlight a distinction that needs to be made even more explicit. This is the reminder that we must not become so absorbed in the violation of individual human rights that we fail to deal with violations of social human rights. The two are finally inseparable, but for discussion purposes let us separate them for a few moments.

It is violations of individual human rights that get the most attention: the arrests, torture, and often murder of individuals, who are denied due process, a fair trial, adequate defense, and a public hearing. What is outrageous is that their humanity is denied; they are treated like objects and their unique worth is obscured and negated. We rightly are appalled when this happens, and we try to counter by insisting that everyone is entitled to the right to speak, dissent, move about freely, and assemble with others.

But there are other human rights that are systematically denied to the great majority of the human family. These are what we usually call social human rights: the right to a job, to decent housing, to education, to sufficient food, to health care. In our own country, such rights are usually defined as privileges. You can have all those things (education, a good job, decent housing, health care, and so on) if you have the money to pay for them. It's a Catch 22 situation for the poor.

4. All of this has some subversive consequences for us. It is initially easy to be concerned about human rights. Who, after all, is going to go to bat for torture? Who wants to propose that it is okay for detainees to be held indefinitely without charges? But once we cross that threshold, things are more complicated. We learn that Latin American dictators are taught sophisticated methods of torture by our own government police academies, in Panama and Washington. We learn that one reason there is no land reform in desperately poor countries is because it is in the interests of our multinational corporations to keep the economy under the control of a few landowners with whom they can cut deals rather than with the peasants who won't be so malleable. We learn that a country that takes political prisoners thereby avoids "unrest" and promotes the "stability" that business enterprises from overseas demand if they are going to invest there.

To commit ourselves to responsibility for human rights, in other words, can easily become a highly subversive operation. Taking on human rights issues may be injurious to your health, unless you define health as wholeness, and realize that it is what our word "salvation" means and that maybe our only true salvation is a salvation secured in concert with those who are victims.

5. Let me turn now to a few more explicitly theological comments.

Our Christian understanding of human nature has several components. One of them is the belief that all people are made in God's image and are therefore of infinite worth. We cannot, within that perspective, opt to be concerned only about a few people. Whatever their skin color, their religion, their political affiliations, if their rights are being denied, they are our concern. We also affirm that all people are sinners, that we distort and shame our high calling. This means that while we may be shocked by what some violators of human rights do to others, there is a sense in which we can never be surprised.

Our affirmations about God are also relevant here. No one has the full story on God. Different times and places call upon us to emphasize different parts of the divine mystery. And what we are rediscovering in our time and place, largely from fresh exposure to the biblical story, is that God makes a preferential option for the poor: God has a special concern for the victims, the oppressed, the marginalized, the people whose human rights are denied. So where, today, are we going to find God at work? Among the poor, the oppressed, the victims. It is part of our historical faith that when God chose to enter into the human story and share it, God came not as a white Anglo-Saxon with good connections to the world of commerce and high finance (which is convincing evidence to me that God is not a Presbyterian), but as one who shared in the life of the poor of the land, a member of the working class, part of a race that is habitually persecuted by the rest of the human race. And it is that God with whom we are called upon to identify in our current struggle for human rights for all. It won't ever be easy, but then God never promised us it would be.

FAITH IN HUMANKIND

This address was given at a conference held in conjunction with the opening of the United States Holocaust Memorial Museum in Washington, D.C., on September 18–19, 1984. The venue was the State Department.

In the summer of 1979, I was part of the Holocaust Council group that visited Europe to get ideas for an appropriate Holocaust memorial in the United States. We went to Warsaw and Treblinka, to Auschwitz and Birkenau, to Ba Har in Kiev, and to Moscow. Final destination: Israel. But we had a curious routing—from Moscow to Jerusalem, by way of Copenhagen. Even a rudimentary acquaintance with geography will suggest the illogic of such an itinerary. But the designers of the itinerary were invoking a higher logic than the logic of geography. It was the logic of the human heart. For during the earlier part of the trip, first in Poland and then in Russia, we saw only monuments of dead stone, reminding us of human degradation. But in Denmark we encountered monuments of living flesh, reminding us of human goodness. For as we know, it was the Danes who reversed the normal experience of Jews in countries occupied by the Nazis. Thanks to them 95 percent of the Jews in Denmark survived the war.

And my question, like that of everyone else in the group, was "Why?" Why did these people side with the victims and shelter them, when most Europe did not? I met some of them—heroes and heroines now in their seventies and eighties—and asked them why. And every time the response was the same. They refused to be labeled "heroes and heroines." They discounted the notion that they had done anything exceptional. Their answer to my question was another question: "Wouldn't you have helped your neighbors if they had been in trouble?"

And the deeply disturbing thing is that I don't know. Would I have tried to save another life if it had meant risking mine? Most of us become cautious in the face of such a question. When the price is potentially too great, we find reasons to excuse ourselves from involvement. But the Danes did not.

About three weeks after my return, a friend at Harper & Row sent me a book about to be released, Philip Hallie's *Lest Innocent Blood Be Shed*. I read it in a single sitting that took all day, and I am grateful for that book which not only reminded me of the horror of those years, but also highlighted the tiny moment of human splendor that Le Chambon[20] revealed. What struck me in my reading was that, hard on the heels of that time in Denmark, there was another group of people who had reacted as the Danes had reacted: they not only protected those in need, but they too refused to see anything wonderful or unusual in what they had done. What, after all, they insisted, is so strange about helping the stranger in need?

The question remains. Why did some see it as a matter of course to risk their lives for Jews, while most, if they ever had such impulses, efficiently curbed them so as not to run afoul of the Nazis. I cannot share an answer, but I will share some probings.

A TEMPTING ANSWER for one like myself, whose professional and personal life centers on the relation of theology and ethics, is to respond that people rise to heights of moral greatness, however modestly they may disclaim such achievements, because of their religious beliefs. Let me make a few comments on that.

There are surely some times when this is so. André Trocmé was, after all, a French Reformed pastor, and many who worked with him were members of his congregation.[21] Some of those Danes, at least, must have retained vestiges of the Lutheranism that had informed their national history. Another example: while in Poland, I had the privilege of going with Eli Zborowski to visit the Catholic family that had sheltered his family and saved their lives. I asked the mother of the household why, in a town and culture that had little use for Jews, her family had taken in the Zborowskis. A very simple, unlettered woman, she gave a direct response: "I do not understand," she said, "why the rest did not hide Jews. We are all Catholics here. How could anyone refuse to hide Jews when our Lord told us that we should help those in need?"

It is a shared resource in Reformed, Lutheran and Catholic faith (and in Jewish faith as well) that all people, without exception, are made in God's image, and must therefore be treated as infinitely precious. They must be afforded whatever protection and defense are necessary to save their lives, to guard them from exploitation, to spare them humiliation. Jeremiah told King Jehoiakim that to act justly by taking up the cause of the needy was the same thing as to know God (Jer. 11:13–17), and Jesus, building on his Jewish tradition, told Christians what Jews already knew, that the commandment to love God and to love the neighbor are identical (Matt. 22:36–30).

Would that the discussion could stop there, with the comment, "Case proven!" But we know that the discussion cannot stop there. The case is not proven, it seems to me, for at least two reasons: (1) There are simply too many people who act on behalf of the endangered without any explicit religious belief for us to claim that their actions are religiously motivated. Our president [Reagan] is wrong when he says you can't be moral if you're not religious. (2) The track record of religious people, whose faith asserts that to believe in a just God means challenging injustice, is abysmally weak. When we cite instances, as I have just done, where religious faith has led to protecting the weak, we are describing the few brilliant exceptions to the general rule of cowardice, or apathy, in the face of human need. We Christians, I insist, cannot let the occasional Alfred Delp,[22] Bernhard Lichtenberg[23] or Dietrich Bonhoeffer, go bail for the failure of the rest of us. "The good that I would, I do not," St. Paul cried out in a passage in which Jews and other non-Christians can certainly find descriptive truth, "and the evil that I would not, that I do" (Rom. 7:19). That describes the immoral majority.

The value of the appeal to religion in this discussion, it seems to me, is that it provides a way of challenging members of the religious community with a moral yardstick before which they can expect to be held accountable, reminding them, in Johannine terms, that "If any persons say they love God and hate their brothers and sisters, they are liars" (1 John 4:20). But I do not think religiously inclined people can very convincingly offer religion as an explanation for righteous behavior to those not so inclined. "By their fruits you shall know them" (Matt. 7:16) is an awesome, and yet justifiable, criterion for testing the authenticity of any religious claim. We are to be judged by the quality of our actions rather than the quantity of our affirmations, by the immediacy of what we do, rather the intensity of what we say.

PROPOSITION 187— AND THE FEARS OF CHILDREN

Proposition 187, passed overwhelmingly by California voters in 1994, was an early version of anti-immigrant legislation that has since been implemented in other states. Strongly pushed by Republican Governor Pete Wilson, it stripped undocumented immigrants of rights to public education, public health, and other services. It was struck down by a federal court before it could be implemented, and Wilson's Democratic successor, Gray Davis, put an end to any further appeals. As this brief essay reflects, Brown's concern was not only political, but deeply personal. Earlier, in 1964, he had vociferously opposed Proposition 14, which was designed to codify racial discrimination in the sale of real estate in California. That proposition passed, but was struck down as unconstitutional by the California Supreme Court.

His name is Akiyoshi. He's a fifth grader in California Public Schools, and he's frightened—not so much for himself as for his friends. Early this fall he began to hear about Proposition 187 and soon gathered that if it passes, he and three hundred thousand other school children might be gathered up by the U.S. and, with their families, expelled from the United States of America.

It has been explained to him that neither he nor his family will suffer such a fate. But it is also part of his family history that his Japanese grandmother was sent to a detention camp during World War II, even though she was an American citizen. So the argument from history is not reassuring.

Akiyoshi remains fearful, fearful of the unknown, especially for his friends, many of whom, in California's marvelous inter-racial system, are Latinos, or have dark skin, or speak "poor English," or maybe just don't look "American" enough. That they should be punished just for being who they are both mysti-fies Akiyoshi and strikes him as unfair. He feels that fairness will go to the winds as, under the terms of Proposition 187, state employees start coming into classrooms to remove certain stu-dents or pick suspicious-looking individuals out of Aki's friends going home from school or interrupt the middle of a ball game on the playground to haul off the second basemen for question-ing—without any explanation of what is happening.

So it is the uncertainty that inspired the fear. Aki doesn't know whether his friends might be taken. He doesn't know what he ought to do if uniformed men corral his friends. It's a pretty poor legacy to offer children in the name of democracy.

Yes, he knows that Proposition 187 is already in the courts and that it may be declared unconstitutional. But he knows that the governor of the state enthusiastically endorses it, that the governor wants its immediate implementation, and that if the process is put on temporary hold, it will soon return in some other form. So although Akiyoshi will not be expelled, the odds are that before long many of his friends will not only disap-pear from school, but from their homes as well, when they are forcibly escorted over the Mexican border. And Aki realizes that for years he might have to carry an identity card or "proof of citizenship," simply because his facial characteristics are Asian rather than Caucasian. Punish the children is Governor Wilson's bottom line.

Akiyoshi's full name is Akiyoshi McAfee Ehara, and he is my grandson. We share the same middle name. He has an older brother who faces the same perplexities that Aki does. And even though Colin Masashi Ehara has had more years to deal with being part Japanese, he knows that many of his friends, too, may be part of the forced exodus of three hundred thousand children.

My connection to Akiyoshi and Colin has made me very angry with the governor of California. I am particularly incensed that he still insists that Proposition 187 has no "racial components." Let me say very bluntly: anyone who cannot see the racial components of Proposition 187 must be willfully blind.

So to Aki and his friends, I say: "While you may despair of the governing officials in California, do not give up on the people of California. Take heart from the brave statements of those teachers and educators who have already publicly declared that they will not cooperate with a law that is one clear step toward a police state. Remember that there are other citizens who see Proposition 187 as a denial of democracy and are already working on your behalf so that you can continue to go to school every day without fear. No matter how ruthlessly the governor of the state may fear you, you still matter infinitely to the rest of us. And we will continue to struggle on your behalf."

GAY AND LESBIAN PEOPLE IN THE CHURCH

Brown's writings reflect a sensitivity to the situation of homosexuals in the church and in society, gained from conversations and counseling of homosexual students in the seminary. This led to an ever deepening understanding of and inclusion of LGBT people in his roster of those who have been oppressed and who seek liberation in the form of equal rights, starting in the church itself. The following is an edited excerpt from Brown's Introduction to Called Out With: Stories of Solidarity in Support of Lesbian, Gay, Bisexual, and Transgendered Persons, *edited by Sylvia Thorson-Smith, Johanna W. H. van Wijk-Bos, Norm Pott, and William P. Thompson, published by Westminster John Knox Press in 1997. The issue at hand is the ordination of LGBT people in the Presbyterian Church USA, but the deeper issue is the theology and bigotry that had up to that time character- ized refusal to ordain them. The PCUSA did finally approve the ordination of LGBT people in May 2011, almost ten years after the death of Bob Brown. While he addresses the issue of ordina- tion here, Brown promoted the full dignity and rights of LGBT people in both the church and society.*

Where do we go from there, in what are now the 1990s? There are a good many suggestions that don't help much anymore. A lot of the intervening discussion has become threadbare, worn out by unappealing conversation that has lost the power to con- vince. Look briefly at a few responses:

1. The typically Presbyterian approach to any problem is to refer to the witness of Scripture. I am not about to dismiss Scripture as a vehicle for seeking the truth, but I do point out, from experiences over many years, that on these issues Scrip- ture has pretty well been run into the ground and that we must not claim too much for continued plowing over the same ter- ritory. It will not do any longer simply to rehash the power of Scripture if we are already committed ahead of time to how much we will put for grabs and how much we will insist upon keeping in our use of Scripture. Exegesis has become eisege- sis—not so much what we draw *from* Scripture as what we impute *to* Scripture. Only to the extent that we are honestly and daringly ready to listen for new insights can we use Scrip- ture as a creative resource for a position on sexuality. That is not a "No" to the use of Scripture. It is a "No" to irresponsible use of Scripture.

2. A second arena of investigation has been tradition, the appeal of which is that of endless material, most of which we have not yet read, save as we have skipped through the Church Fathers or the Reformers or even the mystics, looking for proof- texting possibilities.

Here we encounter a problem in our quest for certainty. The tradition, much to our initial dismay, is not carved in stone. Different portions of the tradition have had different meanings at different times. We would not claim that the tradition is absolutely clear and unchanging on, say, war or racism, let alone sexuality or ordination. It is only within the lifetimes of many of us that we have discovered that the tradition does not forbid the ordination of women. If we can find what we need to sustain an argument in Scripture, how much more can we do so with mountains of tradition at our disposal. And how much more precarious does the position become, the more heavily we lean upon it for our doctrinal explorations.

3. But let us not be unnecessarily iconoclastic. For when we talk about the authority of conscience, and genuinely mean by it the authority of an informed conscience, we are beginning to see beyond immediate horizons that hide more than they reveal. It is a short step to realizing that Scripture, tradition, and an informed conscience remain as helpful tools, provided the adjective "informed" remains central. We need a new sense of care concerning all avenues that lead us toward truth, and I propose that in our new situation a good test would be for each of us to entertain, with true seriousness, the possibility that the positions we have already arrived at must be rethought *in toto*, entailing true risk and an acceptance of vulnerability. In a phrase that always makes us a bit nervous, Oliver Cromwell remarked, "By the bowels of Christ, I beseech you to consider that you may be wrong."

4. Perhaps at this time in history we must listen first of all to our contemporaries and especially to the gays and lesbians within our midst. Otherwise the dialogue will be wooden and unhelpful. Let us take seriously the theme of this book and the personal experiences recounted herein so that as heterosexuals begin to listen to and reflect on the experiences and the stories of lesbians and gays, our dogmatically impermeable walls will begin to confront new ideas, we will find stereotypes crumbling and encounter a new level of sharing of the deepest things of the Spirit.

5. But what if we come to the conclusion that significant change is not going to come, at least not quickly enough to justify our staying within the church? At some point along the way, we have to weigh the merits of "staying in" or "getting out." In principle it is conceivable that the institutional church has strayed so far from what we believe to be the truth of the gospel, that we can no longer give it our support. It has happened many times before that men and women have had to decide, with P. T. Forsyth, that "a live heresy is better than a dead orthodoxy"— and act on the conviction.

We must at least be sure that we are asking the right question from the right place. Indeed, it may be, as Luther and Calvin and others have taught us, that we have misunderstood the true "location" of the church in our time, which may not be for the moment within the traditional institution, but "out there" somewhere, waiting to be rediscovered.

No one can make a decision to leave or stay solely on the advice of another, and we must honor the fact that different individuals may have different timetables. What is appropriate or even mandatory for one, may not be so for another. Past history suggests that the burden of proof is initially, at least, on those who decide to leave and that it is important to work within existing structures as long as it is possible. Nor do we wish by default to grant more power to the opposition by surrendering our voting power. But for all of us, the question of leaving or staying is finally the province of the informed conscience, and the overall question must remain a real question.

Ordination—And a Few Roadblocks

Let us examine some scenarios for gays and lesbians seeking ordination and trying to use the available structures.

Whatever advances my own thinking has made have come not so much from reading books or attending lectures, but from ongoing contact with gays and lesbians in the interval. Most of my ministry has been in seminary classrooms, and the issue of ordination began to be raised with increasing intensity during that period.

The scenario I have experienced as a teacher is that fears about lesbians and gays do not appear quite as formidable within the seminary as elsewhere. To put it bluntly: I sense more trust and support among seminarians of whatever background than is liable to be found in a denominational church. My education on this matter became clearer as I had classes with gay and lesbian students enrolled. I learned most when I offered a seminar on something like "The Church and the City," or "Spirituality and Justice." In the latter seminar there were nine of us, three of whom were gay.

What did this do to the atmosphere of the classroom? It did not produce an atmosphere like "gays take over" or "every discussion of social justice ends up as a discussion of lesbian ordination." What did happen, in a very creative way, was that in addition to the "regular" topics of discussion, the same issues were seen in a new way, through the eyes not only of straights but of gays and lesbians as well. The dominant atmosphere (and I have searched long and hard for the right word) was increased sensitivity: sensitivity to the pain through which all sorts of people in the inner city were going; sensitivity of the fact that standing for justice almost always gets you in trouble; sensitivity to the spillover of a reality like unemployment in the lives of children; sensitivity to proposals for shared Eucharists; sensitivity, too, to a thoughtless comment that had an unfortunate double entendre at the end; sensitivity to the fact that "spirituality" could be an in-group activity for either straights or gays and lesbians; sensitivity too, to the fact that the close friendships would become fragile when they were in competition for the same post-seminary jobs; and, of course, deep fear on the part of almost everyone that those who had not come out of the closet might be exposed without one's intention of doing so.

The above comments are not offered to suggest that gays and lesbians are somehow 100 percent gentle and thoughtful and sensitive compared to the boorish straights who ride roughshod over others, but to suggest that because of what they have gone through, the chances of sensitivity and understanding on the part of gays and lesbians are remarkably high. It is one of the ironies of the situation that in banning homosexuals from the pulpit and pastoral world, the church is denying itself a vast number of ordinands whose pastoral instincts are often higher than those whose instincts have not yet been tested in the crucible of pain.

But one cannot remain forever in the supportive atmosphere of the seminary classroom. Students are soon seeking jobs, and it is often with pastoral search committees that the deepest wounds are inflicted. Here is a student with manifold gifts—a warmth of personality, a good mind, outstanding organizational ability, creativity in the pulpit, empathy at the bedside. All is going well, and then, in one form or another, the issue of homosexuality arises and if the candidate reveals that he or she is gay or lesbian, that is the end of the love feast. Period. The institutional response by the pastoral search committee is absolutely clear: gays and lesbians are not going to be ordained. "If you reveal your sexual identity," they are told, "there is no possibility of ordination. Can't you find a job within the church that does not require ordination? Otherwise you will be hurt."

The student, sensing the injustice, may want to press the issue. The most sympathetic response goes, "If you are irrevocably set on ordained ministry, then whatever you do, do not reveal your sexual identity. You must keep you sexuality a secret. You must, quite literally, 'play it straight.' Pretend to be what you are not. Deceive your denominational leaders. Your only hope is to lie convincingly. Then you can become an ordained servant of the one who said 'I am the truth.'"

(I have been told on more than one occasion that putting the case in such a way sounds judgmental and harsh. My response: "The position is judgmental and harsh. It will remain so until a majority of voting church members come to agree with the assessment and change it.")

It is a scandal for us to claim to be an open and inclusive community with room for all when we are not. We make a distinction between "membership" and "ordination," denying the priesthood of all believers in a most un-Reformed way; we pretend to ourselves that to welcome to membership but to deny ordination should be considered a satisfactory resolution of the problem. Such talk gives grounds for hypocrisy in what we mean by membership. The church's stance is to rest comfortably or uncomfortably with the present situation and expect a homosexual to believe that offering a second-class citizenship is sufficient. It is not.

There are no words, in my vocabulary at least, to describe how destructive and un-Christian this seems to me. There is a total inversion of values. If such demands were made on a "Christian marriage," we would be aghast at the conditions demanded in order to "regularize" what had been a creative union between two people. At some point, things went badly askew in our church, and we must hope that the rejection of the proposed "solution" to gay and lesbian ordination will start us on a new course.

What is the hurt that we inflict most deeply on gays and lesbians who are rejected for ordination? It is not that we accuse them of such things as corrupting the youth, though such charges have been present in some Presbyterian discussions. Our real sin against them, I believe, is that we depersonalize them; we reduce them to something less than full personhood.

Two Conclusions

Two matters still need attention. The first I raise with some fear and trembling, lest I be misunderstood. But the importance of the issue transcends my trepidation.

1. For many of us, heterosexuals as well as lesbians and gays, the matters under discussion here have assumed such unquestioned priority in our lives that the raising of other issues is sometimes looked upon as a betrayal. This is appropriate, given the intensity of hurt that needs to be overcome, and those who have been targets of the church's homophobia are entitled to offer rebuttal and present their own convictions in a positive light.

But all of us who are participants in the discussion need to remember that sexuality is not the only ethical issue deserving attention. A case can be made that issues of justice must be our basic concern, and that gender issues are most convincingly explored as one of the justice issues, but not the only one. To some, such a claim appears to propose that less attention be accorded to issues of sexuality. That is not what I am suggesting. What I am suggesting is that concern about sexual issues as a clear example of injustice within the church and the world can be most creatively discussed and acted upon in that context.

In a complex world, none of us is entitled to be "one-issue" persons, to the exclusion of concern for other issues. We find that as we work on gender issues, their relevance to other issues becomes more and more apparent, and our understanding is enriched. The more we explore our own central concern, the more our sensitivity to other issues is deepened. We are not finished with sexuality until such issues as hungry and starving children, racism, patriarchal culture, and the biblical interpretation of poverty, have captured our attention as well. What is being proposed is an enrichment, rather than a diminishment of ethical concerns. There is no honorable way to isolate one of them and exclude the others from discussion.

2. Finally, over the past few years, as we have struggled with the issue of sexuality in relation to ordination, there have been many harsh words, many bitter statements, and much impugning of the motives of others. Let no one pretend it is not so.

Where is any acknowledgment in this process that the church itself has sinned, and sinned grievously, in its judgmental attitude toward those who, with genuine "calls" to ministry, have found doors of our churches slammed in their faces? Let a healthy dose of the culpability of heterosexuals also be acknowledged in subsequent treatment of this issue. Let us begin to spend less time cataloguing the sins of others and focus on our own corruptions of the faith, even when we may not like what we find.

At the end of the day, this can be efficacious only when all of us submit our prayers and petitions to God and seek the divine forgiveness, without which any words we utter, any deeds we do, will lack power. But as we rediscover that it is only the divine power that avails to forgive sin, perhaps we can begin to seek, and even begin to find, the forgiveness for which all of us stand in such need, and emerging from our recent baleful treatment of our brothers and sisters, begin to find ways to rebuild our lives, and the life of the church, not separated, but together.

4

Peacemaking

Brown started out his life in the church as a pacifist. A conscientious objector, he took a draft exemption in 1943 to study divinity at Union Theological Seminary in New York. There, under the tutelage of Reinhold Niebuhr, he gradually modified his stance to one of selective pacifism: there may be circumstances, such as those presented by Hitler, where participation in a war may be justified. Under this rationale, he enlisted as a Navy chaplain in 1944. It was this modified position that he carried forward into his antiwar activities during the Vietnam era and that led him to support conscientious objectors. This section begins with a very early sermon that shows the marks of a prophetic voice that would become sharper in the years ahead, but is still remarkable for its time and audience. The rest of the chapter reflects the fact that a massive portion of Brown's papers are devoted to his activities against U.S. involvement in the Vietnam War. It concludes with one of his last public expressions about war, a prayer given on the eve of Desert Storm. After that war's conclusion, he called for amnesty for all conscientious objectors.

THE SPLINTER AND THE PLANK

The following sermon was probably given in 1944, just after Bob and Sydney Brown were married, most probably on Bob's summer assignment to a small parish in Higgins, North Carolina.

At this point, he was still a pacifist, though struggling, and the general public did not yet know of the horrors of the Holocaust that had been unfolding under Nazi rule, nor the full scale of Japanese atrocities. This excerpt reveals a courageous sermon for its time, pointing out that the United States itself was not free of guilt. References to racism and anti-Semitism in American life are common in Brown's early sermons, and this one includes reference to the internment of Japanese-American citizens after Pearl Harbor, which few if any public voices were addressing at the time. The texts are Psalm 51 and John 7:53–8:11.

On New Year's Day the leader of one of the great nations now engaged in this war addressed his people over a nationwide hookup, saying this to them in effect: "We are engaged in a life and death struggle against evil powers who would like to conquer and rule us. We did not want this war, but they have brought it upon us. We desired nothing so much as peace with the rest of the world, but they have forced us into deadly conflict. They have threatened us from without and within. They have brutally attacked our outlying defenses; they would destroy our religion, setting up gods in whom we do not believe. In the year ahead I call upon you to sacrifice and sacrifice, that our righteous cause may prevail over these, our treacherous foes, and we may rid the world of their evil ways."

That's good propaganda, you say. Paints the picture clearly, shows how we represent the force of light, trying to conquer the forcers of darkness. That would go well with a Bond Rally. But of course that speech was given in Germany, and the speaker was Adolf Hitler. At which you say that it is a pack of lies. At which I say that I agree with you. But at which Jesus says to both of us that it is a bad speech no matter who gives it. We recognize the hypocrisy in such a speech when it is delivered by Adolf Hitler; but we applaud when it is given by one of our leaders, and therein do we reveal how completely we are searching for the splinter in the other person's eye, while neglecting the plank in our own. We are perfectly willing to see all the evil in the Nazi philosophy, as we should. A Jew cannot own a store in Berlin. "How terrible!" we cry. We must stamp out that sort of inequality, so we raise slogans about freedom for all peoples. But why do we always stop there? It never occurs to us to examine our own national policies in the least bit of a critical manner. When a Negro minister and I are forbidden by law to sit together in public, there is something wrong with *our* idea of equality. And while such things go on we cannot paint ourselves as pure and undefiled, while making Germans out to be totally wicked.

Another of our favorite national pastimes is to tell each other how Japan and Germany started the war, how innocent we were of any part in it. It is so easy to forget that until Pearl Harbor we were shipping war materials to Japan so that she could bomb China, that we made impossible demands on Germany after the last war, so that in the despair of the German mind, in the midst of depression and ruinous war debts, Adolf Hitler seemed like a savior. Probably many do not even know that nine months before we declared war on Germany the United States attacked a German outpost in the north Atlantic, an act as morally unjustified as Japan's attack on us, since we were still not at war with Germany.

Do not misunderstand me. I do not cite these examples to try to show that there is no distinction between the cause of the Allied and the Axis nations. I think there is a real distinction, but I do not think the distinction is black and white. It's not that we are good, and our enemies bad; it is that both of us are evil—perhaps we are a little less evil, and therefore of the two we have more moral justification for waging war. But while we must make these relative distinctions between shades of gray— not between white and black—let not this blind us to the evil of our own cause as well as the evil of the enemy's cause. In looking for the splinter in their eyes, we must not forget the plank in our own national eye. For it is very large. It is large enough for the Japanese to see, and they call us to task when we expel thousands of our own Japanese citizens from their homes and herd them into barbed wire encampments just because their ancestors were born in Japan; and yet we are so busy condemning Japan that we fail to see the injustice that was wrought by the evacuation of the Nisei from the West Coast. Japan is guilty of the same thing, too, and to a much greater degree, but let that not blind us to the mistakes our country makes.

LAST WINTER I SAW a sign in a New York bus that went like this: "Get ready for the big celebration. Come in and let us help you prepare for Victory Day. When the war finally ends, be well stocked up. Gus's Liquor Store." What a tragic prospect; tragic not so much for the emphasis on drinking as for its complete lack of realization that there was anything wrong with war. Victory will of course be a time for rejoicing, rejoicing that at last the war is over, but it must also be a time for deep repentance, both individual and national, for a realization that we have had to commit terrible wrongs for which we must ask divine forgiveness. President Roosevelt's D-Day prayer suffered from this same lack—there was no note of penitence in it, no plea for forgiveness, no avowal that we too have had to commit many wrongs in this great war.

Why? Repentance leads to a new humility. A person who repents, who acknowledges before God and before others that he or she is a sinner, and that we are unable ourselves to effect a change in ourselves, such a person can no longer have such a high and mighty opinion of oneself. [And], as repentance leads to humility, so humility, acknowledging the need of divine assistance, begets new power.

TURNING IN THE DRAFT CARDS

Brown's resistance to the Vietnam War included counseling of conscientious objectors, including people like himself, who were "selective" in their objection in that they judged this war to be unjust. Brown was arrested on more than one occasion for opposition to the draft. The following talk was given at the Federal Building in San Francisco on December 4, 1967. The original plan had been to hold a service in Grace Episcopal Cathedral and to turn in draft cards at the offering time. However, at the last minute, the use of the cathedral was denied them. The ecumenical context is evident in his attempt to include people of all beliefs.

Originally we had hoped to have this service in Grace Cathedral, and we were disappointed that your request to make an act of highest moral commitment was denied such a clear symbolic setting. But as I reflect upon it, I begin to believe that it is a good thing we are not in a cathedral, that the time has come to take our faith out of buildings and express it in the marketplace, not to confine it within cement walls but to express it on cement plazas. So although the church today would not support you with its buildings, many church people today support you with their bodies.

Those of you who are going to turn in your cards are engaging in this act from a variety of presuppositions. For some of you, the allegiance you express is to Yahweh your God, and you are today responding to God's first commandment, given to your people on Mt. Sinai, "You shall have no other gods before me"—not the god of nation or ideology or war machine or draft. Others of you are acting on your conviction that, as the earliest Christian confession put it, "Christ is Lord," denying thereby that Caesar is Lord, denying that the state is Lord. You are saying by your action, in conformity with another early Christian utterance, "We must obey God rather than mortals." Still others of you, who believe neither in the God of Abraham, Isaac, and Jacob, nor in the God and Father of Jesus Christ, nevertheless also affirm your belief in something or someone more ultimate than the whim of General Hershey,[24] or the power of a draft board, or the god of nationalism. You give this allegiance different names: conscience, integrity, honor, decency. It represents for you, too, an ultimate loyalty you cannot define but which your action affirms, and what you do speaks so loudly that we do not need to hear what you say.

All of you, therefore, are affirming with Martin Luther, "Here I stand, I can do no other," even though many of you may not want to go on to add, as he did, "God help me." Will you be offended if I, from where I stand, make that prayer on your behalf and mine?

We have been accused of "anarchy" and "extremism" by the governor [Reagan]. The president of our land [Johnson], in tones that border on contempt, calls us disruptive and virtually disloyal. But I believe that we are acting today not because we hate our nation and its processes, but precisely because we love this land, because we love it so much that we cannot remain idle and complacent when we see it destroying its moral fiber, and in the process threatening the destruction of all humankind. It is because we believe in law that we must challenge a particular law. It is because we trust the body politic that we must on this occasion challenge the body politic. It is because we are committed to justice that we must be prepared to be the recipients of injustice. And if this be "anarchy" and "extremism," then so be it; we must wear that label proudly. I rather choose to believe that what we do today is not an act of disloyalty but an act of a higher loyalty, an appeal from an ill-informed America to a better-informed America, an appeal to our national leaders to recover sanity before it is too late, an appeal from the law of conscience, a law that the highest court in the land can never overrule.

Let me address a few pastoral words to those of you who are about to turn in your cards. The deed you do today must be your own. It cannot be a decision someone else has made for you or forced upon you. It must be a deed about the rightness of which you are convinced in your innermost being. For you make a decision today to endure not only the first event but also the last in a predictable sequence of events—a sequence that will move from turning in the card, to receiving a delinquency notice, to reclassification as 1-A, to an indictment notice, to arrest, to trial, to conviction, to imprisonment. You must be ready to follow that course to the end. If you are ready, if the decision is yours, then know that your act today is a moral act of the highest consequence and that you make it not alone, but with the support of a community of concern beyond just yourselves—ministers, priests, rabbis, lay people, Catholics, Protestants, Jews, humanists. By our presence here we pledge to you our support, and many of us by such action place ourselves in the same legal jeopardy as you and, sharing your convictions, offer to share your incarceration for those convictions.

In facing that kind of future, I remind you of the words of a hymn written in a similar situation of great travail: "You Fearful Saints" (and I remind you that "saint" does not mean a holy person but simply a believer):

> Ye fearful saints, fresh courage take;
> The clouds ye so much dread
> Are big with mercy and shall break
> In blessings on your head.

Let's face it. There is no one here today who is not fearful. No one cavalierly or complacently sets himself against his government, his friends, his family. But let us not acknowledge only fear. Let us also believe that courage comes to the fearful, let us also believe in the mercy and blessing that the hymn describes, recognizing that with all the turmoil that precedes a decisive step, there can indeed by a strange and wonderful serenity, once the step has been taken.

A news reporter asked me a few days ago if it was not sacrilegious to use the offering for an act of lawbreaking. I could only remind him that the offering is an offering of the self, and that it is an offering one makes to the highest one knows. If there is a conflict between the law and the highest that one knows, the offering must nevertheless be made, whether to Yahweh, Christ, conscience or all three. You are saying through your act that even though you government orders you to kill dark-skinned people seven thousands miles away, you will refuse to do so, whatever the cost to you personally; that in the face of a terrible evil, America's war abroad, you will here and now seek to wrest something good out of that evil—a witness to an ultimate loyalty that no human being and no government can coerce.

Your depositing of the card in the offering plate can be a powerfully symbolic expression of wresting good out of evil. The card you now hold has become for you a symbol of a system of coercion and force, of killing and destruction. But the moment you place it on the offering plate it becomes transformed into something else; it is transformed by that act from a symbol of force into a messenger of peace. It will immediately go in the mail to General Hershey's office, there to be transmitted to the FBI, and thence perhaps to your local draft board. At each stage on that journey, it will be a messenger of peace. It will say to Selective Service, to the FBI, to the local draft board, to the whole country, that there are those who believe that they may not kill their fellow human beings, and who are willing to pay a price in order to recall our nation from a policy that forces people to do just that. It will be a messenger proclaiming that a person must follow one's highest loyalty openly, cleanly and without equivocation. The card remains a card, but your act endows it with a message. It becomes a messenger of peace.

Dietrich Bonhoeffer, the German martyr executed by the Nazis, once said, "Only the one who cries out for the Jews has the right to sing Gregorian chant," thereby tying religion and politics together indissolubly. He also said, in words I likewise wish to make my own:

> One asks: What is to come?
> The other asks: What is right?
> And that is the difference
> Between the slave and the free man.

God be praised that today you are not asking the enslaving question, "What is to come?" but are asking the liberating question, "What is right?" and are offering your own unequivocal answer.

CHRISTIANITY AND VIOLENCE

As protests against the war in Vietnam occasionally grew violent, especially following the 1968 Democratic convention in Chicago, serious discussion developed on college campuses about whether violence could ever be justified in the pursuit of peace and social justice. A similar debate was unfolding in Latin America among priests and others in Latin America who were asking the degree to which they could be drawn into the most violent aspects of social revolution. This sermon was given at Stanford Memorial Church on November 22, 1970 The texts, all related to peace and violence, were, in order of their reading: Isaiah 2:4; Matthew 5:21–22 and 43–44; Amos 5:11–12; Matthew 21:12–13, and 10:34, 36–39.

My purpose in reading the various passages you have just heard has been to make clear that there is a vision—a very beautiful vision—of a world at peace, and there is also a vision—a very disturbing vision—of a world of injustice, of a world in which force often seems necessary to right wrongs. Those who simplistically opt for violence need to be reminded that they may be jeopardizing the vision of peace, while those who simplistically opt for nonviolence need to be reminded that they may be ignoring the cry for justice that is wrung from the hearts of the oppressed.

WITH THESE CAVEATS in mind, let me first suggest three assumptions that seem to me beyond question about the world in which we make our own decisions about the use of violence.

1. The first of these assumptions is that the problem of violence or nonviolence is subordinate to the problem of power and deals with whether we will use power responsibly or irresponsibly, creatively or destructively. Violence has been linked to the problem of power from earliest times—since Cain and Abel. (If I may employ a modern translation: "Thou art an effete snob." "Thou are a rotten apple and I shall remove thee from the barrel.") It is particularly important for Americans to remember how central the issue of power really is, since we have the most power and since we have proven particularly adept at abusing it—witness this morning's account of heavy bombing raids over North Vietnam. That power can be exercised by the use of violence is, I believe, self-evident. That power might also be exercised by the use of nonviolence may deserve a new kind of attention.

2. A second assumption is the recognition that we live in a revolutionary era, in a time of radical change, meaning by "radical" changes that go to the very *radix*, or root, of things. The most fundamental structures of our society and our world are being called into question, in the name of justice and in the name of love, and increasing numbers of the peoples of the world are insisting that those structures must be changed—not just tinkered with around the edges, but radically altered. And in this situation, the question we face is no longer, "Will fundamental change come or not?" but much more simply—and more starkly—"Will the change come violently or nonviolently?"

John F. Kennedy's epigram gets truer each day: "Those who make peaceful revolution impossible will make violent revolution inevitable."

3. The third assumption is that we have heretofore defined violence in far too narrow terms. We have confined the term "violence" to overt physical destruction against persons or institutions. What we have failed to realize is that there is also what recent World Council of Churches documents have called covert or hidden violence built into the very structures of our society. It can be described as "the violence of the status quo" of a society whose structures are so rigged in favor of the middle class that minority groups don't really have a chance to make it; or it can be described as the "institutional violence" represented by zoning laws that condemn certain groups to inferior housing or bad education. I think it is not an irresponsible but a responsible use of language to refer to the "violence of the slum" or the violence of trade agreements so designed that they help the rich nations get richer while the poor nations get poorer—systematically, year after year.

Now it seems to me that such realities as these—that we live in a world where covert violence is rampant, so that fundamental and revolutionary change is mandatory, and that change comes through the creative (or destructive) use of power — force us to pose our own question: In rooting out the structures of covert violence in the world today, are we justified in using overt violence? From now on, in talking about violence, I will be referring to the more limited definition of overt violence, the open use of physical force, as destructive as may finally be deemed necessary to change the direction and nature of our society. I think we must accept that the direction and nature of that society needs changing. The question then becomes one of means or tactics; is the change to come violently or nonviolently?

In frustratingly brief fashion, let us look at the case for each answer.

THE CASE TODAY for the Christian approval of overt violence grows out of a recognition that the covert violence of our society is so deep-seated, so powerfully entrenched, that there is no way short of overt violence for removing those from power who exercise their power so despotically. It is indeed intolerable that in a given country a military dictatorship representing 5 percent of the people should totally control the destinies of the other 95 percent. This covert violence is so bad that overt violence is not only permissible to overthrow it, the argument would run, but is demanded in the name of social justice, equality, and love. To shrink from overt violence on a relatively small scale means supporting or at least condoning covert violence on a massive scale. As a Brazilian sociologist puts it: "I do not hope for violence. It is forced upon me. I have no other choice. If I opt for nonviolence I am the accomplice of oppression."

What are the kinds of questions to be raised about our own adoption of this position?

One danger is an extrapolating too quickly from a third world situation of military or economic dictatorship to our own situation and insisting that the two cases are parallel, so that what is appropriate in one case is appropriate in the other. The degree of seriousness with which one argues for violent revolution here will depend upon the degree to which one does or does not believe there are other options for change still available in the United States. And let us be sensitive at this point: If I say I believe there are other options short of violence, I have to be very careful that I am not merely betraying a comfortable white, middle-class set of reflexes. Blacks and members of other minority groups may long since have come to feel that the string of alternatives has indeed been exhausted. But with as much at stake, we must be very careful in drawing parallels too easily.

Another question to be raised about the Christian espousal of violence is that any attempt to achieve social change must count very carefully the cost of the particular methods its advocates employ. I can believe that in some parts of the world a violent coup might really strike a blow for justice, but I am staggered by what seems to me the romantic unrealism of those who feel that a similar movement in the United States could now succeed. I am very fearful of repression from the right. I am not happy living in a state where the governor [Reagan] can say of the students, "If they want a bloodbath, let's give them one right now." And I am impressed by the fact that at the famous New Haven weekend last May, it was the Black Panthers themselves who kept things from getting violent. For they knew who would pay if there was bloodshed; it would not be idealistic college revolutionaries who would go back home on Sunday afternoon, but the blacks who would still be in New Haven on Monday morning.

Yet another question to be pondered is what the use of violence does not only to those who are its victims but also to those who employ it. There is an extraordinarily slippery slope from the *violence-against-property-but-not-against-people* point of view to the *violence-against-people-here-is-okay-because-there-is-more-violence-against-people-somewhere-else* point of view. There is always greater violence somewhere else, and the ugly grip violence gets on people can increasingly undermine the most idealistic ends to which it is being dedicated. And before long, all restraints are gone. The theme of so many of Ignazio Silone's[24] novels—that when the persecuted seize power they always become the persecutors—is a theme we must never underplay.

SUCH CONSIDERATIONS AS THESE are already part of the case that is made by those who opt for nonviolence as the proper Christian stance—a stance that seems to me to be expressed in two main ways. There is first the position of absolute pacifism, which insists that there are no circumstances under which the use of overt violence is justified. The position has the advantage of being very clearly rooted in the New Testament and the early church—so that the initial burden of proof is always on the Christian who rejects it rather than on the one who affirms it—even though it very soon began to be diluted and compromised. As the vocational witness of a minority, it has exerted a creative restraint on other less single-minded individuals and institutions far out of proportion to the numbers of its adherents. I have found myself increasingly attracted to it as an overwhelmingly necessary position for some to adopt in a world that increasingly and more and more unthinkingly opts for overt violence. My own inability to take the full step it represents is my fear that on occasion the pacifist stance may enhance the short-run triumph of injustice, however effective it may be in the long run, for I feel that Christians must be constrained about the short-run consequences of their actions as well, particularly when those actions determine the degree of justice or injustice that may be possible for others than ourselves.

THE OTHER POSITION on nonviolence argues that violence can never be more than the last resort, to be used only if it is crystal-clear that all other options are absolutely futile, and that one must develop criteria that will help determine when it might or might not be appropriate to resort to violence. The process resembles the approach of the tradition and until recently discredited Roman Catholic criteria for determining a "just war"—discredited since they have historically been used to declare all wars "just" that theologians wished to support.

I find it useful to take those criteria and apply them not just to international war but to the entire matter of violence, and I find myself coming out a "selective conscientious objector" to most uses of violence. Let me give just two examples. One such principle would be that the employment of violence must have a good chance of success, i.e., that it will clearly lead to greater social justice and that it will not lead to indiscriminate slaughter (particularly of innocent bystanders), or to greater injustice and repression than we now have. And I simply am not persuaded that domestic violence can be justified on such grounds. Another principle is the apparently abstract notion of the principle of proportionality, that the means used must be in harmony with the ends sought, and that the good end hoped for must be assured of producing greater benefits than the evils that will be entailed along the way toward that good end by the use of violence. That is no longer abstract when I view it in relation to human lives and recognize that on the American scene a resort to widespread violence is likely to be grossly counter-productive, particularly against those who are the greatest victims of injustice.

I do not believe that I am entitled to tell a minority American or an oppressed Brazilian what his or her stance on violence must be—though I am greatly impressed that César Chávez has made nonviolence the key to the whole struggle of Mexican-Americans for social justice, and that Archbishop Hélder Câmara,[25] a revolutionary if there ever was one, has insisted that a new order in Brazil can come only by nonviolent means. They make clear that nonviolence need not be the moral cop-out of the middle class, and I think we must respond to the pleas of Hélder Câmara who calls for "fit instruments to perform the miracle of combining the violence of the prophets, the truth of Christ, the revolutionary spirit of the gospel—but without destroying love."

But I think I am entitled to try to push the vocation of nonviolent militancy on white middle-class comfortable Americans of which (God help me) I am certainly one. In a world and in a nation getting more and more accustomed to violence as the easy answer to all problems, it may be our special vocation to try to take on the role of nonviolent advocates of social change. I cannot yet pretend to spell out all that this might mean. I do not think it simply means imitating Gandhi or Martin Luther King, but it will mean looking for new ways and means to incarnate a love that is not devoid of the most passionate concern for justice. It will mean attacking all the structures of injustice and covert violence in our social system, but not in ways that transform us into precisely the kind of people and structures we are trying to replace. It will not mean an attempt to escape tension but an attempt to deal with it creatively in new ways. And it will further mean certain risks. Martin Luther King told blacks in the 1960s to be nonviolent against angry white mobs. We loved that! If he were alive in the 1970s, I have a feeling he might be telling whites to be nonviolent toward angry black mobs. We don't relish that quite so much. But quite apart from going out to seek suffering, we must embrace a role that might entail suffering.

CHRISTMAS EVE 1972

The Vietnam War escalated to unimaginable proportions in 1972, climaxed by the bombings of Hanoi on Christmas Eve. This sermon was delivered in Stanford Memorial Church, following a rally in downtown Palo Alto, after which the crowd, in the hundreds, and coming from various faiths and beliefs, processed up mile-long Palm Drive to the church. There was standing room only, and people who could not enter the massive sanctuary stood outside. The sermon was reported on Bay Area radio and engendered much controversy. At the time, Brown was Acting Dean of the Chapel. The text was John 1:5: "The light shines on in the dark, and the darkness has never quenched it."

I'm sure some of you are saying to yourselves, "I hope this is one time he leaves politics out of the pulpit."

A fair enough request. This is, after all, the night of the angel's song, the shepherds' journey, the holy family at the manger. This is the night for tenderness and joy, for beautiful carols and soft candlelight.

I agree. Oh, how I agree! How much I would like to leave it that way. When we planned this service, we thought, very foolishly, that by Christmas Eve a peace treaty would be signed. I had even prepared a story about some auto mechanics and computer specialists bearing gifts to the infant son of Joe Millstein and Mary Cohen Millstein of Milpitis, California—a son who was born in the garage behind a motel on U.S. 17 because there was no room in the motel. Maybe I'll tell that story some other Christmas Eve. But not this one. For the promised peace treaty has been replaced by the ugly insanity of the most massive bombing raids in history.

FIRST A WORD about "Christmas and politics." I remind you that when I speak from the pulpit, as I do on this occasion, I am not simply indulging in a few reflections that might be entitled "Bob Brown looks at life." No, when I speak from here, I am trying to bring the weight of the Jewish and Christian traditions, as contained in our Scriptures, to bear on the events of the time in which we live. So although I would like to ignore politics tonight in dealing with the Christmas story, I cannot—for the simple reason that the Christmas story itself is all wrapped up in the world of politics.

How does Luke begin the Christmas story? With references to two politicians: "In those days a decree went out from Caesar Augustus that all the world should be enrolled. This was the first enrollment, when Quirinius was governor of Syria." And how does Matthew begin? With reference to another politician: "Now when Jesus was born in Bethlehem of Judea in the days of Herod the king . . . " Herod, indeed, figures prominently throughout the entire Matthew story. He is extremely worried that his power might be challenged. So he enters into secret negotiations with a group of wise men from the East, but he is using the bargaining table only to trick them. He will use them to get what he wants. They are warned by God to have no more to do with him, and so, after having visited Bethlehem, the three heads of state return home another way.

There is more to that story, and Herod's insane use of power, as we will see in a moment. But for now, the point is that the Christmas story, for all of its winsome beauty, is set firmly in the midst of a political situation—a situation in which the brutal power of Herod is pitted against the apparent powerlessness of a tiny baby. We sentimentalize that story if we ignore the brutal context in which it is set, just as we would sentimentalize its retelling tonight if we ignore the brutal reality in which its retelling is set, the most massive bombing raids in history, being conducted in the name of our country. If the Christmas story made no sense back then apart from its political context, it can make no sense now apart from our political context.

In that original context, the juxtaposition of the story with the political situation tells us at least two things. The first is a word of judgment, and the second is a word of joy. We will come to the joy, before we leave tonight, but we can come to it authentically only through the route of judgment.

So HEAR FIRST the word of judgment. The Christmas story confronts us with an either/or, not a both/and. It confronts us with a choice.

To see how that choice is spelled out, follow the Matthew story a little further. After the wise men have left, Herod is incensed that he has not been able to get his own way with them. As a result, Jesus, Mary, and Joseph have to flee the country; Herod's wrath has made them refugees. Matthew tells us that Herod "was in a furious rage, and he sent and killed all the male children in Bethlehem and in all that region who were two years old or under." Not having gotten his own way at the conference table, he lashes out vindictively at people who had no part in the dealings at the conference table. Not being a modern ruler with napalm or bombers at his disposal, he resorts to swords. But the intent and the result are the same—death. Since he can't get the baby he wants directly, he will destroy all the other babies in the area, and maybe if he spreads the net wide enough, who knows? He might get the one he's really after. It is exactly the logic of the B-52 raid.

The story is called, in the Christian history, the "slaughter of the innocents." It is an ugly tale. It has been repeated many times in human history. It is being repeated this very minute as the modern "slaughter of the innocents" goes on.

So the Christmas story presents us with an emphatic either/or: either Christ or Herod. Spell that out any way you like: Either truthfulness or deception. Either love or rage. Either the power represented by a baby's birth or the power represented by military might. Either/or. You can't have it both ways. You can't affirm the power of the manger and also the power of Herod. You can't both tell the truth and deceive. You can't combine love and blind rage. You can't say, "We really believe that the Prince of Peace is in that manger," and then argue that you are pursuing the way of peace by indiscriminately destroying not only two-year-olds, but women, children, and the aged, as well as embassies, hospitals, and POWs, with a reign of terror from the skies.

So let me say it as plainly and as unambiguously as I have ever said it in my own life, bringing all the weight I can bring of the twenty-eight years as an ordained minister who has devoted his professional and personal life to try to understand the meaning of the Christian heritage:

To those of you who are Christians, I assert categorically that from the standpoint of the Christian faith, there is no possible way to justify this insane escalation of the bombing. It is the way of Herod, not the way of Christ.

To those of you who are Jews, I do not bring the authority of an ordination you acknowledge, but I do bring at least the authority of a lifetime of study of your Scriptures, and I assert categorically that from the standpoint of the God who commands us to act justly and to love mercy and to walk humbly with God and humankind, there is no possible way to justify this insane escalation of the bombing. I do invoke the authority of my dear friend Rabbi Abraham Heschel, who died yesterday, and who said to me on the phone only three days ago, "The new bombing is an unspeakable outrage against human dignity."

To those of you who call yourselves neither Christians nor Jews, but who participate in a perspective in which everyone in this chapel participates, the perspective of a commonly shared humanity, I assert categorically that from that perspective like- wise there is no possible way to justify this insane escalation of the bombing.

So I say, considering well the implication of what I say, that if you approve of what our country is now doing, you forfeit the right to call yourself a Christian or a Jew or a human being. If you call yourself a Christian or a Jew or a human being, then you must not only cry out in opposition to what our country is doing, so that your voice is heard across the land and across the world, but you must find whatever ways are in your power to demand an end to the grotesque contrast between the Christmas season and the way our nation is celebrating that Christmas sea- son. The Christmas message from the sky was, "Peace on earth, goodwill to all people." The American message from the sky is "Death, death, and still more death." Either/or.

Either/or. If you attempt to combine those messages—the message of Christmas and the message of Herod—you are guilty of duplicity and lies, as are the leaders of our nation. Jer- emiah described such people centuries ago, in words that could have been written for the past week. Listen: "Everyone deals falsely . . . saying 'Peace, peace,' when there is no peace" (Jer. 6:13–14). Every presidential appointee with a shred of moral integrity should resign in protest over the double-dealing of this administration.[26]

So the Christmas story is a stern judgment on what our nation is doing, engaging in barbaric destruction, in wanton and insane fashion—the largest nation on earth petulantly flexing its muscles and telling a tiny nation that we will have our way with it no matter how many of its people we have to destroy.

WE'VE USUALLY CHOSEN HEROD. And when we don't, we have to reflect that the cards seem pretty well stacked in Herod's favor. After all, he's got the bombers. What power has a baby against a bomber? What chance has love against hate? What chance has truth against lies, particularly when the tellers of the lies have control of the media? What chance has compassion when power-hungry leaders appear to go berserk? It is enough to lead us to despair.

I agree. It is enough to lead us to despair, to the very edge of despair. But only that far. For there is still joy in the Christmas message as well as judgment. And the final word, after the word of judgment, has to be that if we will truly confront the judgment, we can also, this night, embrace the joy. We can sing, and mean it, "Joy to the world." We can say, and mean it, "Merry Christmas." We can sing, "Angels We Have Heard on High."

Why? What kind of crazy logic makes it possible, in the face of the darkness we so clearly acknowledge, to talk this way, to act this way? The answer is found in the affirmation we heard a few moments ago in the reading from John, about the meaning of the presence of love and hope and joy in the world that is so very dark—love and hope and joy symbolized by the theme of light. What does John say? Listen: "The light shines on in the dark, and the darkness has never quenched it." That is why we can go on, that is why we are not entitled to the luxury of despair or inaction, that is why we can affirm joy: because "the light shines on in the dark, and the darkness has never quenched it." Incredible! No, not "incredible," but rather the only thing worth investing with credibility in this time of darkness.

It is a time of thick darkness. I believe myself that it is worse now than it has ever been in the long history of this war. But, says John, there is a light in the darkness. No matter how thick the darkness, it is not all-engulfing. No matter how close it comes to destroying, it cannot totally destroy.

What is the nature of this light? The Christian sees this light focused in the Messiah who has come. That is what we have been singing about all evening. The Jew sees the light focused in the Messiah who is still to come. For both, Jew and Christian, the light has been from the beginning; it is at the very foundation of all things, and for both Jew and Christian in the end it will be all in all. For those who call themselves neither Jews nor Christians, there is still the light that is unquenchable in the human breast, the light of tenderness, hope, joy, compassion, love.

Those things seem very frail, in the light of the ancient Herod's swords and the modern Herod's B-52s. But we are called upon to make the affirmation that their apparent frailty is stronger than all the B-52s, all the diplomatic deceptions, all the lies, all the broken promises, all the cries of "Peace, peace, when there is no peace." "The light shines on in the dark, and the darkness has never quenched it." The gamble I ask you to make again tonight with me is the gamble that is true: that the light does "shine on," as John says. It did not just shine once, it still shines; and also that "the darkness has never quenched it," nor will it ever do so. The baby is finally more powerful than the bomber.

That is the gamble—or to call it now by its right name, that is the faith—that has sustained the Jews through millennia of darkness, through catastrophe after catastrophe; it is the faith that has sustained Christians when they were derided as naïve and foolish sentimentalists; it is the faith that can sustain all human beings who will forfeit their easy securities in naked power and B-52s, and affirm instead, that the other things the Christmas story talks about—joy and hope and love—are those things that are most worthwhile, and most enduring, because they are, as the choir will now remind us, "Of the Father's love begotten, ere the worlds began to be," and, that being so, are eminently trustable. Amen.

RECONCILIATION:
A CHRISTIAN APPROACH

Toward the conclusion of the Vietnam War, which ended in April 1975, Brown participated in a forum of the Fund for Reconstruction and Reconciliation in Indochina, a project of the World Council of Churches, held in Vientiane, Laos, February 23–26, 1975. Here are excerpts from his contribution at that conference:

How Christians Understand Reconciliation

What does it mean to be reconciled? It means that a situation of enmity, of alienation, of disorder, has been overcome. It means that those who were divided have now been brought together. It means that those who were wounded have now been healed. It means that those who were estranged have now come back into creative relationship. Christians assert that the basic enmity, alienation, or disorder, has been that between God and the world, and that in the life, death, and resurrection of Jesus Christ the chasm has been bridged, and reconciliation has taken place.

It needs to be made clear that the Christian concern is not only that we should be reconciled to God, but that we should be reconciled to one another as well. Indeed, reconciliation with God is not real so long as there has been no reconciliation with one's fellow human beings. Jesus puts it bluntly: "If you are offering your gift at the altar, and there remember that your brother has something against you, leave your gift there before the altar and go; first be reconciled to your brother, and then come and offer your gift" (Matt. 5:23–24).

The Risks of Reconciliation

There has been deep enmity created between Americans and Southeast Asians because of what Americans have done. How, in that circumstance, can reconciliation possibly take place? Here we have to be careful not to answer too quickly. It will not do to say simply, "Oh, God has already reconciled everything, so it is going to be all right." Christians, at least, will have to look a little more carefully at the model of reconciliation that has been given to them in Jesus of Nazareth and see what things might be learned from that definitive act of reconciliation that could be transferred to contemporary attempts to engage in "the ministry of reconciliation." It is the hope of the writer that although non-Christians will start somewhere else, we might emerge close to one another in terms of the conclusions to which we would come. Here, then, are at least a few things that would be involved in thinking through the risks of reconciliation today:

1. *Reconciliation itself is a risky and costly process.* It is never cheap and easy. For Christians, the cross is the reminder of how costly it was for God to reach out in reconciling love. And there are no guarantees that contemporary attempts at reconciliation will not also be costly; we may try to reach out to one another in reconciling love and find ourselves rebuffed; we may discover that one party is trying to "use" the other; Southeast Asians may suspect that American attempts at reconciliation are only a new form of imperialism, designed to regain by bread a toehold on a continent Americans could not gain by bombs. Americans, coming individually with genuine good will, may find their motives misunderstood by Southeast Asians or discover too late they have been co-opted by American business or governmental interests that will "use" their attempts at good work for other ends. The list of risks and costs is endless. Anyone concerned about reconciliation should be aware of them.

2. *Reconciliation, rather than initially making things better, may initially make them worse.* For Christians, the coming of Jesus did not initially usher in sweetness and light; it brought division, setting brother against brother, as people had to decide for or against the message of the Kingdom, and it produced chaos in Jerusalem when Jesus finally confronted the Roman authorities and forced everyone to take sides. The point is that matters which otherwise remain just below the surface come to the surface when people genuinely confront one another and try to be honest with one another. The American may have to learn that Southeast Asian resentment of Americans is much deeper than he or she had previously realized and be able to absorb that disturbing truth before genuine reconciliation can begin to be established. Both may have to endure the suspicion of their own motives by the other. So initial attempts at reconciliation may seem to make things worse rather than better.

Another and perhaps more positive way to make this point would be to indicate that only as the breaches and alienations that are actually there can be openly acknowledged is there a possibility of overcoming them. Until both sides are aware of their deep need for reconciliation, no reconciling can take place.

3. If those steps can be taken (a recognition of the risk and cost, and an acknowledgment that at first things may appear to get worse rather than better), what then? It would seem to be the case that *those who have been wronged will have to reach out to initiate the possibility of reconciliation.* For Christians, it is God who had been wronged in the broken relationship between himself and humanity. And it was God who reached out toward humankind. Humankind did not start the process; humankind could respond only after God had started the process. The initiative in restoring the relationship came from God. Similarly, in restoring broken human relationships it would seem that the initiative must come from those who have been wronged.

Here is where a burden is put upon Southeast Asians, as those who have been wronged by Americans. Can they really take such a first step? Can they reach out toward those who have wronged them and say, in effect, "We wish to be reconciled. We do not want to remain at enmity"? If they are not willing to do this, reconciliation cannot take place. They can cut off the possibility, if they choose, by refusing to make the initial gesture that would make it possible.

4. Should the wronged be willing to initiate the process, then *the response on the part of those who have inflicted the wrong must be one of genuine repentance and a desire to make whatever amends are possible.* For Christians, God took the initiative in opening up the possibility of new relationship, but for the relationship to be fully established there had to be a response of repentance and a willingness to live in new ways—no longer denying God's love but acknowledging it and trying to embody it.

Here is where a burden is put upon Americans, as those who have inflicted the wrong. Can we really acknowledge our responsibility for the evil that has taken place? Having tried in many ways to evade that responsibility, can we now turn about (i.e., repent) and say, "We have done wrong, terrible wrong. Are you able to forgive us so that we can begin again together in a new way?" And more important than such words, can we engage in actions that will show that we mean what we say about a fresh start and a new relationship?

5. There is another burden for the American. For if there are risks in even approaching the issue of reconciliation, it is a further part of the truth that *acts of reconciliation may involve their doers in suffering.* For Christians, not only did Christ suffer as the reconciler, but those who affirmed him and became the reconciled also suffered. They in their turn had to endure shame, pain, and frequently death. That was simply part of what being reconciled entailed. (There is another side to this, in that Christians affirm an ultimate resolution and conquering of suffering in the ultimate victory of God, but that is not our concern at the moment.)

In the present situation, "suffering" may seem too strong a word to apply to most Americans, when it is the Southeast Asians who have done the real suffering. But let it point toward a dimension of concern that must not be absent from the discussion. It will not be appropriate or right for Americans to escape too easily in this matter. And while this "suffering" is not in many instances going to involve physical pain, there must be some genuine costliness involved, or no new situation will be created, and we will shortly lapse back into our callous ways. What Americans must face is whether or not we are willing to give and share to an extent that might threaten to lower our "standard of living," whether or not we are willing to challenge the unchanged direction of American foreign policy that created our brutal military presence in Southeast Asia and could easily do the same thing in some other part of the globe tomorrow. Whether or not we can do things like this will be the measure of how genuine is our word of repentance.

But let us push this matter further. If we really mean repentance (turning about), it will be a matter of working to see that the past sins are not repeated in the future. And this is where the real "hurt" might come and where we will discover if Americans are really serious. We will have to see, in other words, that truly radical "conversion" is called for, a reordering of our priorities, a willingness to acknowledge not only our past guilt but also our ongoing complicity in much of the evil that goes on in the world today. This, then, is the "suffering" that reconciliation will involve for us—a willingness to lose face, to relinquish some of our power, to stop trying at all costs to remain "number one."

6. Another part of the risk of reconciliation is that, along with our acknowledgment that some are much greater perpetrators of evil than others, *there is also a sense in which we all finally stand under judgment.* No individual, and no nation, is finally so pure that it does not need to receive the gift of reconciliation as well as offer it. The reconciliations we achieve among ourselves, in other words, are finally related back to the basic act of reconciliation achieved on our behalf by God. We can deny that fact and continue to live alienated lives, or we can accept the reconciling love that continually reaches out to us and thereby be reborn daily. We will, of course, do this in different ways and with different vocabularies. Buddhists will not accept the Christian version of it, and Christians cannot demand that of them. But however we put it, the sense that we stand accountable to something or someone beyond ourselves would seem to be the only true basis for a kind of humility that will enable us more openly and more trustingly to reach out toward one another.

MEMORIAL FOR THOSE WHO DIED IN VIETNAM

In this memorial address at Arlington Cemetery, delivered during one of his peace missions to Washington, Brown offered the following reflection. Its words resonate in a way that is indeed timeless. The text he chose was Isaiah 11:1–9, 2:1–4.

We gather here with strict instructions: there shall be no special pleading in this place. These are instructions to the living, which we the living gladly heed, for others can plead our cause more nobly than ourselves.

In this place there is no need for us to plead a cause. The dead plead for us in our stead—their silence eloquent beyond all speech of ours, their stillness more compelling than our movement, the rest they have eternally a more powerful practitioner than all the motions of frenetic men.

Can we listen to the cause they plead? Can we hear the words that speak across their silence? Can we be open to the message that cries out from this vast grave, that shouts to us from every Cross and every Star of David?

Let us learn from the terrible fraternity of the dead the awful lesson that the only place on earth where human beings have true equality is in the graveyard. Let us hear their anguished witness that only the sod does not distinguish black from white, Northerner from Southerner, Jew from Christian, bond from free. Earth folds her children to herself and gives them in death the gift that they deny themselves in life—a full equality, but purchased at too great a price.

We have not learned to heed the lesson that they teach us. Instead, we still reverse the ancient dream and beat our plough-shares into swords, our pruning hooks into spears, our research into warheads, our insights into bombsights; nation still lifts up sword against nation and we learn war once again. Can we not hear the voice of Cross and Star? Can we not honor our dead and their silent, shouting plea to us that enough have died, and that instead of being able to honor only those who find equality in death, we must learn from them to grant equality in life?

And so we, who have not heard their lesson, mourn this day all those who died long since and here are buried—from Chateau Thierry, Dunkerque, Iwo Jima, Panmunjon. But even more we mourn all those who die today, most of whom will never rest where we now stand. We mourn all soldiers dying in a sure conviction that their cause is just. We mourn the soldiers bewildered by conflicting aims, those torn apart as much by inner strife of spirit as by bullet, shell, or shrapnel-burst. We mourn the peasants whose land and homes all sides have ravaged and whose bodies have become incinerated hostages of brutal war. We mourn the children, cowering in mute or shrieking horror, whose last remembered sound was but a bullet or a curse. We mourn the loss of hope bequeathed to all who find them, bind them, carry them, and bury them, and we mourn the sorrow borne by those condemned to live a living death, psychically destroyed by all that has been done to them.

No, we are not the ones who plead this day. The ones who plead are those for whom we mourn. They speak from here but not alone from here: they speak from crosses row on row in Flanders Field, from far beneath the tumult of the Coral Sea, from the rotting stench of jungles in North Vietnam, from decay along the rivers of the Mekong Delta, from the sulfurous hell that is the DMZ. Their voices are American, but also German, French, and Russian; voices from Haiphong and from Ben Suc, of generals and privates, of friends and enemies, of women and children. They plead with us for a world in which the lion may dwell with the lamb, in which the leopard may lie down with the kid, in which the daughter of Saigon and the son of Hanoi may love one another, in which the American soldier may plant rice rather than destroy it, in which the N.L.F. guerilla may offer friendship rather than deceit, in which an airplane may drop life-giving food rather than fragmentation bombs, in which people may approach a mountain not to bomb or despoil it, but so that the dream of the prophet may be fulfilled: That "they shall not hurt or destroy in all my holy mountain, for the earth shall be full of the knowledge of the Lord, as the waters cover the sea" (Isa. 11:9).

Is such a dream no more than a naïve illusion? Must we dismiss those who yearn for that? Are we doomed only to make a desert and then call it peace?

We dare not leave this place believing so. If we can scarcely dream of more, we dare not work for less. There will be other moments for the formulas, the programs, and the plans. Those must come. Those shall come, but only if we have the will to make them come, only if this can be our moment of high resolve that the dream of peace remain a dream no longer, since we dare not close our ears to all the silent voices shouting from beneath the ground on which we stand. They will not be honored if we swell their ranks. They will be honored only if we pledge, with the fervor the dead can demand of the living, that there shall be no need for fresh-dug graves in Arlington, that we today will pay the utmost price for peace that those in other days demanded that we pay for war.

GULF WAR PRAYER

*The First Gulf War of 1991–92 ("Desert Storm") was the larg-
est declared military intervention since Vietnam, and triggered
some familiar responses among those committed to peace and
peaceable solutions to conflict. Brown was drawn again into the
public square, in Palo Alto and elsewhere, to stir the consciences
of his fellow citizens to action. At the conclusion of one of these
rallies, he offered this prayer:*

O God, you are the God of all your children, and we believe that
your heart is pained, as our hearts are pained, by what we are
doing to one another. We pray for peace, without knowing just
what that peace will look like, and implore you to empower us
to work for peace with justice even in time of war, so that sooner,
rather than later, we may turn from destructiveness to creativity.

Keep us from hatred and vindictiveness, and give us the courage of patience so that we do not lose perspective.

Guard and protect all those we love who are in the Middle
East in places of insecurity and danger, and extend your loving
protection as well to those whom we presently call the enemy
but whom we recognize, at our best, to be our sisters and brothers within your overarching human family.

Be with us all in the frightening days and nights ahead so
that, amid great personal confusion, we can continue to love
and serve you, and through that love affirm the worth of all your
children everywhere.

Amen.

5
Interfaith Solidarity

The Second Vatican Council, convened in 1962, was an epic event, opening the Catholic Church to the wider world and setting the stage for changes in the Christian ecclesiastical landscape, especially between Catholics and Protestants. Brown is remembered as an ecumenical pioneer, not only because he was an official Protestant observer at the Council, but because of his unique abilities to translate the Catholic world to the world of Protestantism at the time. However, Brown's seemingly natural ecumenism was the result of a gradual evolution, and that process continued beyond the days of the Council to tap into the original meaning of the word: oikumene, *or the whole inhabited world. Thus, it was natural, in keeping with Brown's fusion of faith and politics, that ecumenism would find its concreteness in the work for justice in the world. At the same time, "ecumenical" concerns extended beyond Christianity to Judaism, and eventually to consideration of the religious and cultural pluralism of the world we currently inhabit.*

UNITING THE CHURCH
FOR A FRACTURED WORLD

Twenty years after the Second Vatican Council, Brown's ecumenical interest had evolved, toward a greater humility about the whole project of Church unity and a focus on the ends of ecumenical endeavors, which in his mind had always to be

179

related to the ends of the gospel itself, in service of the poorest and in pursuit of social justice, thereby uniting a fractured world. Church unity for its own sake could in fact become the occasion for a pride that has nothing to do with the gospel. This sermon was delivered at an ecumenical service held at Trinity Episcopal Cathedral in San Jose, California, on March 11, 1984. The text is Matthew 4:10: "You shall worship the Lord your God, and God only shall you serve."

We are celebrating the twentieth anniversary of the Vatican Council's Decree on Ecumenism, and it is once again a tribute to the progress we have made, that twenty years ago it seemed like a revolutionary document, whereas to read it today produces among some ecumenical veterans almost a ho-hum reaction: so what else is new? For the decree has admirably served its purpose, which was, whether stated or not, to outdate itself—to point in new directions in such a way that as they were explored they wouldn't be new anymore but increasingly taken for granted.

I had the privilege of being at the Vatican Council as a Protestant observer, and heard most of the conciliar discussion of the Decree on Ecumenism. And I will impose on this occasion just a couple of reminiscences from that rich and exciting time. Even within the four-year history of the Council there were extraordinary advances in ecumenical understanding. Before the Council, of course, we Protestants were routinely described by the phrase "schismatics and heretics." If you have forgotten the meaning of those words, take it for granted from one who knows that they were not terms of endearment. But at the Council, thanks to the new atmosphere created by Pope John XXIII, we observers were—in the conciliar terminology which was exclusively Latin—the *fratres seluncti*, the separated brethren. That is now a sexist term, but we didn't know it was a sexist term then, and since all the observers were males anyway, it didn't matter—something that will surely not be true of Protestant observers at Vatican III. (In fact there is a Catholic joke, not appreciated by all those in authority, that at Vatican III the Catholic bishops will bring their wives, and that at Vatican IV they will bring their husbands— which suggests at this stage of ecumenical history that it's going to be a long time between councils.)

Within the various drafts of the Decree on Ecumenism there were notable advances. The first time around, Protestants were described by the sociological term "communities" rather that the biblical word "churches." But a couple of drafts later we were being described as "ecclesial communities," i.e., communities in which at least something of the *ecclesia*, the church, "subsists," and that's what the final draft says. It has been a twenty-year exegetical struggle to figure out just what it means to say that the church "subsists" within our Protestant ecclesial communities, but on any reading it beats being a schismatic, and is an acknowledgment that however defective various branches of the church may seem to others, we are no longer reading each other out of that arena in which Christ's body dwells and in which Christ's work continues to be done.

By the end of the Council, the atmosphere had grown so friendly, and the range of those included within the orbit of God's concern had so widened that one of the American bishops said to me, "When we get home we won't be able to preach about the devil anymore; we'll have to call him 'our separated brother'"—which actually isn't too bad a description of one who is usually described theologically as a fallen angel.

I HAVE TAKEN as the text out of which to ponder our theme of "Uniting the Church in a Fractured World" the words with which the ecumenical lectionary lesson concludes, in which Jesus says to the devil in words that have their echo in the Jesuits and Calvin: "You shall worship the Lord your God, and God only shall you serve." Jesus is quoting here Deuteronomy 6:13, which is an extended commentary on the first commandment, "You shall have no other gods before me."

I want to concentrate on this verse in the context of the third temptation, but say something also about the other two temptations. So let us look at the passage in terms of how it acts out certain ecumenical temptations in which we are likely to fall if we do not take Jesus' repudiation of them seriously.

1. In ecumenical terms, the temptation to turn stones into bread is the temptation to unite around a gospel of ecumenical success. We are tempted to make our Christian message read "become a Christian and things will go well with you. You'll have enough food to eat, you'll make a good living, material satisfactions will come your way." And, we cannot help reflecting, how much better we could implement that message if we were united instead of divided. But Jesus will have none of that sort of thing. No easy guarantees, no smooth paths. People are not to come to the fellowship for rewards, but to know God and find God in the midst of God's children.

But we, who for the most part are well fed, need to be careful not to do spurious "spiritualizing" of this episode. We must not confuse the proper realization that the gospel is about more than bread, with the diabolical suggestion that the gospel is not about bread at all. The gospel is about bread, and later, you will remember, Jesus makes a big point reminding us that the real test of Christian living is whether or not we feed the hungry, visit the sick, and clothe the naked. The verse he quotes back to Satan in responding to this final temptation, does not read, "Persons can live without bread." It reads, "Persons shall not live by bread alone." More is needed. If I were living in a third world country, I would have the agenda of daily bread high on my list of church concerns, and I have it high on my list here also in terms of the demand that we who have more than enough bread share it. Jesus is reminding us that that's a legitimate part of the gospel but not the whole of the gospel. Our temptation will not be to say, "Give them bread but give them bread as a means of keeping control over them." Or, "Give a little land reform but send them arms as well and keep the Marines close at hand in case they get obstreperous."

2. In ecumenical terms, it seems to me that the temptation to jump down from the temple is the temptation to unite as a way of proving how right we are and how wrong the others are. Once we get back together, then we show the world how great we are, then we can demonstrate the power of our message. Look at the charts and statistics—we're getting bigger and bigger all the time. The conversion curves are on the upswing after a long slump. You don't believe that God is behind all that we are doing? Just look at our statistics. We are a winning proposition. Don't you want to be on the winning side? Join our community, our ecclesial community, our church. It's where God is. And just as God looks out for us, God will look out for you. Don't worry about the odds. God has legions of angels to come to your rescue. Don't worry about Armageddon—the Christians are going to be saved.

Would that I were caricaturing. For that is not only the message of the TV evangelists, but in more subtle ways it is our message whenever we think that ecumenism is the vehicle by which to demonstrate how much God cares about us.

And, of course, when we look at the places in the world where the church really is vital and powerful, there isn't any of this demonstration of invincible success around at all. This is an era of Christian martyrs like almost no other era in Christian history. In Latin America, South Africa, the Philippines, South Korea, El Salvador—everywhere, ironically, that United States guns and diplomacy are keeping the modern Herods in power— Christians are paying for loyalty with their lives. And Jesus' response to the suggestion that he give a demonstration that God will take care of him even in defiance of the laws of gravity, is to quote again from Deuteronomy, "You shall not tempt the Lord your God."

To be ecumenical these days is the farthest thing from demonstrative proof that the gospel works to save its adherents. It means taking chances, siding with the poor rather than the successful, taking up the cause of victims of plant closures rather than lining up with the folks on top who close the plants—in other words, running risks.

3. And all of this comes to focus in the third temptation—worship the power of evil and you can rule the world. "See all those kingdoms out there, all those people that you can help, for whom you can do good things? I'll give it all to you," Satan says, "if you'll just worship me."

Now doesn't that really seem a bit far-fetched? Who is going around these days worshiping Satan? What church is putting on an ecumenical push in order to let the devil get the upper hand? What does it mean in our ecumenical situation, in our world today, to face this temptation?

Let us get at it by looking at the response Jesus makes. His response, you remember, goes: "Begone, Satan, for it is written, 'You shall worship the Lord your God and God only shall you serve.'"

It is surely our supreme duty as Christians to worship God alone, to give to no other idea, no other principle, no other power, the devotion we are called upon to give to God. And it is my clear belief that in the years just ahead the greatest temptation we are going to face, both as individual Christians and as churches, will be the temptation to give to something else the allegiance and devotion that Jesus tells us is to be given exclusively to God.

Jesus is shown the nations; they can be his if he will bow down to Satan. In our day, it is the nations who most tempt us to the kind of loyalty and devotion that ought to be given only to God. When we accept such things as normal, we are saying that we give final and uncritical allegiance to the nation, that we will serve the nation no matter what it says or does—and that is a far cry from Jesus' reminder, "You shall worship the Lord your God, and God only (not the nation) shall you serve."

I think that's pretty clear on an individual level. And it needs to be clear on our corporate, ecumenical level as well. We need to see to it that our churches remain places where such issues can be raised, else we too have succumbed to the worship of false gods. We need to see to it that our churches confront us with the plight of victims of our nation's, or any nation's, economic and political ambitions, else we too have succumbed to the worship of false gods. We need to see to it that those among our numbers who take risks for unpopular causes are protected and supported by the rest of us, else we too have succumbed to the worship of false gods. We need to see to it that the united forces of our churches in ecumenical coalitions are voices raised on behalf of all God's family, and not just that portion that are United States citizens, else we too have succumbed to the worship of false gods.

So if we are really serious about our theme of "Uniting the Church for a Fractured World" we will see that no lesser vision than the giving to God alone our ultimate loyalty will suffice. We will not serve a fractured world by adhering to the standards and patterns of that world, for it is just those standards and patterns that have fractured it—all nations insisting, "We must be number one," or this group insisting that we must "stand tall" at the cost of cutting down any rivals.

It is a tall order. The struggle has been going on for a long time and will continue. But we can take heart today, not only because we can hear afresh the words that Jesus speaks to us, but also because, in a way that was not possible even twenty years go, we can hear these words—together.

VOCATION AND THE THEOLOGY OF WORK:
RESOURCES FOR DEALING WITH A NEW SITUATION

Bob and Sydney Thomson Brown jointly delivered the presti-
gious Earl Lectures at the Pacific School of Religion in Berke-
ley from January 31 through February 2, 1978. Sydney Brown,
founding director of New Ways to Work, had by this time
become an expert in issues of labor and women in the work-
place and was later to become director of the Northern Califor-
nia Interfaith Council on Economic and Environmental Justice.
The full text of all lectures is yet to be drawn together from the
papers of both Bob and Sydney Brown, but what we have here
is a version of one of Bob Brown's lectures, later given in other
forms at other venues. It is included here because of its criti-
cal appropriation of Protestant and Catholic understandings of
work and, in a broad ecumenical spirit, undertakes a critique of
the Protestant contribution.

The need for a new theology of work can be highlighted by a
story about Pope John XXIII. As he walked through his new
headquarters in the Vatican, a reporter observing the Swiss
Guard, the myriad of monsignors, clerks, titular bishops, and
other bustling bodies, asked the pope, "How many people work
here?" The pope responded: "About half."

LET ME BEGIN with a couple of arbitrary definitions that are the
framework for what I want to say.

The normative word for our discussion, the biblical and
Christian word, it seems to me is *vocation*. *Vocatio, klesis,*
Beruf, means "calling," our "calling" as Christians. What we
are called to, of course, as Christians, is discipleship, "following after," a life lived in its wholeness under God. Vocation is
thus an all-inclusive term for the totality of our human lives
as Christians. Our work, our job, on the other hand, is a more

restrictive term. It refers to part of the way we fulfill our calling or vocation. It is what we do, for sufficient or insufficient remuneration, during a portion of our waking hours. It fills, if we are lucky, about a third of our lives. Looking around the world we see that many people are not lucky. They are either overworked or unemployed.

Let me develop the contrast between vocation and work by signaling, very sketchily, four characters of our vocation, our calling, as it is developed in Scripture.

1. It is community that is called—first Israel and then the church and, only after that, individuals. It is Israel-as-a-people whom God calls to live in covenantal relationship with God, and it is only with that corporate understanding of calling that individual callings are perceived. First Israel, and then within Israel, Moses, Miriam, Joseph, Rachel, you and I, are called—not the other way around.

2. Those called are called to be instruments for the doing of God's will—which, whatever else it means, surely in shorthand terms involves the embodiment of love through concern for justice. Vocation thus has the purpose of drawing people together, and destroying walls of separation. The word "reconciliation" is a good descriptive term. This would seem to be God's vocation, too—through divine love and justice to achieve reconciliation with us, so that we, through human love and justice, can share that reconciliation with one another.

3. Vocation is for the sake of all people. Israel's calling is not just for the sake and benefit of Israel—one of the most pervasive misunderstandings of the biblical view of election. It is so that all may be brought into fellowship with the one God who is not only the God of Israel but also the God of the Egyptians and Assyrians—and Sandinistas and Palestinians. Israel is to be light unto the Gentiles, God's "polished shaft" shot into the darkness. The result of being so called is not special privilege but special responsibility.

4. Finally, God's call is not just to the worthy or to the people with the best social credentials. Put another way, it is not hierarchical. No one receives God's call in ways that separate him or her from others. As Deuteronomy makes clear, God chooses Israel not because Israel has special merit but simply because God loves Israel. The one whom God chooses to address the people of Bethel is not a great leader, but a country boy, a dresser of sycamore trees. The one who tells off David in God's name is not another king but a local prophet named Nathan; and Jesus— let's face it, in terms of the social realities of the first century—is a "nobody." "Can any good thing come out of Nazareth?" "Of course not." There is a great leveling process involved in the biblical notion of calling or vocation. It is finally sheer gift, an act of grace.

Now in light of that sketchy review of the biblical understanding of vocation, our problem becomes: Can we express and fulfill our "calling," our vocation, in our work life? Is there any congruence between the two? If all is going well, our work should be a significant means of expressing our calling and vocation.

But the fact of the matter is that all is not going well. For all but a handful, it is difficult, if not impossible, to enhance our Christian vocation through our day-to-day work. The two are at war with each other. Consider the people in your parishes, or your parents, or your college friends. What are they? Real estate salespeople, brokers, munitions manufacturers, caterers, maintenance employees, rising young executives, women trying to survive in the old-boy network while thrust into what is now being called the "mommy track." Are their jobs really ways of fulfilling their vocation as Christians?

Think again of those four characteristics of vocation in relation now to jobs and work.

1. Vocation is communal: Do the jobs in our society foster the well-being of the whole community or only of the few who make it to the top of the heap? Do they contribute to a better life for all or only to those lucky enough (or ruthless enough) to squeeze out their competitors? Do they spread the benefits of technology widely or limit those benefits to those who can afford them? Does "the American dream" benefit blacks, gays and lesbians, women, Mexican migrant workers in California and Puerto Ricans in New York, or are they exploited that a few of us can reap the benefits?

2. Our vocation is to effect God's will through the exercise of love and justice. How many people in our society can see that as a result of the jobs they do in the workplace? Pretty tough if you work for a tobacco company or manufacture munitions or produce exclusively luxury items or work for a corporation that moves its assembly plants over the border in order to exploit cheap labor, get around collective bargaining, and avoid minimal health conditions for workers.

3. Vocation, calling, fulfillment, is for all people. What segments of the human community prosper from the work we do at the expense of others?

4. Vocation leads to nonhierarchical patterns. Is it possible to have work places with nonhierarchical patterns? Is there an inevitable pecking order in the office? Doesn't feminization of poverty make a mockery of equal pay for equal work? What about an economic system in which, as has been demonstrated again in recently released studies, it is manifestly the case that the rich get richer while the poor get poorer and that, by any ethical analysis, it is clear that the rich get richer at the expense of the poor?

The tension between our vocation, our overall calling as Christians, and our work life is so strong, that only the most romantic and unrealistic appraisal of the work most people do can relate them to their vocation in a significant fashion. In most instances we work against, rather than for, the quality of life that vocation is supposed to enhance. And even if some of our individual jobs are creative, they are often part of an overall system that is mainly destructive.

BEFORE LOOKING AT the classical ways Catholicism and Protestantism have tried to deal with that problem, let me offer a few comments about a biblical understanding of work. Our situation is so different from the biblical situation that we must not try to squeeze too much out of Scripture to solve work problems today. But there are a few hints and pointers.

1. It is clear from the earliest biblical accounts that God is a worker—God does things, in contrast to Greek or philosophical deities who see the deity in terms of unchanging eternal perfection. God's self-definition in Scripture is not "I am the unmoved Mover," but rather, "I brought you up out of the land of Egypt."

2. God works, God creates, and human beings, made in God's image, are therefore likewise called upon to work, to create. The primitive image was to till the earth, to tend the garden, to make creative use of the created order, in other words—and we have got to begin to find some ways to translate that into the world of silicon chips.

But from these two starting points on, it seems to me, it's a mixed message, or at least a message that is intensely difficult to decipher. On the one hand, there is the positive evaluation of work we have just outlined: work is mandated before the Fall, part of the glorious possibilities given by God to human beings, basic to what it means to be a person. But, on the other hand, and in the other creation story, work very soon comes under a cloud. It is seen as a punishment for sin, and it is because of sin that we must work "by the sweat of our brow," be driven from the garden—all the glorious possibilities nullified.

In the wisdom literature, work is still praiseworthy; indeed it is commanded, and the idle are admonished. Ants receive greater commendation than [lazy] human beings.

The prophets make pretty clear that if God's work is to "do justice," then our work is to do justice too, especially toward the poor, for whom God shows partiality—a theme that has recently re-emerged in the Latin American bishops' documents at Puebla and in the North American bishops' letter on the economy, in both of which the church is to emulate God by making "a preferential option for the poor." So in these terms, work that helps alleviate the misery and dehumanization of the poor and empowers them is work that is pleasing in God's sight. Which is a fine theme and a worthy goal, but if that is the yardstick of human fulfillment and divine approval, not many people are going to be cheered by the news.

The same themes are confirmed in the Christian Scriptures, where Jesus himself is identified as a "worker," and we need to be clear that this is not simply as one who does what theologians call the cosmic "work of redemption," but that he is also identified with on-the-job work consisting of nitty-gritty manual labor in a carpenter shop. And the social class to which he belonged was the *am-ha'aretz*, the poor of the land, the working class, blue-collar at best. It counts in our discussion of work, I think, that the one in whom we most transparently see the divine in human life, is not a king or a potentate or a captain of industry, but a worker who shares the common lot and so indicates that it can be an arena of redemption for all of us.

THE CHURCH GRADUALLY developed an approach to work and vocation that came to its clearest focus in the Middle Ages in Catholicism, and in the Reformation in Protestantism. Let us remind ourselves briefly what those two classical positions were.

The medieval solution resembles the worldview presented in the British TV series, *Upstairs-Downstairs*, which depicts life in England before and during World War I. "Upstairs" live the people who run society, make crucial decisions about the future, do important things; they are the folk who really count.

"Downstairs" is the locale of the servants—the people who light the fires, draw the drapes, make the beds, cook the meals, and clean the grounds. Their role is subordinate, circumscribed, designed to make life easier for the folks upstairs, but not to be involved in the important tasks.

That's an analogy for the view of Christian life in the Middle Ages. "Upstairs," truly fulfilling a Christian vocation, were the A+ Christians, those who were living significant lives, withdrawn from the menial world, following the "evangelical counsels" of poverty, chastity, and obedience—the monks and nuns. They were, in a familiar bit of later Protestant lingo, engaged in "full-time Christian service."

"Downstairs" in the medieval order on a subordinate level were all the ordinary folk, the B- Christians, doing "secular" things like being butchers, bakers, and candlestick makers, and counting on the A+ Christians to intercede on their behalf and get them into heaven. There was no question which group contained the "better" Christians, the ones who were fulfilling their vocation in their day-to-day work. It was the monks and nuns.

Notice what has happened here: the idea of "vocation," of life lived under God, has been extended in one direction, to include the "religious" calling; but it has been denied in the other direction, life lived in the secular world. Work in the secular world was not to fulfill one's vocation. If you want to demonstrate a true Christian vocation, "get thee to a nunnery," as Shakespeare said so well, yet who would have no part of it himself.

Now to be sure, that presentation is oversimplified, for those within the monasteries and convents did "work" hard, manual work—and the Benedictines had a clear view of its importance, as did St. Thomas Aquinas, who spoke not only for the Dominicans, but for just about everybody else. Nevertheless, the fullness of the meaning of vocation was available only to those in religious orders.

Now it was the initial virtue of the Reformers to challenge that dichotomy, and the strength of their position was to insist that one's vocation could be achieved fully within the world rather than by withdrawal from it. One need not be a monk or a nun to lead a life pleasing to God, for (as Luther put it) one could praise God at the shoemaker's bench just as fully as at the altar. All jobs could be vehicles through which God could be praised and one's vocation exercised. Luther did acknowledge that he had a bit of trouble with thieves and prostitutes—though none, apparently, with hangmen who were praising God in their calling by seeing to it that order was maintained in the state. So the refrain went, "Glorify God in your calling,"—"calling" in this instance meaning your work in the daily world.

Notice the contrast: whereas the medieval view had narrowed the meaning of "calling" to the religious life, the Reformation view extended the meaning of "calling" so that it became virtually synonymous with what we call "work."

Ernst Troeltsch[27] described this Protestant view in a famous phrase, as "intramundane asceticism." That is to say, it was "ascetic" in the sense that devoting one's life to God in a monastery apart from the world was "ascetic," with the difference that now the ascetic life was to be pursued in the world rather than in the monastery. The whole world, so to speak, became the monastery, the place where one's vocation could be fulfilled.

As this was elaborated in later Calvinism and in English Puritanism (cf. Tawney, Weber, Troeltsch, Walzer),[28] a curious anomaly cropped up. Calvin, not unexpectedly, I am afraid, developed the stern side of the biblical view of work, namely that it was a consequence of the Fall and a penalty for sin, so there was a systematic discipline (a favorite Calvinist attitude) of labor. However, this very Calvinist exaltation of hard work had the unforeseen consequence that hard work led to increased production, and increased production led to the creation of consumer goods, and the creation of consumer goods led to the expansion of the economy, and the expansion of the economy led, very frequently, to wealth—to which good, disciplined, intramundane ascetics were certainly not supposed to aspire.

The ascetic virtues of the monastery were supposed to be practiced in the *monastery-that-was-now-the-world*, which meant that one must work hard, be frugal, shun earthly distractions, and above all, avoid laziness, since idle minds might spark the imagination in unwholesome directions, of which, on the Calvinist moral road map, there were an infinite number.

NOW LET US CONCEDE, mixed messages aside, that it was initially a great emancipation to be told that we could glorify God in whatever we did with our daily lives, and that is the enduring value of the Reformation view. But there are shortcomings as well to this view, in relation to the world of work today, and I want to highlight three of them.

1. An initial reason for dissatisfaction is simply that the traditional view has become anachronistic. However valuable it might once have been, it doesn't fit our world.

The major reason this view has gone out of date, of course, has been the Industrial Revolution and its stepchild, modern technology. We live in an era of complexity undreamed of by the Reformers—an era of mass production, specialization of labor, separation of ownership from management, the preemption of profit as more important than human need, the replacement of persons on the job by computers and robots, along with consequent diminishment of the number of available jobs, and (in the United States at least) an economy so top-heavy with weapons production that services to the poor and unemployed are recklessly cut back at the very time they are needed most.

Add to all that the fact that the natural resources of our planet are finite and are being exploited faster than we can replace them, and that our industrial expansion is contaminating the planet by pollution, and the point should be clear. (In underdeveloped countries, the message goes, "Don't drink the water," while in highly industrialized countries, the message goes, "Don't breathe the air.")

In the face of all this, it is sheer romanticism to talk about the shoemaker at his bench praising God with every blow of the hammer, for today shoes are mass-produced on machines that seldom require the intervention of a single human being. And it is cruel, and therefore theologically sinful, to tell people to glorify God in their daily jobs if conditions are such that, through no fault of their own, they can't even get a job.

We must push this first point about anachronism one step further. The Reformers did not have to take the global consequences of their position into account. At most, they had to consider the effect of their work ethic on a small portion of Western Europe. We have to see the consequences of work in a global perspective.

2. A second and much more serious criticism of the traditional Protestant work ethic is that it does not challenge the social structures that define our jobs. It leads to an easy acceptance of the status quo and to complacency in the face of what may be very unjust working conditions. The Reformation position, stated most succinctly, is an attempt to fit us in to the existing social structures, rather than challenging those structures and asking whether they are just or not. The imperative for change is dulled. Luther even argued that the desire to change one's form of employment was a sign of pride, a pretentious implication that God, in the providential ordering of things, had somehow goofed (Gardner, *Biblical Ethics*).

So society is effectively stratified, in the Reformation view, and left that way. The doctrine becomes an effective bulwark against social change. The rich are fortified by what providence has dealt them, and the poor are to accept their lot without complaint. Notice the curious thing that has happened: A Reformation doctrine that initially contained the good news of an equality of all persons before God—breaking the medieval "double standard" and putting kings and commoners on the same level—became a way to perpetuate inequality between persons, who are told to accept their lot, whether high or low, rich or poor, and stop complaining. That's not dialectical; that's diabolical.

3. This suggests a third inadequacy in the traditional work ethic. It is not simply anachronistic and reactionary; it can also (perhaps for those very reasons) be positively harmful, dooming people to continue uncreative, unjust work lives. Emil Brunner saw this a full generation ago:

> The disappearance of joy in work, which is so evident at the present time, is not due mainly to the fact that individuals no longer regard their work as a Divine calling, taking it from the hand of God; on the contrary, the actual conditions of labor often make it practically impossible for individuals to accept their calling from the hand of God. (*The Divine Imperative*, slightly altered by RMB)

The root cause of all this, I believe, is that products are now deemed more important than persons. In the encyclical *Quadragesimo Anno* (1931), Pius XI offered a description of modern work life that could become an epitaph: "Dead matter," he wrote, "leaves the factory ennobled and transformed, where workers are corrupted and degraded." The priorities have been exactly reversed: It is supposed to be that the workers who leave the factory at the end of the day be "ennobled and transformed" by the fact that they have done useful work, but in the modern world it is those same workers who are "corrupted and degraded." John Paul II makes the same point, more conceptually than imagistically, in his 1997 encyclical, *Laborem Exercens*, one of the basic themes of which is that capital should be for the sake of labor and that the trouble with the present economic arrangements is that labor is now for the sake of capital. Another inversion of priorities.

This devaluation of the person is surely at the heart of what is most harmful about contemporary views of work. Workers today have little control over their work lives and few opportunities for self-expression. This is true not only on the assembly line (which is gradually disappearing under the impetus of automation), but in middle- and upper-management as well, as any pastor counseling middle-class parishioners knows full well. At one time in our history, labor unions challenged some of these kinds of arrangements, accumulating enough collective clout to give some power to workers. Today, not only has the decline in influence of labor unions been one of the tolls of Reaganomics, but the unions have themselves become subject to many of the same hierarchical and impersonal structures within their own organizations.

So today there are a lot of reasons why we cannot easily affirm the Protestant work ethic the way our forebears did. In light of all these factors, it is clear that there is need for a new theology of work.

A PROTESTANT CRITIQUE OF A CATHOLIC PASTORAL LETTER

One consequence of Brown's growing involvement in the ecumenical movement in the years immediately following the Second Vatican Council was a deepening of his reading into and grasp of Catholic social thought and teaching, so much so that he was called upon by Catholics to help them understand some of the implications of their own doctrine. But he was also an able bridge from the Catholic world to the Protestant world on such matters, as we see in this address, which was delivered on April 29, 1987, at the New Brighton United Church of Christ in New Brighton, Minnesota.

The letter under discussion, "Economic Justice for All: Pastoral Letter on Catholic Social Teaching and the U.S. Economy,"

was issued in November 1986 by the National Conference of
Catholic Bishops. This letter followed upon another, issued in
May 1983, "The Challenge of Peace: God's Promise and Our
Response," which dealt with the ethical implications of the
arms race. Brown was understandably optimistic that these let-
ters marked a turning point in the methodology and substance
of Catholic social teaching. Despite his knowledge of pockets
of resistance to these letters from conservative Catholic com-
mentators, and to growing retrenchment by the church from the
progressive stances of the Second Vatican Council, he remained
optimistic.

Roman Catholics, who do not appreciate their bishops rehears-
ing such issues as nuclear weapons or the state of the economy,
frequently ask themselves by what right the bishops presume
to speak on "secular matters." "If they want to write a pastoral
letter," the complaint goes, "why don't they do one on prayer?"

We need not linger long on rebuttal. From the very beginning
of both Christianity and Judaism, adherents, whether bishops
or not, have had this irritating conviction that religion and politics and economics do mix, that the message is not just about a
blissful eternity somewhere else, but about a conflictive earthy
existence right here. In the Hebrew Bible, Abraham Heschel[29]
reminds us, the word for earth, *eretz*, occurs five times as often
as *shammayim*, the word for heaven. And if your leader tells
you to render certain things to Caesar, that means that certain
other things are not to be rendered to Caesar, and the theologi-
cal/political pot is already boiling.

In 1891 came the first of the so-called "social encyclicals" of
the popes, Leo XIII's *Rerum Novarum*, and at stated intervals
ever since there have been follow-ups in which, with remarkable
specificity, a series of popes have addressed such problems as
collective bargaining, the evils of socialism, the evils of capitalism, the rights of the workers, the immorality of great wealth in
the hands of a few when the hands of most are empty, and so on.

Over the years since 1891 the strictures against capitalism have gotten more severe, and (dare we say it?) the strictures against socialism have diminished. The process of relating the church to such matters received strong impetus when not just one bishop, the bishop of Rome, but twenty-three hundred bishops at Vatican II, gave their signatures to a document called "The Church in the Modern World," which continued this relentless exposure of the political and economic world to the searchlight of the gospel. Three years after Vatican II, the Roman Catholic bishops in Latin America did the same thing in a conference at Medellín, Colombia, which has become a landmark in forthright episcopal exposure of the shortcomings of modern political and economic life. They did the same thing eleven years later at Puebla, Mexico, in 1979.[30]

How did the document come to be? Not in the old-fashioned way, with a bishop and some bright theologians closeting themselves and producing a document in which the faithful, properly instructed, would toe the line in the future. No, this document, like its predecessor, was the product of a tremendous number of consultations, in which the six bishops entrusted with creating an initial draft did not go and lecture, but went and *listened*. They listened to all sorts of people: religious, lay people, theologians, priests, business people, labor leaders, Catholics, Protestants, so-called "secularists"—but not, unfortunately to many poor people, which is a criticism of the process. (I had the privilege of making a presentation at one of these sessions, and I tell you that it is a heady experience for a Presbyterian to have six bishops sitting there taking notes on what you say.) Out of this process, a first draft was created, released for response, discussion, and feedback, out of which a second draft was created, similarly critiqued, and then, but only then, a third and final draft was created and voted on.

The whole process was so threatening to conservative Catholics that a number of business people, plus such eminent Catholic theologians as General Alexander Haig and Clare Boothe Luce[31] formed a committee to create an alternative document. They released that "answer" to the bishops' first draft even before the first draft appeared, which gives some indication of the theological paranoia that was invading high places in American corporate, military, and diplomatic life. This letter, however, almost immediately sank into oblivion and has scarcely been referred to since. Much of the criticism elsewhere, however, was responsible, and the final document was markedly strengthened by the resultant exchanges, even if at some points it adopts a more cautious tone than might otherwise have been the case.

So we have a 188-page letter—not much in bulk in comparison to the writings of Thomas Aquinas or John Calvin or Karl Rahner, but still a meaty document. Let's do a little digesting.

1. I first comment briefly on the tone and posture of the letter. It is not a "treatise on economics" about which the bishops can claim no special competence; it is, they say, an attempt to "look at economic life through the eyes of faith," about which they can claim a great deal of competence. They begin with a look at the world; what is going on, what is asked, what must be changed. After this, they examine the biblical heritage in terms of the relationship of faith to economic life. Although the biblical material had to be somewhat condensed from the earliest draft, I think it is one of the strongest parts of this document, and it is, naturally for Protestants, one of the places where we can be fully attuned to what is going on. The biblical section is followed by a laying out of broad ethical and cultural norms on which rational people can agree, whether they are Christians or not. And then, after all that, the letter discusses four specific areas of economic trouble in the world today.

Although the letter is not a third world document, and nobody except a paranoid conservative is going to accuse the bishops of being liberation theologians, it is interesting, and significant, that an important methodological principle of liberation theology has been employed, what Gutiérrez encapsulates by saying that "theology is always the second act." The first act is commitment, commitment to the cause of the struggling poor, which means finding out what is going on, becoming informed, taking sides; and then, out of that situation one reflects theologically, bringing the insights of faith to bear on the specifics of the situation. This method is followed in the overall document, for in each of the specific areas, the first section is a crash course in statistics, sociological data, human experiences, etc., so that one is exposed to the depths of the problem before prescribing ways to deal with it.

2. I mention this matter of methodology and approach because my second point, which is an attempt to isolate the dominant theme of the document as a whole, is deliberately appropriated from third world concerns, and in particular the reflections of the Latin American bishops at Medellín and Puebla. At every important point throughout the letter, the bottom line in looking at economic problems is (in a phrase borrowed directly from Puebla) that the church must make a preferential option for the poor. The phrase is open to misunderstanding, but when one sees it in many different contexts, the bishops' point is clear. It is so clear, in fact, that this was a theme the conservative critics were most determined to have excised from the final draft. It is a tribute to the integrity of the drafters that they refused to bend and the phrase, and all that it points to, is much more in evidence in the final draft than in the first. In the biblical material, for example, the discussion of the jubilee year reminds them that throughout the Bible there is "a special concern for the vulnerable members of the community." Widows and orphans, were the most disadvantaged of all, and Yahweh continually enjoins concern for them. Jesus' teachings also have a special thrust toward the poor. Throughout the letter, the bishops weigh every proposal, every policy, every suggestion, in the light of whether it will or will not help the poor to escape from poverty. The question is never "how can the rich hold on to what they have?" but "how can the poor attain what rightfully belongs to them?" "The fulfillment of the basic needs of the poor is the highest priority" (89). Such statements would be duplicated a dozen times over throughout the text.

But that is not the only thing. Even more important is the bishops' recognition that the task is not to "help" the poor by doing things for them, or seeing to it that they get the requisite handouts for survival. No, the basic concern is to work for the *empowerment* of the poor, so that they can help themselves, so that rather than being the recipients of the largesse of the affluent, they can become the architects of their own destiny, no longer be objects but subjects, in control of their lives.

That's what is really "radical" in the document, and that is what is fantastically scary to those who are presently running the show, for it would mean sharing the running of the show with all kinds of folks who ought to have been content to stay at the bottom of the heap and look up gratefully when crumbs were dropped to them from the economic table.

One more word about the church's "preferential option for the poor." The term is not proposing an exclusive option for the poor. It is not saying God loves only some people (the poor) and hates all the rest. It is saying that in working toward a better society, your first attention, your preferential option, must be directed toward those most victimized, those most oppressed and destitute. Certainly the church is concerned about liberty and justice for all. How do you get there? Not by a preferential option for the rich, on the theory that if they have more, a little bit will trickle down to the poor, but by a preferential option for the poor, for if their basic needs are met, society will, to that degree, be more just, and there will be more liberty and justice for all. It is also important to remember that the chapter in the Puebla document, after "The Preferential Option for the Poor" is called "The Preferential Option for Youth," it being recognized that in an unjust society the children particularly are the victims, and that we must ask, finally, about how proposed changes will affect the children of the poor, those who are most vulnerable and most in need of special attention.

I think this basic, bottom-line perspective is absolutely on target. I cannot imagine that one could read the Bible and emerge with any other conclusion, and I am very hard put to retain much sympathy and charity for those who take issue with this emphasis.

3. A third important theme stresses that when we talk about human rights, we are not only talking about political rights, but economic rights as well. We do reasonably well as a nation on the right to dissent, the right to assemble peaceably, the right to freedom of expression, of movement, and so forth, and our original "Bill of Rights" in the Constitution guarantees such concerns. What did not get sufficient attention then, and what the bishops insist needs more attention now, is an *economic* Bill of Rights. For in our society, such things as jobs, education, clothing, housing, and health benefits, are really privileges rather than rights. That is to say, if you have enough money you can buy an education that will enable you to get a good job, so that you can have adequate clothing and housing, pay for health benefits, etc. The bishops are saying that human rights must include economic rights as well. Simply because of the fact that people exist, they are entitled to education, health care, employment, a place to live—whether they can pay for them or not. If we have work, and it is adequately compensated, we can, of course, pay for the other things, so the right to employment is a crucial right, not a privilege, which society must provide.

Immediate knee-jerk reaction by millions of people: but that's socialism. Actually, the bishops are not invoking socialism. They are invoking justice; they are invoking the gospel. If we are indeed made in God's image, we have infinite worth, and people cannot be thrown on the economic scrapheap, which is also the moral scrapheap, for that is saying to them, "You are not worth anything. You do not deserve to survive. If you can't stand the competitive heat, get out of the kitchen." Only, the door out of this particular kitchen is always the garbage dump.

4. The specter of socialism, however, has been raised, so let us turn to that. The key concept in dealing with this problem is a concept that is almost as important as "the preferential option for the poor." This is the concept of *partnership*. The word sounds either tame or Sunday-schoolish or both, but it is helpful in dealing with the document. For the overriding concern is that all segments of society, in partnership with one another, have an obligation to create a more just society. The private and the public sectors must work together, as must the church and individuals within society. This will please the doctrinaire from neither the right nor the left. But let us first be clear about what is being urged:

> The church's teaching opposes collectivist and statist economic approaches. But it also rejects the notion that a free market automatically produces justice. Therefore, as Pope John Paul II has argued, "One cannot exclude the socialization, in suitable conditions, of certain means of production." There is, as he said on another occasion, "a social mortgage on all private property."

The capitalists have plenty to worry about if the bishops get their way, but so also do the socialists. For the document is calling for "a mixed economy," which in terms of this country is probably the only reasonably feasible position. We are not going back to pure laissez-faire capitalism, and we are not, in the near future, going forward to socialism. But in the mix, the bishops give an important place to government. There are no panaceas, no party line solutions, but a recognition that a partnership of all segments of society is the only way we can go. The document is "centrist" rather than extreme, but also "realistic" rather than encouraging utopian hopes, either left or right.

When dealing with how we divide up the partnership tasks, how much to government, how much to labor unions, how much to business, etc., a venerable Catholic social principle is invoked, the principle of subsidiarity, which states that control is always to be kept at the lowest and smallest and most localized unit possible. If the matter can be handled on a town level, don't turn it over to the county; if at a county level, don't have it done by the state; if the state can handle it, don't let it be adjudicated on a national level, and so forth. Here is a built-in protection against "bigness" and over-bureaucratization that should provide some relief to those who fear that everything is going to end up in some Washington office. But there is another thing to say. Subsidiarity must be regulated by the norm of justice. If civil rights for blacks or women are violated on a local level, the county, the state, or the federal government may need to become the appropriate enforcement agency.

5. A fifth emphasis, never developed in detail, but frequently mentioned, is a recognition that expenditures for the arms race play havoc with the achievement of justice in the economic order. The reason the matter is not developed in detail is, of course, that what the bishops have to say is already in print in their previous pastoral letter on nuclear weapons. But their repeated references to the arms race in the present letter are important, for they show how interrelated are all such issues of public policy. Along with all the horrendous long-term consequences of continuing to build nuclear weapons are the equally horrendous short-term consequences. Money that goes into weapons cannot go into housing projects, or job-training programs, or child care centers. "The arms race kills, even without war," is the way Dorothee Soelle[32] puts it. This is just another reason why the bishops need to rethink a crucial portion of their earlier letter. They come to the edge of an argument that goes: Since it is always wrong to use nuclear weapons, it is morally wrong to possess them, since possession tempts toward use; consequently it is also morally

wrong to manufacture them since manufacture leads to possession, which tempts toward use. At that point they drew back
and concluded, provisionally, that possession is morally justified
if it leads to serious attempts to get rid of nuclear weapons. We
must hope the Catholic bishops will consider going the whole
way, as the Methodist bishops have done, and condemn outright
the use, possession, and manufacture of such lethal instruments.

6. A sixth characteristic of the letter is a great strength: its
specificity. It is not reducible to grand moral exhortations. Particularly in Chapters 3 and 4, which deal with four specific
areas of concern—employment, poverty, food and agriculture,
and our relation to the global economy—the bishops have
done their homework and pass the results on to us. In addition to data, statistics, and bibliographies, there are practical
suggestions for getting out of the binds we are presently in.
I particularly appreciate the attention to new strategies and
experiments. For example, dealing with the problem of unemployment, they propose more widespread adoption of what are
still such related priorities as job sharing, flex time, a reduced
work week, abolishing compulsory overtime, refraining from
hiring part-time workers who do not receive benefits, establishing pay equity between men and women, etc. Later, dealing
with workers, they advocate profit sharing, enabling employees
to become company stockholders, cooperative ownership of
firms, and greater employee input into company policies such
as the conditions of work. These are examples of taking the
theme of partnership seriously.

7. A final characteristic of the document is the acknowledgment that if the church is going to make recommendations for
economic justice in the world, it must address all such admonitions and proposals to itself as well. The church is, among other
things, an economic institution, with budgets, workers, hiring
policies, salary scales, etc., and the bishops acknowledge that its
track record in these matters is far from exemplary. "The Church

as an Economic Actor," the title of this section, recognizes that the church must set an example if it expects to be listened to. Such items as the following need immediate domestic support: adequate pay, the right of employees to organize and bargain collectively, the need to overcome existing discrimination against women, the imperative to invest its funds responsibly, the use of church property for the good of the entire community, and special vocation to serve the poor. We can expect lay employees to hold the church accountable in these areas, and if the one about discrimination against women is taken seriously, ordination will have to be part of the package. Speed the day, is my Protestant comment on that. But my pastoral advice is: don't hold your breath waiting.

I AM NOT OVERLY impressed by critics on the far right who seem to have been so conditioned to expect a socialist document from these far-out bishops that they see indications of the death of private enterprise in every paragraph. The critics on the left, of course, want much, much more than the bishops have given them. Their basic question, loudly trumpeted, is also my question, voiced more quietly: Is capitalism as "reformable" as the bishops believe? The bishops do not argue for drastic change, or urge the masses to rise up and smite the imperialistic oppressors; they appeal by and large to those with power and influence to humanize the system. It will be wonderful if this works. I personally doubt that it is going to work very well. I see few instances where those with power—whether economic, political, military, or ecclesiastical—voluntarily relinquish it, or let appeals to "the common good" run the risk of depleting the size of the stockholder dividend for the current quarter. We must continue to make such appeals; in our own church constituencies it is mainly those in middle management to whom we cater, and we must not give up on the possibility of change along those lines. But lack of responsiveness will push us in more radical directions.

And there is a "sleeper" in the document that has the potential to lead to more radical change. This is the recognition that concern for the rights of the poor does not aim to give them goodies or placate them with palliatives, but to empower them. The point is for the poor to assume control over their lives rather than leaving it to the rich to control their lives for them.

There is a phrase in World Council of Churches documents and in speeches by Pope John Paul II that I used to affirm but with which I am now uneasy. It is the image of the church as "the voice of the voiceless." That now seems to me patronizing. "Never fear," we are saying to the poor, "we will take up your cause for you. You will have a champion in us; just leave it to us." No, our place is not to be "the voice of the voiceless" but to be the place where the voiceless can begin to speak on their own behalf and begin to take control of their lives. That is the excitement of, and the potential threat of, the notion of a "preferential option for the poor." That is why even the innocent-sounding word "partnership" is a radical notion, for we have not had partnership before, except among a few people at the top of the heap.

How much are we willing to be open to the new situation such proposals would create? The bishops state it uncompromisingly: "The question is not whether the United States can provide the necessary funds to meet our social needs, but whether we have the political will to do so." Do we have the political will? We will not answer that question by the kinds of things we do inside the church, but only by the kinds of things we do outside the church.

An old Catholic salutation is *Deo gratias* (Thanks be to God). I repeat that, coupling it with another salutation I am still somewhat surprised to hear coming from my Calvinist lips: "Thanks be to the bishops."

ELIE WIESEL:
A JEW'S MESSAGE TO CHRISTIANS

Brown was deeply committed to the Jewish heritage of his own Christian faith, and especially in light of the Holocaust, to Jewish people and the Jewish faith itself. Some of this was further stirred by the remarkable friendship between Brown and Elie Wiesel. Together they worked on the United States Holocaust Memorial Commission, and through the years exchanged many thoughts about the relationship between Judaism and Christianity. In some ways, Wiesel was also a source of spiritual consolation for Bob. The following sermon was given at First Presbyterian Church, Palo Alto, on March 13, 1983. Brown was a frequent preacher at his home church both before and after retirement.

For the last ten years, Elie Wiesel has been the central person in my life—with the notable exception of Sydney Brown.

Quite apart from his intrusion into the domestic life of the Brown family, a number of you may legitimately ask, "Who is Elie Wiesel?" Let me spend a couple of background moments responding to that question.

Elie Wiesel was a very pious Hasidic Jew from Hungary who in 1944 at the age of fourteen was deported by the Nazis, along with his family and every member of the Jewish community of his town, to the death camps of Poland. He was in Auschwitz, Birkenau, Buna, and Buchenwald. Six million Jews did not survive, including Wiesel's mother, father, younger sister, and almost all the friends he had known in his growing up. The very first night in Birkenau he saw a dump truck unloading objects onto an open fire. The objects were babies, only a few of the one million children the Germans exterminated in their effort to wipe all Jews from the face of the earth. On that night, Wiesel lost his family, most of his friends, and his faith. The God of his childhood was gone forever, and his own life became, as he put it, seven times cursed.

How does one deal with such evil? Wiesel has spent his life coping with that question. Some people, he realized immediately, get no choice; they are victims. That is the reality he describes in his autobiography, *Night*. A second book, *Dawn*, a novel, explores the possibility that in a world of victims and executioners it might at least be better to be an executioner than a victim. But that doesn't work. When the young Jewish protagonist kills a British soldier in the postwar struggle for Palestine, he discovers that he has destroyed himself; murder, Wiesel concludes, is a form of suicide. In the next novel he explores the alternative of suicide directly. It doesn't quite work either and leaves the surviving protagonist more despairing than before. What other options? Go mad; simply opt out, resign from community, create your own self-sealed world, insulated from reality. No good. And then, the most appealing and devastating option of all. In a world of monstrous evil, choose to be a spectator; disengage, refuse to take sides. To Wiesel, that is even worse than being an executioner. The spectator becomes less than human, refusing to care, refusing to take sides. Furthermore, spectators aren't really neutral; they are actually casting their votes for whoever has power at the time. To be a spectator in Germany was not to be neutral, but to support Hitler and become complicit in genocide. A troubling conclusion. The other options don't particularly tempt us most of the time. But who is not tempted by the spectator role?

There are a number of steps on Wiesel's journey upward from such depths. Let me simply describe the turning point, which occurs at the end of the fourth book, *The Town beyond the Wall*. Michael, a death camp survivor, is in a prison cell, captured for going back to his home town behind the Iron Curtain after the war. His only companion is another prisoner, who is in a catatonic state, totally out of touch with the world around him. He does not speak, or respond, or betray emotion on his face or in his person. Before being arrested, Michael had encountered Pedro, who had broken through Michael's own self-protective shell and established a relationship, the first person since Auschwitz whom Michael had been willing to trust. And it was a healing thing. When Pedro and Michael parted, Pedro said, "Now when someone asks you your name, you can say, 'I am Pedro,' and I, Pedro, will say, 'I am Michael.'" So close have they become that neither can be defined any longer without reference to the other.

Michael has discovered the blazing truth that selfhood is never achieved in isolation but only in sharing, only in community. And Pedro further points out that God is found at the point where two lives intersect. It would be too bad, he reflects, to look for God everywhere else, and find out too late that God was in the next-door neighbor.

Armed with that strength of friendship and sharing, Michael is not content to sit alone in his prison cell. Indeed, he realizes that unless he can break through the shell of the other and establish relationship, it will not be long before he is like the other, himself living in a totally enclosed world, no longer a true self. The vision of Pedro comes to him, and Pedro says to Michael, about the Silent One across the cell from him, "Cure him. He'll save you." And in those five simple words, "Cure him, he'll save you," we have the key to what Wiesel has discovered: If Michael really extends himself to the other, not only can the other be cured, but Michael himself can be saved, saved from a similar isolation and madness.

As the book ends, they are still in prison, but the beginnings of salvation have come, for the Silent One is beginning to respond, and Michael is saying to him, "Someday someone will ask you your name, and you will say 'I'm Michael.' And then you will know the taste of the most genuine of victories." And in this investment in another human being, Michael has begun, once again, to be aware of the presence of God.

There is still a long way to go but, building on this one-on-one relationship, Wiesel goes on in later books to explore the reality of wider community as the place for the full flowering of humanity. In so doing he begins to recover for himself the whole heritage of his own community—the songs, the stories, the prayers. In his most recent writings, he is retelling the stories of the biblical figures—Jacob, Abraham and Isaac, and Jonah and Jeremiah, whom he calls, in one book, *Messengers of God*. And he has discovered that in retelling those old stories he is now retelling his *own* story in a new way.

AFTER THAT BRIEF ACCOUNT of his pilgrimage, let me indicate a few things out of Wiesel's present affirmations about God that speak to me and I hope speak to you.

For Wiesel *faith is a constant struggle with God*. I choose the word carefully. We can believe in an evil world apart from God; no problem. We can affirm the reality of God apart from an evil world; no problem. It's when we are called upon to acknowledge both the reality of an evil world and the reality of God that we've got problems—big problems. Richard Rubenstein, a rabbi for whom the Holocaust made belief in God impossible, once said, "It is so hard trying to live in the world without God." Wiesel, next on the program, said, "Dick, let me tell you something even harder than living in the world without God: living in the world *with* God." The real agony, the agony of trying to figure out where God was during the Holocaust, why God was silent, is the agony of the *believer*. To believe doesn't necessarily make things easier; it can make things harder.

But to do so is at least to take God seriously. Michael, to whom we have referred, says on one occasion to Pedro, "I lift my voice against God, I shake my fist at God, I scream at God, I blaspheme—but even my blasphemy is a form of prayer. It's an acknowledgment that God is there, that I have to deal with God." Dealing with God is a serious business. As Wiesel says,

"Whenever, in a biblical story, an angel comes as a messenger of God and says, 'Fear not!' you'd better start worrying."

Wiesel tells of the beadle in a synagogue in a town overrun by the Germans: "Master of the Universe," he says defiantly, climbing into the pulpit the morning after the Germans have entered the town, "I have come to tell you that we are still here."

A few days later, the Jews are forced into a tiny ghetto area, and a few days after that the deportations to death camps begin. Once again the beadle mounts the pulpit: "Master of the Universe, I have come to tell you that we are still here."

Finally, everyone has been deported but the beadle. He climbs into the pulpit one more time. "Master of the Universe," he says in a voice full of pathos, "I have come to tell you that I am still here. But you, Master of the Universe . . . where are you?"

Another tale Wiesel recounts out of the Hasidic tradition begins to deal with that question. The scene is heaven. Word has just been received that the Jews have escaped across the Red Sea and Pharaoh's army of Egyptians have drowned. There is rejoicing. How often in history has there been a Jewish victory to celebrate? So the angels are singing and dancing. And then the archangel Michael notices that God is not singing or dancing, but weeping. He approaches the divine throne and says, "Master of the Universe, there has been a great victory. Why are you not singing and dancing with us? Why are you weeping?"

And from the divine throne comes the response: "Why should I not be weeping, when so many of *my* children have drowned?"

WHAT ABOUT VIOLENCE in God's world? We read Joshua for our Scripture reading. In his lecture on Joshua, Wiesel describes how for years he stayed away from the book, not wanting to acknowledge it as part of the Jewish heritage, because of the bloodshed and vindictiveness and cruelty. And besides, he says, it has no poetry. And then he tells the story, recounting the bloodshed and vindictiveness and cruelty, after which he says: "And so

I'm glad there is no poetry in the book of Joshua. Poetry should never be used to glorify violence and deceit. That which is beautiful should never be used to exalt what is unbeautiful and ugly. We may sometimes have to fight, even to kill, but let us never glory in it, let us never write poems about it, let us never exalt in it, let us never make of it something in which God rejoices. So there can be no holy wars, no crusades, no evil done exultantly in God's name."

What then do we do with all of the evil, all of the violence, all the suffering we have endured or inflicted? Wiesel has an answer. We must, he says, talk about it. We must tell the story (in his case particularly the story of the Holocaust) so that never again will people act in such a way.

In one of his novels there is a pogrom. All the Jews, save the one who survived to tell the tale, are killed, but so great is the frenzy that is built up, that the killers can't stop and they begin to turn on one another, brother against brother, son against father. Finally a house is set afire in which Christians, not Jews, have been locked. The narrator watches with horror. And then, he says, "All of a sudden I knew the reason for my horror. I had just glimpsed the future."

The episode encapsulates a truth Wiesel has observed in history, that what human beings first do to Jews they later on do to themselves. In the Holocaust, six million Jews were burned to death. So, repeat the tale, keep it alive, never let it be forgotten. Why? Because otherwise there could be a second holocaust. The second holocaust, a nuclear holocaust, would be the burning not only of Jews but of everybody. The great tragedy in the first holocaust was that people did not realize until too late that Hitler meant business; they ignored the telltale signs, they refused to act in time. Let us learn that lesson, Wiesel says, so that we will not, now in global terms, fail to notice in time that weapons are constructed to destroy, and that this time the destruction would be global. We must tell and retell the story of the Jews' destruction, so that we will not repeat it on a magnitude that will make it the story of the world's destruction.

WHAT ABOUT JESUS? There are many things that unite Christians in a shared heritage with Jews. But doesn't that all founder when we make our radically different assessments of a particular Jew, Jesus of Nazareth?

For Wiesel, it is not so much Jesus who is the problem; the problem is what Christians have done with him. Not so much, perhaps, that they have exalted him and divinized him, but that they have slaughtered, tortured, and killed in his name. To Christians the cross is a sign of divine love; to Jews it is a sign of human hatred. In his hometown, Wiesel says, "On every Easter the Jews trembled," for they knew that Christians, inflamed by the stories of the passion week, would descend on Jews with the cry, "Christ-killers! Christ-killers!" and beat them up. And that has happened in capital letters across two thousand years of history.

Concerning Jesus himself, Wiesel feels, there is much to learn and much to admire. In one book, a major character, Jewish, is twice described as having a handsome, Christ-like face. Amazing. One of the characters in *A Beggar in Jerusalem* describes Jesus as the prophet who had only one word on his lips: love. The same character says that the real tragedy of the crucifixion is that Christians use it as a pretext to deny the love for which Jesus lived and died and use his name to foster hate against the people from whom he came. In one bold utterance, Wiesel suggests that perhaps the Christians betrayed Jesus more than the Jews did.

I think we have to take such assessments very seriously. I think we *have* betrayed Jesus, again and again. And Wiesel himself would counsel us not to forsake our Jesus but to be more faithful to him.

As we look at the evil in the world, we can understand the anguished cry of the Jews, "The world is so evil; why does the

Messiah not come?" But if that is the Jewish question, we cannot so simply say that we have an easy answer, for our answer turns out to have within it a further question, and it is the opposite of the Jewish question. We Christians also have to cry, with similar anguish, "The Messiah *has* come; why is the world so evil?" We both acknowledge evil and we are both messianic faiths. We simply have different timetables. And we could begin to work together on what it means to struggle against evil together.

AND IT IS IN the sharing of that common struggle that I have learned most from Elie Wiesel. All of us stand in a heritage; we are the inheritors of a faith, and it is a faith that can empower us. We are not alone on the journey. We have each other, and we have the God who is on the side of laughter and compassion and sharing, and who seeks with us to oppose bitterness and cruelty and shame. To affirm such a God is not to be exempted from pain and suffering but to be able to deal with pain and suffering, and turn even those things into vehicles by which we can move more sensitively into the lives of others, with compassion and even, sometimes, with healing power. And, I must say it from a Christian pulpit, I see God at work in a Jew in our time, Elie Wiesel, a Jew who does not acknowledge, as I do, that God was uniquely embodied in a Jew of another time. I am no longer disturbed by the discrepancy. I am only grateful to know such a one, to learn from his books, and to give thanks that at no time and in no place is the God we worship left without a witness.

So I end with a story. In his youth the great Rabbi Napthali was confronted by a skeptic who said, "Napthali, I'll give you a gold coin if you can tell me one place where God can be found." And Rabbi Napthali replied, "And I'll give you two gold coins if you can tell me one place where God *cannot* be found."

Amen.

ON SPEAKING ABOUT ISRAEL:
AN ONGOING PROBLEM
FOR JEWS AND CHRISTIANS

Among the complications of this attraction to the Jewish roots of his heritage were the increasingly controversial policies of Israel toward the Palestinians. This was an issue over which Brown struggled mightily, particularly in light of his friendship with Wiesel. This article is adapted from a talk given at the fifteenth conference on Christian-Jewish relations, held in Minneapolis, in November 1987.

Recent events in Israel, particularly relating to violence in the Gaza Strip and the West Bank and the threat of escalating violence elsewhere, shove to the forefront a series of questions most American Jews and Christians would prefer not to face. The questions, however, are not going to go away; indeed, they are only going to become more demanding, and their evasion is only going to become more difficult. They are all variants of the same overall question: How are we, Jews and Christians, to talk creatively with one another about the state of Israel?

With whatever significant gains have been made in Jewish-Christian dialogue in the last decade—and those gains have been impressive—there still seems to exist an invisible barrier that no one wants to cross when the state of Israel is mentioned in such a way as to imply that a criticism might be forthcoming. There are some good reasons for this which I presently want to explore, but they do not, for reasons I also want to explore, justify the ongoing chill in the atmosphere that all of us have experienced when some comment about the Middle East implies even a veiled critique of Israeli policy.

I raise this issue, I need to say, with a certain fear and trembling, hoping that I do not overspend whatever capital I have been able to build up over the years within the Jewish and Christian communities. But we do ourselves no favors by keeping silent about matters of importance, and I want to break through what has been, in the case of many of us, a kind of quasi-silence on the delicate and complex issue of how we begin to initiate this new dimension of the dialogue.

For Jews, the existence of the state of Israel is a glory, but a very fragile glory, its existence continually under threat. For Christians, the state of Israel is sometimes a glory but more often a perplexity. How do we deal with it? How are we to react to what it does? Is it a state like other states or is it something more? Is the atmosphere inevitably poisoned when questions are raised about the appropriateness or inappropriateness of certain of its actions? Can Jews criticize the state of Israel without being perceived as disloyal Jews? Can Christians criticize the state without being perceived as anti-Semitic?

We all live with these questions, though we are reluctant to discuss them openly with one another. Are we not at a place where we could begin to do so? I want to test the waters for the possibility of beginning that discussion. So let me begin by listing a few expectations that each side should be entitled to receive from one another, and see whether they enhance or erode the possibilities for further exchange.

It seems to me that there are at least four things that Jews have a right to hear from the Christians as preconditions for responsible discussion:

1. Jews have a right to hear from Christians an unequivocal affirmation of the right of the state of Israel to exist and prosper. What a foreboding state of affairs that such a condition need even be mentioned! Do we Americans demand from Germans such an assurance of our right to exist when we are working on the provisions of a trade agreement? Must Denmark's survival be made a precondition for export negotiations with the Dutch? And yet, the survival of the state of Israel is so precarious and threatened from so many directions that Jews are entitled to be assured that whatever is said by Christians is not a subtle attempt to weaken the state of Israel and make it more vulnerable to attack. This is particularly true when Christians take up the cause of the Palestinians—where there is surely a justice issue worth discussing—and thereby appear in Jewish eyes to be proposing policies that would strengthen the convictions of the P.L.O.[33] that the state of Israel has no right to exist, let alone to prosper. So Christians have an obligation to be unequivocal about the permanence of the state of Israel.

2. Jews have a right to hear Christians disavow Armageddon scenarios. These are popular among certain Christians, and their articulations offer present support to the state of Israel, not because Israel has an inherent right to long-term survival, but because Israel is destined to play a central role in the apocalyptic projections that designate it as a site for the battle of Armageddon, the outcome of which will be a world ruled by Christ—a world in which there will be no Israel, no more Judaism, and no more Jews. The issue is important since Armageddon theology is not only affirmed by fringe groups in the population, but has been publicly endorsed by Ronald Reagan, and thus represents the perspective from which he views the Middle East struggle. Jews have a right to be assured by Christians that they are more than pawns in Christian eschatologies illicitly extracted from Ezekiel or the Book of Revelation.

3. Jews have the right to hear from Christians that Christians understand why Jews equate the state of Israel's survival with Jewish survival. The destruction of the state of Israel would be seen by Jews as virtually the equivalent of their own destruction—a tragedy of even more vast proportions than the destruction by Hitler of six million Jews. A greater tragedy than the Holocaust? How can one imagine such a thing? Christians need to realize that every living Jew can imagine it, can interiorize it, can be daily threatened by its possibility. Jewish destiny and

Israel's destiny are now forever linked by Jews, and the importance of that linkage must be acknowledged by Christians.

4. Jews have a right to hear from Christians that Christians understand why Jews of the diaspora are reluctant to be publicly critical of the state of Israel. In the face of overwhelming tides of criticism of Israel from Israel's enemies, Jews living elsewhere are surely entitled to think, "Israel needs more critics?..." When so much of the criticism is angry and false and often openly anti-Semitic, it is natural for a diaspora Jew to have no interest in swelling a chorus of hate. There is also an understandable reluctance to criticize Israeli Jews who are on the very battleground itself, when other Jews are removed from the immediacy of physical combat.

There are surely other things Jews have a right to ask of Christians, and Jews can state them more poignantly and compellingly than any non-Jew can do. Let that be one of the subjects of the ongoing dialogue.

What about the other side of the coin? What things have Christians a right to ask of Jews in discussions about the state of Israel? Here let me propose three things (three is a very big number in Christian thought).

1. I back into the first point by sharing a personal dilemma that has bothered me for years, For both physical and moral reasons, I do not believe that any form of assistance should be given to the government of South Africa, since any such support bolsters the continuation of the policy of apartheid. I am publicly against this aid, whether it comes from the United States or Japan or Germany, and I should be able to be publicly against such aid when it comes (as it has) from the state of Israel. Similarly, I have argued for many years that it is wrong for the United States to fund the contra forces in Nicaragua, whether such funding is proposed by Ronald Reagan, George Shultz, Oliver North, or Pat Robertson.[34] And I believe that in the political arena I should be permitted to deplore it publicly when such aid is given to the contras (as it has been given) by the state of Israel.

So out of such concerns, which are initially political, I formulate my first point: Christians have a right to hear from Jews that Christians can be critical of this or that political action of the state of Israel without automatically being labeled anti-Semitic. It must be a rule of political life that we can be critical of Israel, or supportive of Israel, in just the same way that we can be critical or supportive of any other state. For a Christian to be a friend of Israel cannot mean giving Israel a political (or military) blank check in advance, saying in effect: whatever you do, we will support you, or at least we will not oppose you.

And yet it is one of the painful facts of American political life that Christians often find that any public disagreement with political policies of the state of Israel is interpreted by Jews as at best a political betrayal, and at worst an insistence of subtle or not-so-subtle anti-Semitism. When such voices are raised, Christians have a right to hear other Jewish voices countermanding them.

2. Christians have a right to hear from Jews that Jews understand that Christian disagreement with certain policies of the state of Israel is not just a political matter but a theological matter as well. We need to be clear about what this does and does not mean, and it will take a few paragraphs to avoid possible misunderstanding. I am not proposing here to theologize about the state of Israel. Early in my own theological life I learned from extended exposure to Amos, Micah, Isaiah, Ezekiel, and Jeremiah that the worst sin is idolatry, i.e., giving uncritical allegiance to human constructs that can never be worthy of uncritical allegiance. The greatest candidate for idolatry is always the nation.

And I learned from the Hebrew prophets that no nation— whether Assyria or Babylon or Egypt or Persia or Judah—is entitled to uncritical allegiance. I learned in Hebrew Scriptures that the first commandment is not only first numerically, but also because all the other nine flow from it: "You shall have no other gods before me."

That has been an axiom throughout all of my theological and political life (two entities that I am unable to separate), and one reason why I am sometimes perceived as overly critical of my own nation is because our perennial temptation in the United States is to assume that our nation is God, i.e., that any criticism of it is unworthy and unpatriotic.

And if, from the stance of Hebraic prophetism, I have seen and continue to see idolatry in my own nation, I saw it also in the German nation in the 1930s and 1940s, where there were six million silent verifications of that appraisal, shouting to us by their very silence; and I see it in the South African nation today, wreaking havoc on 18 million blacks. The common factor in the posture of those governments (and in Russia and Chile and El Salvador, to name only a few more) is: no criticism. The state is above criticism. You are disloyal if you criticize. You forfeit your right to a place in the civic community if you challenge the policies of the state.

I submit that the prophetic tradition is one long No to such attitudes. And I submit that it is not part of the prophetic tradition to say: there can be criticism of all states save one, in this case the state of Israel. To be sure, there are rampant differences of degree in the extent of and the kinds of idolatry present in the states I have mentioned. But whenever, and by whom, the principle of no criticism is raised to the level of guiding axiom, there, especially, must there be criticism.

It is important once again not to be misunderstood on this point. I am not urging people to hold a magnifying glass over the state of Israel and look for things to criticize, while applying less exacting standards elsewhere. But I am saying that in the ongoing critique that we must make of all political constructs in the name of the first commandment, it may sometimes be the case that one of those constructs will be the state of Israel.

Let me try to clarify this further by emphasizing another insight from the prophetic tradition. To refer again to the image of the magnifying glass, the magnifying glass should always be focused on the nation of which one is a member; the basic critique, the initial critique, is always self-critique. I am amazed at how faithful the Hebrew Scriptures are to this fact, where judgment after judgment is piled up against the various political actions of the Jewish nation. I am even more amazed that the ongoing critique is not put on the lips of enemies of the Jews, but on the lips of the Jews themselves, most notably the prophets. And I am most amazed of all that these unflattering descriptions are not preserved for us in the annals of the enemies of the Jews, but in the sacred Scriptures of the Jews themselves. Those are staggering realities, and exceedingly impressive ones, reminding us that we are not entitled to locate the "evil empire" only somewhere else. We must first of all see the evil empire within ourselves.

And from that initial self-critique, the net must be cast widely. No one will escape, for no nation is God, no matter how much its leaders claim exemption from judgment.

So Christians need to hear from Jews that critique of every nation, no matter what its name may be, even if its name is Israel, is a part of the prophetic tradition Jews and Christians share, and not a deviation from that tradition.

3. Something follows from this: Christians can hope that Jews will speak critically of political policies of the state of Israel if injustice is being done. I realize that such a plea may sound insufferably arrogant to Jews who hardly need instruction from Christians on how to behave Jewishly. So let me indicate some of the things this might mean.

I am saying first that the prophetic tradition lays upon us all, Jews as well as Christians, an imperative to speak against injustice wherever it is found, even when it is found within that political configuration we most admire, nay, especially when it is found within that political configuration we most admire. It is in relation to those things we most admire that we must be especially on guard to see that idolatry does not blemish our admiration.

Second, I take it as a sign of great interior health that there has always been tremendous internal criticism within the state of Israel itself, and never more than in recent weeks. There, if anywhere on earth, it is true that if you have two Jews arguing you get three options. Let us press the point further: the vigor and sharpness of the internal debate within Israel would be a model for every state on earth and a liberation to all of us to say in our own situations whatever needs to be said.

Third, I note that there are some Jews outside of Israel who do speak up, who lament certain policies, who work for change in those policies. How they do this is their business, not mine. All honor to Elie Wiesel who says, "When I want to criticize Israel, I go to Israel"— and who goes to Israel frequently. All honor to those who do so within Jewish periodicals or at Jewish gatherings. Christians need to remember that Jews pay a price; I once said to a Jewish activist that it was painful to be accused of anti-Semitism whenever I offered even a mild criticism of some action of the state of Israel, and he replied, "You think it is painful for you, on the outside? What do you think it is like for us, on the inside?"

Fourth, when all has been said by Christians, there is no inherent reason why those in the state of Israel should listen to, or take seriously, the admonitions of the *goyim*. What have we ever said to them in the past that has been a blessing for the Jewish future? Consequently, when there are specific policies in the state of Israel that need challenging, the challenging words are far more likely to be heeded when they come from the lips of Jews rather than from lips of Christians.

To conclude with the most important word of all: in such discussion about the state of Israel, there is reason for a special concern and tone. Howard Singer, of the Anti-Defamation League, speaks a needed word to Christians. "Jews," he consoles us, "are not really as defensive as they appear. But they know that true critics, like true prophets, are those who criticize with love."

This is our only valid passport into new territory. We Christians need to take special pains, if there are occasions when we feel compelled to speak critically of Israel, to speak with love, so that we do not give aid or comfort to critics of Israel who seek by their criticism to bring about its demise or weaken its place in the forum of world opinion or who operate from openly anti-Semitic concerns. Let not any words of ours be so couched, in tone or content, that they bring aid and comfort to those who deny Israel's right to exist. Let our critiques of Israel spring from our love for Israel, from our desire that Israel be all she is destined to be and can become, both for her sake and our own, so that new meaning can continue to be given to the venerable phrase, "a light unto the gentiles."

Hers is a light we will always need.

GROUND RULES FOR ECUMENICAL (AND MULTICULTURAL) EXCHANGE

As the various churches and denominations changed through the 1980s and 1990s, the original impetus of the ecumenical movement, church unity, seemed more elusive. The Roman Catholic Church, too, shifted its remaining interest toward relations with the Orthodox and conservative Christian groups. At the same time, the pluralism of cultures and of religions was becoming evident as a reality within which people were living. All of these shifts are reflected in this talk given at the dedication of the Multicultural Center of the Franciscan School of Theology at the Graduate Theological Union in Berkeley, on May 8, 1993. The original "Ground Rules," published shortly after the Council, had a narrower focus and concerned only Catholic-Protestant relations.

I want to begin by saluting the foresight of those who have created the Multicultural Institute and wish them all success in their venture. Multiculturalism is a theme whose time has come; indeed, it is long overdue. The grapplings with this issue on Holy Hill[35] will benefit not only those who participate directly, but all others who are baffled by the issues raised and turn to this Institute for help.

I want, as briefly as I can, to raise some of the issues all of us must face at this time of beginnings, and rather than aim two or three suggestions straight at the bull's eye, I am going to employ a scattershot technique and brashly suggest, without developing them, nine items for our common agenda, hoping that one or two of them will strike home with each of you.

1. *The giving up of humanly definable absolutes.* This is not a coy way of saying that there are no absolutes, or that if there are we should ignore them, but simply a recognition that whatever we know about them, or It, or He, or She, is such a far cry from the real thing that we are not entitled to claim too much for our wisdom. It is folly to equate the divine with our understanding of the divine. I am advocating a modest theology that is quite prepared to concede that old ways of speaking or visualizing may need drastic overhaul, and that we need all the help we can get from all sources.

2. *The surrender of the axiom that my tradition automatically has better insights than your tradition.* This is a safeguard against fanaticism as well as pride. If I have the whole truth, that means that you do not, and since fidelity to the truth means the suppression of untruth, I am entitled to dispose of your ideas (and even of you) if necessary. (Old-timers will recognize that this was the classic defense of the Inquisition, whether practiced in Madrid or Geneva.)

3. *The importance of dialogue without hidden agendas.* Dialogue is rightly a big word in all ecumenical situations, but it often means different things to its practitioners. The chief hidden agenda of such dialogue is the desire to convert: "If I can just get things going the right way, my dialogue partners will see the rightness of my position and the wrongness of theirs." I remember one Catholic poster in the early years of the Week of Prayer for Christian Unity that showed the whole world streaming into St. Peter's in Rome—an interpretation of the consequences of dialogue that did little to mollify Protestant fears of a hostile takeover.

4. *Recognizing the cultural trappings* (not a pejorative word) in which all convictions are clothed, especially our own. There is no sacred book that is not in part the product of what its culture has contributed. Rather than apologize for this and downplay it, we ought to give it center stage, for we have much to learn from the cultural dimensions of the idea, the book, the dance, the painting, the sculpture, the song.

5. *The importance of starting with each other.* Whatever our cultural background, in addition we all share a common humanity across cultural differences—students and teachers alike. We can begin by celebrating this common humanity and sharing whatever parts of our culture illumine that humanity for us. We do not start with a full complement of eternal truths to dispense to one another. (If we do, communication is going to get clogged early in the process.) I am reminded of D. T. Niles's[36] definition of evangelism as "one beggar telling another beggar where to find the bread." We will be helped in this process by recognizing the importance in theological communication of the role of story. We can share stories long before we share theories of atonement. The fact that the stories are always wrapped in cultural garments is a further plus: as we understand the story we come also to understand the other culture. Gain all around.

6. Our need to *receive help from others, not just impart help to others.* We in the West are so ready to give advice and counsel, especially when it gives us a sense of psychological or moral superiority. We need to turn the Scriptural admonition around and realize that sometimes "it is more blessed to receive than to give." Our penchant to jump in and explain things transforms the possibility of enriching dialogue into strident monologue. We also enact the academician's favorite posture of giving a brilliant answer to a question that has not been asked.

7. *We need to learn about other cultures and faiths from their practitioners,* not from our own interpreters. During my college days a whole spate of books appeared about "the world's great religions," all written by Christians and all demonstrating, after a series of comparisons, that Christianity was far superior to all the others in such categories as its view of God, God's relation to the world, and comparative schemes of redemption. Such an approach has no place in the future. We are not engaging in a religious sweepstakes to see who wins, places, and shows. We are trying to get to know one another better. We are trying to have our own faith enriched by drawing on each other's resources.

8. *We need to do things together* in order to learn who we really are. As Gustavo Gutiérrez has pointed out, theology is always the "second act." The first act is commitment to one another and, especially, to the disadvantaged. We work together, we think together, and—this is new for many—we celebrate together. We discover who we are, not just in head trips, but in walking together, on previously untrodden paths, maybe even dancing on the way. We find each other both in projects designed to create social justice, and in fiestas that remind us that we can share the bounty of creation even in the midst of sorrow and heavy responsibilities.

9. Finally, we recognize that *all these matters have desperate urgency.* If you doubt that, think for a single moment about Bosnia[37] and what is going on there even as we are meeting here.

The problem in Bosnia is precisely that so many people cannot yet handle multiculturalism and are determined to blow out the brains of people who disagree or come from a different cultural background. In such situations, the issues are life and death, whereas in a privileged situation like this, we can talk together, play together, work together, share together—without fear. It is an extraordinary privilege. Let today be the moment at which we look at the future in a new way—with resolve, with commitment, with sensitivity, and also with joy.

A Concluding Word:
On Not Knowing Where
We Are Going

This sermon, delivered on October 20, 1968, at Stanford Memorial Church, still resonates in a time when we are uncertain in so many ways about the directions of the future, both in the life of faith and in our societies and the world as a whole. Here Brown dips into the wisdom of the letter to the Hebrews to offer some guidance into the future.

> Now the Lord said to Abram, "Go from your country and your kindred and your father's house to the land that I will show you." (Gen. 12:1)

> By faith Abraham obeyed when he was called to go out to a place where he was to receive an inheritance; and he went out, not knowing where he was to go. (Heb. 11:8)

This is perhaps the tenth or dozenth time I have preached from this pulpit. And while I have not gone back and reread the sermons preached on those occasions—an experience that is shattering even to contemplate—I have tried to recall the things I have said here, and they seem to me to have been variations on a similar theme: the relationship of the life of faith to the life of action, as sparked by such events as the Birmingham riots, the death of Pope John, Proposition 14, the death of Martin Luther King, the escalation of the war in Vietnam, and so forth.[38]

I want, therefore, to attempt something different this morning. I want to think with you about the way we approach these terrifying immediacies of our time, the stance from which we go forth today to face a very precarious tomorrow. We are in the midst of international problems that promise only to become more complex and in response to which our very ambiguous decisions may only exacerbate those problems. We know not what a day may bring and such knowledge as we have is usually more alarming than our ignorance. And we simply don't know which way to turn.

In this situation, the age-old story of Abraham has something to say to us, for Abraham at least faced, in his time, much the same situation we face in ours.

THE POINT AT WHICH we can establish an initial rapport with Abraham is that "he went out, not knowing where he was to go" (Heb. 11:8). Here is Abraham, a man of considerable means, suddenly called upon to take a total gamble. "Go from your country and your kindred and your father's house to the land that I will show you" (Gen. 12:1). Give up all the securities you have had, cast those aside, get moving. Where? No further information; simply, go "to the land that I will show you."

That is surely our situation, if we bracket for a moment the statement that Abraham was called by God to do this. Surely every day we go out, "not knowing where we are to go." It is simply a description of our times. Even though we may not leave our country physically as Abraham did, we surely realize that we cannot remain secure in our country as though it would suddenly shed the turmoil, the change, the frightening passions that are presently tearing it apart.

We go forth, not knowing where we are going. Surely that much is clear.

How, THEN, SIMPLY can we go forth with anything but an esca-lating series of responses on the order of heavy-heartedness, fear, despair?

We have so far glossed over part of the Abraham story. Abra-ham goes out, not knowing where he is to go, but he goes out in response to a call. The Genesis story tells us that "the Lord said to Abram, 'Go from your country.'" And the Hebrews story says, "By faith Abraham obeyed when he was called." Abraham didn't know where he was going, but he trusted that the direc-tion could become clear to him. When you marry, you don't know just what direction your marriage is going to take, but you trust that the direction will be good, and because of that trust you are willing to take the risk. That doesn't make it a sure thing, but it does make it a risk worth taking.

Abraham's response must have been something like that. The fact that God was somehow mixed up in it didn't make it a sure thing for Abraham. He still had to risk everything. Even though *God* called him to go, he still went out "not knowing where he was to go." What a fool his friends must have thought him. But Abraham risked it. It was not simple. He didn't just travel, arrive, and settle down. The New Testament account tells us that he and his family "lived in tents," ready to move at a moment's notice, and it also tells us that Abraham and his descendants "died in faith, not having received the promises." "They lived in the land of promise," the text tells us, "but they did not receive the promises."

Now this is surely a mixed bag. Abraham trusts in God so much that he picks up bag and baggage, sets out on a strange journey, lives in the land of promise, but yet does not receive the promise. What is the point of that?

The point of that is that we do not have the option of risk or no risk. We have a choice among various risks. Like it or not, life comes to me as a succession of risks. You can embrace what could paradoxically be called the risk of security, that is, the risk of trying to arrange your life neatly and predictably, so that your blueprint is gradually completed step by step—but you should be quite aware that your chances of pulling that off are virtually nil in the world we now inhabit. You can embrace the risk of cynicism, a risk many people embrace without realizing that it is a risk—of deciding that the whole human venture is a gigantic waste, that you can't trust "nobody nowhere nohow" and that you must simply get what you can for yourself while it's gettable—and then have the whole thing torpedoed by being the recipient of an act of trust by someone that you can't dismiss cynically, try as you will.

Or, along with Abraham, you can embrace the risk of faith, so long as you don't let that word become a weasel word. Let's try not to, for the New Testament author almost does. He starts out to give an abstract definition of faith, but almost immediately goes on to say in effect: You want to know what faith is? I can't really define it, after all, but I can describe it. Now take Abraham . . . or Sarah, or Moses, or Gideon, or the legions of people who were tortured, imprisoned, stoned, sawn asunder, because they believed in something. Faith is this monumental kind of trust, a trust that does not say, "Fulfill your promises to me and then I'll trust you," but says rather, "Even though the promises can only be anticipated, even though they are not going to be fulfilled in me, nevertheless, I will stake my life on the belief that they are what is truly important."

THOSE TWO STEPS, it seems to me, take us part way—that although first of all we do not know where we are going, we can, secondly, take our steps in the light of certain promises (even if their fulfillment is denied to us). We can live with a kind of creative risk. Can we go a third step? Can we give a little more substance to the nature and relevance of the promise? I think we can. Let me try to do so briefly.

The writer of the letter to the Hebrews describes Abraham's relation to the promise by saying that "he looked forward to the city which has foundations, whose builder is God." He describes Abraham and the other heroes of faith in his chapter as "seeking a homeland." And in the next chapter he offers a model to his readers, exhorting them to look "to Jesus, the pioneer and perfecter of our faith," the one who for his pains gets strung upon a cross but nevertheless can endure it (and get this) "for the *joy* that was set before him." What could those sorts of things possibly mean for us? I think they offer us at least a few important clues.

After reminding us that no one has faith as a "sure thing" that is guaranteed or foolproof in advance (and whatever else the crucifixion means it surely means at least that), the author then says to us in effect, "Very well, in a world like that where the good guys can get it in the neck, where are you going to place your trust—in a belief that the last word is with the crucifiers, that they always destroy the crucified, that love (in other words) is finally at the mercy of hatred, *or* in a belief that one can triumph even through apparent disaster, that love shines through even when it appears to be defeated. Going out into an uncertain world, are you willing to gamble, to risk, that there are such certainties as these, even though you may have to die without having them vindicated in your experience?"

Let me use one unlikely illustration out of the experience of the Christian community that produced the letter to the Hebrews to suggest how the question is answered. The unlikely illustration is the belief of the early Christian community in the return of Christ. Those who had known Jesus in the flesh were firmly convinced that he would shortly return to complete among them the work he had begun. In terms that seem naïve to us, they spoke of his returning on the clouds of heaven or of the living and the dead rising up in the air to meet him or of a time when God would be all in all. That vision did not come to fruition Christ did not return, at least not in the way they conceived he would, and yet their faith and their courage did not die. The vision furnished them instead with a definition of the quality their lives could possess, not just at some future moment of glory, apparently long to be deferred, but in the immediate present. They felt themselves called to live *now* in the light of that kind of vision—a vision in which the purpose of God in uniting all people to Godself and to one another has become reality, in which people are brothers and sisters, in which peace rather than discord prevails, in which one sees that love does in fact prevail and we can dare to live so now, even though save to eyes of faith such a commitment seems naïve.

How, then, can one have hope? Because in addition to all this, we are furnished with the vision, the promise, which, even if we do not ourselves receive it, is there and can be appropriated by us, so that even though we too die in faith not having received the promises, there is a very real sense in which we do receive them. To live in love, even if smitten for doing so, is in a very precious sense to have received the gift of love already, for how can we live in love unless in some sense we already possess it or are possessed by it? We *can* affirm the vision that there are other factors at work than those that immediately discourage us—the factors of purposiveness and love and concern embodied in Abraham and Jeremiah and Jesus, in St. Francis and Martin Buber and Martin Luther King, factors that tell us that even though they may not save us from death, they can enable us to face death unafraid; that tell us that even though compassion may appear to be going down the drain it is still right to live compassionately and thereby perhaps (only "perhaps" but still "perhaps") help to bring about a rebirth of compassion; that tell us that it is nobler to risk ourselves for the highest we know than to seek a premature "security" that will finally betray us; that tell us that even though we may not receive the promises in their fullness, we can live now in their light and thereby make them more real for others.

The great thing in all this is that we can never measure in advance the impact that a single deed may have or the use that may be made of what we attempt. Christopher Fry has written, "The Christian is the one who can afford to fail"—who need not have results to vindicate one's actions.

I give you, to drive this point home, what many of you may consider an extreme example of the way in which the vision of the end can dictate the action of the present. Listen to some words from Fr. Daniel Berrigan, an American Jesuit who is about to spend perhaps ten to sixteen years in jail for pouring napalm on draft board records. I ask you, in listening to what he says in his book *Night Flight to Hanoi*, not to refuse to hear if you simply happen to disapprove of his action, but to be open to the fact that obedience to a vision can give one a strange and winsome and disturbing kind of authority:

> Our apologies, good friends, for the fracture of good order, the burning of paper instead of children, the angering of the orderlies in the front parlor of the charnel house. We could not, so help us God, do otherwise. For we are sick at heart, our hearts give us no rest for thinking of the Land of Burning Children. . . .
>
> The time is past when good people can remain silent, when obedience can segregate people from public risk, and the poor can die without defense. . . .
>
> We wish also to place in question by this act all suppositions about normal times, longings for an untroubled life in a somnolent church, that neat timetable of ecclesiastical renewal which, in respect to the needs of human beings, amounts to another form of time serving.

And he concludes by exemplifying our theme that even though we die in faith without having received the promises, there is in fact a sense in which we do receive them:

Redeem the times! The times are inexpressibly evil. Christians pay conscious—even religious—tribute to Caesar and Mars; by approval of overkill tactics, by brinkmanship, by nuclear liturgies, by racism, by support of genocide. . .And yet, and yet, the times are inexhaustibly good, solaced by the courage and hope of many. The truth rules; Christ is not forsaken. In a time of death some people, the resisters, those who work hardily for social change, those who preach and embrace the unpalatable truth—such people overcome death, their lives are bathed in the light of the resurrection; the truth has set them free. In the jaws of death, of contumely, of good and ill report, they proclaim their love of the brethren.

We think of such people, in the world, in our nation, in the churches, and the stone in our breast is dissolved; we take heart once more.

Let us pray:

Almighty God, help us to take heart once more, we who so often doubt your might and even more your lordship, in this world that seems so devoid of the signs of your presence. Help us to learn that faith in you is not a way to avoid demands, but a way to be confronted with demands and help us also to know that it is in responding to your demands that we become human. Free us from the fear of tomorrow so that in the light of your promise of what you intend for us we may be emboldened to believe that we enter the future not alone, but in company with you and the cloud of witnesses that have come before. This we ask in the name of Jesus, the pioneer and perfecter of our faith. Amen.

Further Reading

Robert McAfee Brown's memoir, *Reflections over the Long Haul* (Westminster John Knox, 2005), was published posthumously. It is an eminently readable and engaging introduction to his life and career. Linda Woods Glenn wrote a very useful dissertation on Brown that takes us up to the year 1988, entitled: *The Theologian as Social Activist: A Study of the Public Career of Robert McAfee Brown* (Denver: Iliff School of Theology, 1988). It contains an extensive bibliography of works by and about Brown, arranged topically. An updated bibliography by Glenn appears in a Festschrift, *The Future of Prophetic Christianity: Essays in Honor of Robert McAfee Brown*, ed. Denise Lardner Carmody and John Tully Carmody (Orbis, 1993). Finally, the website of the Flora Lamson Hewlitt Library of the Graduate Theological Union contains a wealth of material. Consult www.gtu.edu Special Collections, Archives.

Notes

1. Joseph Gélineau (1920–2008), a Jesuit priest and liturgical composer, known especially for his settings of the psalms.

2. Erik Routley (1917–82), a twentieth-century Congregationalist minister, musicologist, and composer of many influential Protestant hymns.

3. Daniel Berrigan (1921–), a Jesuit priest, poet, and friend of Brown and a leading peace activist.

4. The Hebrew word *shuv* has these connotations. It is more or less equivalent to the Greek *metanoia*.

5. U.S. policy in Nicaragua was favoring the "Contras" (from *contra-revolucionarios*), a right-wing paramilitary group opposed to the government of the Sandinistas, who had overthrown the dictator Somoza. Brown was deeply involved in the critique of that policy and remained attuned to U.S. policy in Latin America, notably in Chile, Guatemala, and El Salvador.

6. Abraham Heschel (1907–72), a Jewish rabbi and a personal friend of Brown's. He was a leader of the civil rights movement, active in ecumenical affairs, and the author of many scholarly works, including *The Prophets*.

7. Leonardo Boff (1938–), a Brazilian liberation theologian and a former Franciscan friar.

8. Sister Agnes Mary Mansour (1931–2004) was director of the Michigan Department of Social Services, which assisted poor women in procuring abortions. She left the Mercy order rather than comply with a requirement issued by the archbishop of Detroit that she make a public statement of support of church teaching; Sister Teresa Kane greeted Pope John Paul II in Washington, D.C., with a public call for the opening of all ministries

239

in the church to women and has since been an ardent voice for women's dignity and rights in the church; Sister Margaret Farley is professor emerita of Christian ethics at Yale Divinity School and the author of several influential works on moral theology, sexuality, and ethics. She is a past president of the Catholic Theological Society of America.

9. Brown is referring in particular to the controversy over the position taken by Sister Agnes Mary Mansour on the abortion issue, which generated both sympathy and controversy.

10. Brown is referring to previous assemblies of the World Council of Churches.

11. The phrase is from Bonhoeffer.

12. Jesus enters the synagogue and reads from Isaiah 61:1–2. The reaction of the crowd is one of hostility. Jesus responds that "no prophet is accepted in the prophet's hometown." Indeed, he was driven out of town "so that they might hurl him off the cliff" (v. 28).

13. Ignazio Silone (1900–1978), an Italian anti-Fascist and anti-Communist, and one of Brown's most-cited novelists.

14. The reference is to the Loma Prieta Earthquake of October 17, 1989, which hit the San Francisco Bay Area. It registered 6.9 on the Richter Scale and caused widespread damage.

15. Jon Sobrino, a Jesuit priest and leading liberation theologian, was a member of the Jesuit community in San Salvador, but was absent from the community the night of the murders. He was in residence at Santa Clara in the months following the massacre, and it was during this time that Brown and Sobrino became acquainted.

16. Robert McAfee Brown, ed., *Kairos: Three Prophetic Challenges to the Church* (Grand Rapids: Eerdmans, 1990). Contains: "The Kairos Document" from South Africa; "Kairos Central America: A Challenge to the Churches of the World"; and "The Road to Damascus: Kairos and Conversion").

17. Ita Ford, Maura Clarke, Dorothy Kazel, and Jean Donovan were four American missionaries in El Salvador who were

brutally murdered by military personnel on a roadside on December 2, 1980. Ita Ford and Maura Clarke were Maryknoll Sisters, Dorothy Kazel was an Ursuline Sister, and Jean Donovan was a laywoman.

18. *Gaudium et Spes* ("Joy and Hope"), also known as "The Pastoral Constitution on the Church in the Modern World," was the last of the decrees of the Second Vatican Council, charting a course for the Roman Catholic Church in relation to the realities of the world. It both reflected and advanced the Catholic Church's commitment to social justice and peace.

19. Steve Biko (1946–77), an anti-apartheid activist who was arrested by South African police and brutally beaten. He died in custody from his injuries.

20. Le Chambon-sur-Lignon, a village in southeastern France, which became famous for hiding Jews during World War II.

21. Trocmé was the Protestant pastor in the village of Chambon-sur-Lignon who led the resistance to the Nazis.

22. Alfred Delp (1907–45), a Jesuit priest who was arrested and, like Bonhoeffer, executed for his resistance to the Nazis.

23. Bernhard Lichtenberg (1875–1943), a German Catholic priest who protested the mass exterminations taking place under the Nazi regime. He died in transit to Dachau.

24. General Lewis Blaine Hershey (1893–1977) was the director of the Selective Service System (draft) during the Vietnam War.

25. Dom Hélder Câmara (1909–99), was archbishop of Olinda and Recife, Brazil, and was a great champion of the poor, "the bishop of the slums." He was the target of reactionary forces in both the Brazilian government and the Catholic Church.

26. Brown's brother-in-law, James C. Thomson, Jr. (1931–2002), who worked for the State Department, had already resigned from the Johnson administration in 1966 over the conduct of the Vietnam War. His critique of the war, "How Could

Vietnam Happen: An Autopsy," was published in the *Atlantic* in the April 1968 issue.

27. Ernst Troeltsch (1865–1923), a Protestant theologian most remembered for his contributions to the developing field of the sociology of religion.

28. R. H. Tawney (1880–1962), British economist and educator, wrote *Religion and the Rise of Capitalism* (1926); Max Weber (1864–1920), German sociologist of religion, wrote *The Protestant Ethic and the Spirit of Capitalism (*1905–6); Michael Walzer (1935–), American political philosopher.

29. See note 26.

30. Medellín and Puebla were both meetings of CELAM, the bishops' conference of Latin America. The documents from both conferences were foundational in efforts at evangelization through the decades of the 1970s and 1980s, and, to some degree, contributed to the development of the theology of liberation in Latin America.

31. General Alexander Haig (1924–2010), served briefly as secretary of state under Ronald Reagan and was a prominent conservative critic of the bishops' pastorals. Clare Boothe Luce (1903–87) was a journalist, Congresswoman, Ambassador to Italy, and strong conservative Republican. Both Haig and Luce were Catholics.

32. Dorothee Soelle (1929–2011) was a German political and feminist theologian and personal friend of Bob and Sydney Brown.

33. The Palestinian Liberation Organization.

34. George Schultz (1920–) was Secretary of State from 1982 to 1989 under Ronald Reagan, succeeding Alexander Haig; Oliver North (1943–) was involved in the notorious Iran-Contra affair, which diverted monies from arms sales to Iran to support of the Contras in Nicaragua; Pat Robertson (1930–) is a conservative American television evangelist.

35. "Holy Hill" is a local name for the hill where most of the member schools of the Graduate Theological Union are located, next to the campus of the University of California, Berkeley.

36. Daniel Thambyrajah Niles (1908–70), a Sri Lankan ecumenist.

37. The reference is to the war between Bosnia and Herzegovina, 1992–95.

38. The references are to events that were recent or contemporary then. The Birmingham riots occurred in April 1963. Martin Luther King Jr. was jailed. It was there that he wrote his famous "Letter from a Birmingham Jail." Pope John XXIII, who convened the Second Vatican Council and signaled an era of hope, died in 1963. Proposition 14 was a measure on the 1964 California ballot designed to repeal an anti-discrimination law passed by the California Legislature by amending the California Constitution. It passed, but was struck down by the California Supreme Court. Martin Luther King was assassinated in 1968 (as was Robert Kennedy). And 1968 was the year of the Tet Offensive, a major escalation of the war in Vietnam. (1968 was also the year that Pope Paul VI published the encyclical *Humanae Vitae,* which forbade the use of artificial contraception.)

MODERN SPIRITUAL MASTERS
Robert Ellsberg, Series Editor

This series introduces the essential writing and vision of some of the great spiritual teachers of our time. While many of these figures are rooted in long-established traditions of spirituality, others have charted new, untested paths. In each case, however, they have engaged in a spiritual journey shaped by the challenges and concerns of our age. Together with the saints and witnesses of previous centuries, these modern spiritual masters may serve as guides and companions to a new generation of seekers.

Already published:

Simone Weil (edited by Eric O. Springsted)

Dietrich Bonhoeffer (edited by Robert Coles)

Henri Nouwen (edited by Robert A. Jonas)

Charles de Foucauld (edited by Robert Ellsberg)

Pierre Teilhard de Chardin (edited by Ursula King)

Anthony de Mello (edited by William Dych, S.J.)

Oscar Romero (by Marie Dennis, Rennie Golden, and Scott Wright)

Eberhard Arnold (edited by Johann Christoph Arnold)

Thomas Merton (edited by Christine M. Bochen)

Thich Nhat Hanh (edited by Robert Ellsberg)

Mother Teresa (edited by Jean Maalouf)

Rufus Jones (edited by Kerry Walters)

Edith Stein (edited by John Sullivan, O.C.D.)

John Main (edited by Laurence Freeman)

Mohandas Gandhi (edited by John Dear)

Mother Maria Skobtsova (introduction by Jim Forest)

Evelyn Underhill (edited by Emilie Griffin)

St. Thérèse of Lisieux (edited by Mary Frohlich)

Flannery O'Connor (edited by Robert Ellsberg)

Clarence Jordan (edited by Joyce Hollyday)

G. K. Chesterton (edited by William Griffin)

Alfred Delp, S.J. (introduction by Thomas Merton)

Bede Griffiths (edited by Thomas Matus)

Karl Rahner (edited by Philip Endean)

Pedro Arrupe (edited by Kevin F. Burke, S.J.)

Sadhu Sundar Singh (edited by Charles E. Moore)

Romano Guardini (edited by Robert A. Krieg)

Albert Schweitzer (edited by James Brabazon)

Caryll Houselander (edited by Wendy M. Wright)

Brother Roger of Taizé (edited by Marcello Fidanzio)

Dorothee Soelle (edited by Dianne L. Oliver)

Leo Tolstoy (edited by Charles E. Moore)

Howard Thurman (edited by Luther E. Smith, Jr.)

Swami Abhishiktananda (edited by Shirley du Boulay)

Carlo Carretto (edited by Robert Ellsberg)

Pope John XXIII (edited by Jean Maalouf)

Modern Spiritual Masters (edited by Robert Ellsberg)

Jean Vanier (edited by Carolyn Whitney-Brown)

The Dalai Lama (edited by Thomas A. Forsthoefel)

Catherine de Hueck Doherty (edited by
David Meconi, S.J.)

Dom Helder Camara (edited by Francis McDonagh)

Daniel Berrigan (edited by John Dear)

Etty Hillesum (edited by Annemarie S. Kidder)

Virgilio Elizondo (edited by Timothy Matovina)

Yves Congar (edited by Paul Lakeland)

Metropolitan Anthony of Sourozh (edited by Gillian Crow)

David Steindl-Rast (edited by Clare Hallward)

Frank Sheed and Maisie Ward (edited by David Meconi)

Abraham Joshua Heschel (edited by Susannah Heschel)

Gustavo Gutiérrez (edited by Daniel G. Groody)

John Howard Yoder (edited by Paul Martens and
Jenny Howells)

John Henry Newman (edited by John T. Ford, C.S.C.)